Democracy in Its Essence

Democracy in Its Essence

Hans Kelsen as a Political Thinker

Sara Lagi

LEXINGTON BOOKS

Lanham • Boulder • New York • London

Published by Lexington Books
An imprint of The Rowman & Littlefield Publishing Group, Inc.
4501 Forbes Boulevard, Suite 200, Lanham, Maryland 20706
www.rowman.com

6 Tinworth Street, London SE11 5AL, United Kingdom

British Library Cataloguing in Publication Information Available

Library of Congress Cataloging-in-Publication Data Available

Library of Congress Control Number: 2020944613

ISBN 978-1-7936-0371-5 (cloth)
ISBN 978-1-7936-0373-9 (pbk)
ISBN 978-1-7936-0372-2 (electronic)

Contents

Introduction

Hans Kelsen as a Political Thinker

When mentioning the name of Hans Kelsen (1881–1973), the immediate mental association—like a sort of Pavlovian effect—is with legal formalism, ultra-positivism, with the "purification" of legal science to make it independent from not-legal disciplines like sociology and political science.[1] His name and figure are in fact commonly associated to imposing monographic studies such as *Das Problem der Souveränität* (*The Problem of Sovereignty*, 1920), *Allgemeine Theorie der Normen* (*General Theory of Norms*, 1925), *Reine Rechtslehre* (*Pure Theory of Law*, 1934), and *General Theory of Law and State* (1945).[2] Yet, he was much more: in his long life, he was a constitutionalist theorist, an international law theorist, and an observer of the main events influencing both the history of his country—Austria—and the international environment from the end of World War I to the Cold War. Also, even though he claimed a rigorous separation between Law and politics, the purity of legal science, and so on, his scientific interests ranged from Law to psychology, from philosophy to political theory. According to the American jurist Roscoe Pound,[3] Kelsen was "leading" among the twentieth-century legal theorists. He was however a political and democratic thinker too. He provided us with a theory of modern, representative, and parliamentary democracy, which will be specifically analyzed in this book and which he elaborated through a series of writings, including the two editions of his most iconic and popular work *Vom Wesen und Wert der Demokratie* (*Essence and Value of Democracy*) (1920; 1929).[4] By parliamentary democracy in relation to Kelsen's political theory, I will refer to a specific form of government, which is based on two core principles: On the one hand, on the principle of political representation, that is, the idea that Parliament (the legislative body)—being democratically elected—is the key element for the democratic decision-making process. On the other, on a particular relationship between the Legislative and the

1

Executive power, which means the government needs the approval and the political trust of the former. His legal work has been and continues to be the subject of international scholarships, developed mainly by legal theorists and philosophers of law. Regardless of being supporters or opponents, Kelsen's legal theory has been and is still considered one of the major achievements of twentieth-century European legal thought. In general terms, what clearly emerges is the great amount of monographic studies on Kelsen as jurist. With regard to the German-speaking context, Robert Walter made a crucial contribution to the study of Kelsen's *Reine Rechtslehre* and constitutional theory, while editing—only one year before dying a collection of essays aimed at delineating a broad and articulated view of Kelsen's complex and long-running intellectual production.[5] With a similar purpose, Horst Dreier and Ernst Topitsch have analyzed the interconnections between Kelsen's legal and political thought, whereas Michael Hebeisen elaborated on Kelsen's legal philosophy with a particular focus on his theory of sovereignty.[6]

I would also mention the names of Klaus Zeleny, Clemens Jabloner, and Thomas Olechowski who have coordinated and supervised a series of scholarly works on Kelsen's legal thought and how it spread internationally.[7] More recently, they co-edited a new scholarly work analyzing Kelsen's intellectual biography, as it took shape in the main cities where the Austrian jurist lived and worked: from Vienna to Berkley passing through Köln and Geneva.[8] Similarly relevant is the work of Matthias Jestaedt, who has analyzed Kelsen's legal theory.[9]

Italy has an important tradition of studies on Kelsen as a legal theorist, too. His legal philosophy has been discussed and studied in depth by Renato Treves, Vittorio Frosini, and Norberto Bobbio, just to mention some of the prominent Italian intellectuals of the past century.[10]

The attention and the interest for Kelsen has never ceased in Italy: from Agostino Carrino, who has also edited some of the fundamental Italian editions of Kelsen's legal and political works to Francesco Riccobono, who recently published an interesting volume which is a sort of intellectual map of the way Kelsen's legal theory has been recognized and criticized in Italy.[11]

It is also significant to mention figures such as Mario G. Losano and Luigi Ferrajoli. The former has provided a key-contribution to the understanding of Kelsen's normative theory. The latter, a few years ago, published a highly critical book on Kelsen's legal formalism, including a sharp counter-analysis of Kelsenian constitutional theory, which aimed at highlighting the conceptual weaknesses and limits of Kelsen's theory of the primacy of the constitutional law.[12] Remaining within the Italian environment, a young generation of scholars, such as Tommaso Gazzolo and Federico Lijoi, have returned to critically reflect on Kelsen's legal positivism and more precisely on the dichotomy between "Sein" ("Is") and "Sollen" ("Ought"), whereas Antonio

Merlino has analyzed Kelsen's intellectual heritage within the Italian legal tradition.[13]

In France, Kelsen has been an object of thorough examination over the years. It is worth mentioning Simon Goyard-Fabre's key essay on the neo-Kantian influence over Kelsen, which—in my opinion—remains to this day one of the best works on such a theme and the still fundamental contribution to Kelsenian scholarship coming from, for example, Michel Troper.[14]

If Troper investigated, for example, Kelsen's theory of the State, another French scholar, Olivier Beaud, recently edited a work on Kelsen's theory of constitutional justice, which is particularly useful and fruitful to reconstruct, among many other aspects, the controversy between Kelsen and Carl Schmitt on the function of constitutional jurisdiction.[15]

Over the years, in English-speaking countries, interest for Kelsen has considerably grown. Among the most internationally distinguished scholars of Kelsen, there is certainly the American Stanley L. Paulson. He devoted a considerable part of his scholarship to Kelsen's legal philosophy and very recently co-edited a Horts Dreier's study, in which Kelsen's legal positivism is interpreted—among many other aspects—as the expression of the trust in the enlightening power of science and modern rationality.[16] Within the English-speaking academic world, a relevant scholarly work published recently on Kelsen, with the declared purpose of offering an analysis of Kelsen's whole theory, is that of Lars Vinx. He has more recently focused on Kelsen's constitutional theory, reconstructing his debate with Schmitt on the *Hüter der Verfassung* (*Guardian of the Constitution*) and during the German constitutional crisis of 1932.[17] An example of the increasing interest for Hans Kelsen within the English-speaking world is also the collected works edited by Peter Langford, Ian Bryan, and John McGarry, who have analyzed in depth Kelsen's legal positivism and his complex, critical attitude toward the natural law tradition.[18] Another remarkable example of such an English-speaking revival is undoubtedly the volume edited by the American scholar Jeremy Telman on Kelsen's intellectual production after his moving to the United States. The present work effectively explains the reasons why Kelsen's legal theory was contested and criticized by many prominent American legal theorists during the post–World War II period, while reconstructing how Kelsen's major scientific interests developed in the New World.[19]

Although a little less popular than studies in the German, French, Italian, and English languages, I think that Spanish-speaking and Portuguese-speaking scholarly works on Kelsen as a jurist deserve the attention of those who are interested in his figure and thought. Just to mention some publications, I would refer to Albert Calsamiglia and Juan Antonio García Amado, who have investigated both Kelsen's concept of legal science and the foundations of his legal positivism, as well as José Antonio Sendin Mateos, who has concentrated his attention on Kelsen's idea of *Grundnorm* (Fundamental norm).[20] Another name worth mentioning is that of the Colombian Mario Alberto Montoya-Brand, who has committed to analyzing Kelsen's pure theory of law, while showing a remarkable interest for the more political aspects of his work.[21] Also, I would mention the works published in Portuguese language by José Lamego, Antonio Martins, and João Baptista Machado.[22] Yet, one of the most interesting aspects to underscore is the fact that in the last two decades and in all of the countries mentioned above, scholars (both legal and political philosophers) have shown an increasing interest in Kelsen's political thought and democratic theory too. In German language, a key volume is undoubtedly Robert Christian Van Ooyen's analysis of Kelsen's concept of society and democracy, in contrast to—for example—Carl Schmitt's legal and political theory.[23] Similarly relevant is Tamara Ehs's contribution to a better understanding of Kelsen's personal commitment in support of an appropriate education to democracy and women's civil emancipation, chiefly in early postwar Austria. Ehs's work has the undoubted merit to show how, regardless of his repeated claim to be a man of science far from politics, Kelsen made a clear and personal choice in favor of democracy and democratic values.[24]

In Italy—since the mid-1990s—a series of monographic studies have been published on Kelsen's democratic theory: from Gaetano Pecora and Raimondo De Capua, who provided—in 1995 and 2003, respectively—with two effective overviews of Kelsen's democratic thought to Marco Caserta who has investigated also Kelsen's idea of constitution.[25]

In France, Carlos Miguel Herrera elaborated on Kelsen's concept of democracy already in the 1990s, providing some fundamental contributions to the understanding of Kelsen's political philosophy, whereas more recently the Swiss-French Sandrine Baume published an interesting volume on Kelsen's political thought along with articles on his concept of political compromise.[26]

The Italian but naturalized French scholar Pasquale Pasquino has never systematized his profound interest for Kelsen's political thought in the form of a monographic study, but his essays, for example, on Kelsen's thought in relation to the Weimar debate on democracy represent a major reference point for those who want to investigate Kelsen as a political theorist.[27]

In some cases, Kelsen's political theory—or at least some of its aspects—has become a reference point for critically re-thinking contemporary democracy and chiefly the crisis, in which representative democratic systems seem to be involved, for example, in some European nations, characterized by the resurgence of nationalist and populist movements. Within this context, I would mention the works (mainly published in English language) by Nadia Urbinati, David Ragazzoni, and Carlo Invernizzi-Accetti who have discussed

Kelsen's conception of democracy from the perspective of political theory and political philosophy.[28] At a general glance, Kelsen's thought has been thus investigated from two leading scholarly perspectives: legal philosophy and political philosophy. Also, some of the works mentioned above have, in my opinion, tried—more or less successfully—to integrate in particular the two viewpoints, chiefly those interested in grasping the interconnections between Kelsen's legal and political theory. Identifying the major lines of reflection characterizing studies on Kelsen is particularly relevant to me because it allows me to highlight the fundamental difference between my volume and the main scholarly literature developed so far and of which the above mentioned works represent an important example. My book is based on a well-defined methodological choice which is basically different from that of legal philosophy and political philosophy.

In the present book, Kelsen's political and more precisely democratic theory will be discussed through the lens of the history of political thought, which has some relevant implications in methodological terms.

I will take into account Kelsen's intellectual production devoted to the analysis of representative and parliamentary democracy and its chief characteristics, while historically contextualizing it. His writings on democracy—from the early 1920s to the mid-1950s—will be considered in relation to the concrete historical and political context within which they took shape. Differently from legal-philosophical and political-philosophical approach, which is usually not particularly sensitive to the historical dimension and its impact on the concrete development of theories, I will instead show how Kelsen's democratic theory can be read—in many respects—as his personal, political response to specific political problems and issues. In this sense, I would like to contribute to reconsidering Kelsen not only as a political thinker but also as an observer of the major political changes of his time. I will then investigate and highlight how some of his major works on democratic theory published between the 1920s and the mid-1950s—from the first edition of *Vom Wesen und Wert der Demokratie* to the *Foundations of Democracy* (1955)—could be not fully understood unless we take into account the weight of the historical-political context.

I am referring to the rise of the soviet system, the issue of giving his country—Austria—a democratic constitution after the collapse of the Habsburg Empire, the growth of ultra-right movements as a response to the widespread crisis of parliamentary institutions in early postwar Europe, the crisis of the Weimar Republic, the post–World War II period, characterized by the Cold War and the ideological contrast between the West and soviet Russia, and the need for Kelsen to reinvent himself as a scholar in the United States after leaving Europe because of nazism in 1940.

Thus, contextualizing Kelsen's political theory means, for me, to put his works in an ideal "dialogue" with his time, to stress those aspects of his theory which have a clear reference to concrete political challenges and problems. This also implies understanding how and to what extent Kelsen's works and their political and ideological content reflect elements, issues, inputs coming more or less directly from the historical-political context, within which Kelsen lived and worked.

Moreover, it is just by adopting this kind of perspective that—in my opinion—his democratic theory emerges not only as Kelsen's attempt to critically and personally reflect on the *essence* of democracy—or at least what he thought was its *essence*—but also as its *defense* against specific targets, that is, a series of political movements, figures, theories, which, according to Kelsen, embodied serious intellectual and political threats to democracy as an idea and as a specific form of government. As I am going to argue, such targets have all a clear ideological-political connotation and range from soviet Russia to reactionary forces, from Lenin as the great heir of Marx's theory of the "proletarian revolution" to neo-jus naturalists such as Jacques Maritain and Karl Niebhur, from Carl Schmitt to Eric Voegelin.[29]

Contextualizing does not however imply any attempt to "flatten" Kelsen's political thought, which is incredibly complex and multifaceted. My particular methodological approach and the choice to concentrate my attention on the political content of Kelsen's huge intellectual production does not signify that I will put his legal theory aside—that would make no sense. On the contrary, I will identify and discuss some of the core elements of his legal positivism and particularly his ferocious attack on the natural law doctrine, in order to highlight how and to what extent both represent, in some crucial respects, a conceptual premise to the development of his democratic theory or—at least—some of its aspects.[30]

Given the enormous impact which Kelsen's legal positivism, with its radical critique of the traditional conception of Law, State, and sovereignty, exercised on European early twentieth-century legal thought and the many counter-replies which arose, I will take into account some of the most remarkable anti-Kelsenian critiques, chiefly those promoted by one of his sharpest and most brilliant opponents: the German-Jewish, Social-democratic jurist Hermann Heller.[31]

Just within a logic aimed at avoiding any form of "flattening" of Kelsen's political reflection, my analysis will follow two general directions: on the one hand, I will discuss how all his democratic theory seems to start from the objective to delineate a *realistic* definition of democracy, in order to make it live up to the political challenges of his time. More precisely, I will show how Kelsen's search for such a realistic definition and understanding assumes the recognition of a fundamental hiatus between *ideal* and *real* democracy.

On the other, the book will be divided into four chapters, each of which will be devoted to what I think are some of the chief characteristics of Kelsen's democratic theory (as developed from the 1920s to the 1950s): *pluralism, constitutionalism, relativism*, and *proceduralism*. In other words, I will seek to argue in what sense Kelsen formulates a *pluralist, relativist*, and *procedural* theory of democracy, implying a particular conception of the relationship between *democracy* and the *defense of the constitution*. As I am going to elaborate in detail, by the term *pluralist* I refer to Kelsen's particular vision of politics and society, which he depicts as a complex and articulated dimension made up of a plurality of interests, ideas, projects, and perspectives. By the term *constitutionalist* I refer to his way of interpreting the problem of how to protect the democratic constitution. With regard to this aspect, I will concentrate on the dispute between Kelsen and Schmitt on constitutional jurisdiction, not only to discuss how profoundly contrasting their legal views were about the role and functioning of Constitutional Courts but mainly to argue that behind such intellectual controversy there was an equally contrasting conception of democracy and more exactly of parliamentary democracy.[32]

By the term *relativist* I mean the proper philosophical and epistemological outlook ("Weltanschauung") characterizing real democracy, according to Kelsen. In particular, I will take into account and discuss some of the main objections made to Kelsen's theory of relativism, chiefly the one where his concept and defense of relativism would open the door to a dangerous indifference toward which political and moral aims and values are to be chosen. Finally, by *procedural* I refer to the fact that, in some crucial respects—which I will examine—Kelsen looked at democracy also as a means, a procedure, or a combination of procedures to make political decisions, at very well-defined and particular conditions. Focusing on these conditions in my opinion allows better understanding of his democratic theory and also to critically examine its procedural component. In order to define and comprehend the latter, it will be relevant for me to compare it with that of the economist and political scientist Joseph A. Schumpter, who is commonly depicted as one of the leading exponents of a procedural vision of democracy and whom Kelsen openly mentioned and quoted in his American work on democracy, *Foundations of Democracy*. My intention is to demonstrate that all these major aspects (*pluralism, constitutionalism, relativism*, and *proceduralism*) are profoundly interrelated and intertwined; that is, they imply each other and they also presuppose—in legal terms—a choice in favor of a *positivist* conception of law. While elaborating on the *pluralist, constitutionalist, relativist*, and *procedural* components of Kelsen's democratic theory, I will show that—in more stringent terms—Kelsen as a political thinker faced extremely concrete political and institutional issues such as the conception of Parliament, the meaning of parliamentary representation and the people, the legal and political significance of the democratic constitution, the democratic relationship between the rulers and the ruled, the principle of majority, the relationship between the majority and the minority within parliamentary dialectics, the voting system and the granting of fundamental rights, and so on. I will try to prove how all these issues were essential for Kelsen to define the significance of a modern, representative, and parliamentary democracy in contrast to its exact opposite: autocracy. Historically speaking, the latter was identified by Kelsen with soviet Russia, nazi Germany, and the fascist regimes that took shape in Europe during the early postwar period. Analyzing the contrast between democracy and autocracy as elaborated by Kelsen will allow me to highlight the relevance of the problem of freedom within his political theory and also how the former is interpreted by Kelsen in *liberal* and *democratic* terms. By *liberal* I refer to that political and ideological current of thought affirming the existence of fundamental and individual rights of freedom which have to be legally granted and which represent *per se* a bulwark against the potential abuses committed by the government or by the majority against the minority. By *democratic* I refer to that political and ideological current of thought which theorizes the people as "sovereign" and which—from such an assumption—makes freedom coincide with the equal political right to participate in the formation of political will directly or indirectly. In general terms, liberalism as a political theory thus assumes the primacy of the principle of freedom, while democratic thought assumes that of equality. For the former, being free essentially signifies recognizing a space of personal freedom which the government is not allowed to abuse or violate; for the latter, being free fundamentally means obeying laws which the citizens—all considered politically equal and thus provided with the same political rights—have directly or indirectly established. The former emphasizes the private connotation of being free, whereas the latter emphasizes a public one.[33]

Historically speaking, these two principles, that is, the liberal and the democratic, have been separated and in a reciprocal antagonism for a long time, at least until the outbreak of the American and French Revolutions. Yet, in Europe, from the end of the French Revolution (1799) until the mid-nineteenth century the relationship between liberalism and democracy continued to be controversial. Liberal thinkers in fact advocated constitutional government and the respect of individual rights and minority freedoms but were firmly against the democratic right to vote. To them, democracy seemed a radical thought because it assumed the political equality of all citizens—including those coming from lower classes—and because it seemed to sacrifice the respect of the individual and minorities to the principle of people's sovereignty. For liberals—such as, for example, the Swiss-French political thinker and constitutionalist Benjamin Constant—the risk was that a democratic government would turn into the government of an oppressive majority, in which there would have been no room for dissent. Like all European liberals of the early nineteenth century, Constant was thinking of the Jacobin democratic phase of the French Revolution (1792–1795), which had resulted in the dictatorship of the Public Safety Committee. Constant's critique of democracy represents one of the best examples illustrating the anti-democratic prejudice characterizing European liberalism at that time.[34] As a result of the massive political and social changes occurring in many parts of Europe—including the spread of the Industrial Revolution through the Continent, the rise of a modern working class, and the birth of national emancipation movements—liberalism started to open to democratic theory, that is, to the concept of the people's sovereignty. Within the European context, a consistent liberal-democratic theory began to take shape and develop in particular since the mid-nineteenth century. The encounter and compromise between the liberal tradition of thought and the democratic one was the outcome of a complex historical and political transformation. Liberalism accepted, for example, universal suffrage and thus the importance of granting citizens—regardless of their socio-economic status—the right to vote. In his two volumes on *De la Démocratie en Amérique* (*Democracy in America*) (1835; 1840), Frenchman Alexis de Tocqueville depicted political democracy and society democratization as an unrestrainable process, although he warned of the tyranny of the majority as the tyranny of common opinion and conformism.[35]

Moreover, between the late nineteenth century and the early twentieth century some representatives of European liberalism became particularly sensitive to social issues. In his *Principles of Political Economy* (1848), John S. Mill advocated the necessity of social reforms in support of the working class; in the early twentieth century another British thinker—Leonard T. Hobhouse—sought to conciliate liberal-democratic principles with social demands such as the provision of social services and social insurance for the working class.[36] Liberalism opened to the principle of equality, and by doing that, democratic theory changed itself: recognition of the principle of political equality and greater sensitivity to social issues in fact had to assume the provision and respect of the individual freedoms granted within a constitutional type of government, that is, within a government with limited powers. In this way, democracy opened to the liberal principle of freedom. On an institutional level, liberal-democratic theory—as it developed in Europe between the nineteenth and the twentieth centuries—sustained a representative form of government; that is, it argued that the appropriate realization of a liberal democracy was through the parliamentary mechanism: in other words, liberal democracy could be established in the form of an indirect participation of citizens in public life.[37]

Indeed in early-twentieth-century Europe, liberal-democratic theory and liberal democracy centered upon the parliamentary mechanism were seriously challenged by the development of mass democracy, as a result of political democratization and the assertion of mass political parties. As the German sociologist Max Weber argued, the true subject of political life was not the Parliament anymore, as mass-parties related directly to the mass and interpreted their needs and demands. The typical liberal-democratic belief in the centrality of parliamentary dynamics for the shaping of politics was thus put in crisis.[38] Liberal-democratic theory and liberal democracy were also challenged by those leftist political thinkers and movements who—recalling Karl Marx and socialism—argued that true democracy could be established only by eliminating social injustice and differences. From a liberal-democratic perspective, mass democracy represented the triumph of the Tocquevillian warning about the dangers of social conformism as a threat to individual freedom, whereas the idea of a "ätrue" democracy professed by the socialists was seen as an equally dangerous threat to the respect of individual freedoms and to constitutional government: both could risk being sacrificed and even erased in the name of a perfect social equality.[39]

I am aware of the fact that both liberalism and democracy as political theories are much more multifaceted and that, chiefly since the second half of the twentieth century, liberal-democratic political theory and institutions have been the subject of an articulated reflection by scholars such as the American John Rawls, Ronald Dworkin, and Robert Nozick, as well as by the Indian Amartya Sen and the German Jürgen Habermas, just to mention some internationally distinguished thinkers.[40] Yet, I have deliberately focused on the abovementioned aspects of European liberal-democratic tradition because they are interesting and useful for my analysis. As I am going to argue, Kelsen provides us with a political theory which is liberal and democratic. He wants to investigate the meaning and functioning of democracy, but the true point for me is that by doing so he develops an analysis and a defense of a particular form of government, that is, a liberal and representative democracy. If it is true that liberal democracy assumes a compromise between freedom and equality, it is also true that Kelsen poses himself two relevant problems: to understand how such a compromise can actually be established, while working properly, and to outline a defense of the specific institutional and political form which such a compromise takes. In the following chapters, I will try to delineate Kelsen's reflection on these two problems. By doing so, the present work intends to offer a *reasoned overview* of Kelsen's political theory as it developed from the 1920s until the 1950s.

NOTES

1. See: chapter 1.
2. I will refer to these works in the next chapters of the book.
3. Stanley L. Paulson, *Die Rolle des Neukantianismus in der Reine Rechtslehre: eine Debatte zwischen Sander und Kelsen* (Aalen: Scientia Verlag, 1988).
4. I will refer to both works in the next chapters of the book.
5. See: Robert Walter, *Hans Kelsen. Ein Leben im Dienste der Wissenschaft* (Wien: Manz, 1985); Robert Walter, *Hans Kelsen als Verfassungsrichter* (Wien: Manz, 2005); Robert Walter, Werner Ogris, and Thomas Olechowski hrsg., *Hans Kelsen: Leben—Werk—Wirksamkeit* (Wien: Manz, 2009).
6. Horst Dreier, *Rechtslehre, Staatssoziologie und Demokratietheorie bei Hans Kelsen* (Baden-Baden: Nomos Verlag, 1987); Peter Koller, Werner Krawietz und Ernst Topitsch hrsg., *Ideologiekritik und Demokratiekritik* (Berlin: Duncker & Humblot, 1982) Wilhelm Hebeisen, *Die Souveränität in Frage gestellt: die Souveränitätslehren von Hans Kelsen, Carl Schmitt und Hermann Heller im Vergleich* (Bade-Baden: Nomos Verlag, 1995).
7. See: Clemens Jabloner und Thomas Olechowski hrsg., *Methodenreinheit und Erkenntnisvielhaft: Aufsätze zur Rechtstheorie, Rechtsdogmatik und Rechtsgeschichte* (Wien: Manz, 2013); Clemens Jabloner, Thomas Olechowski und Klaus Zeleny hrsg., *Das internationale Wirken Hans Kelsens* (Wien: Manz, 2016); Clemens Jabloner, Jan Kuklìk und Thomas Olechowski hrsg., *Hans Kelsen in der tscechischen und internationalen Rechtslehren* (Wien: Manz Verlag, 2018).
8. See: Clemens Jabloner, Thomas Olechowski und Klaus Zeleny hrsg., *Kelsen in seiner Zeit* (Wien: Manz, 2019).
9. See: Matthias Jestaedt, *Hans Kelsen und die deutsche Staatsrechtslehre* (Tübingen: Mohr Siebeck, 2016).
10. See: Norberto Bobbio, *Diritto e potere. Saggi su Kelsen* (Milano: Edizioni di Comunità, 1992); Vittorio Frosini, *Saggi su Kelsen e Capograssi. Due interpretazioni del Diritto* (Milano: Giuffré, 1988); Renato Treves, "Intorno alla concezione del diritto in Hans Kelsen," *Rivista Internazionale di filosofia del diritto* XXIX (1952): 117–97.
11. Agostino Carrino, *Kelsen e il problema della scienza giuridica (1910–1935)* (Napoli: Edizioni scientifiche italiane, 1987); Francesco Riccobono, *Antikelsenismo italiano* (Torino: Giappichelli editore, 2017).
12. See: Mario G. Losano, "Il problema dell'interpretazione in Hans Kelsen," *Rivista internazionale di filosofia del diritto* XLV (1968): 524–42; Mario G. Losano, *Forma e realtà in Kelsen* (Milano: Edizioni di Comunità, 1981); Mario G. Losano, "La trilogia su Umberto Campagnolo (1904–1976). Kelsen, il federalismo, la guerra giusta e la guerra europea," *Accademia delle Scienze di Torino* 145 (2011): 45–59; Luigi Ferrajoli, *La logica del diritto: dieci aporie nell'opera di Hans Kelsen* (Roma-Bari: Laterza, 2017).
13. See: Tommaso Gazzolo, *Essere/Dover Essere. Saggio su Hans Kelsen* (Milano: Franco Angeli, 2016); Federico Lijoi, *La positività del diritto. Saggio su Hans Kelsen* (Roma: Aracne, 2011); Antonio Merlino, *Kelsen im Spiegel der Italienischen Rechtslehre* (Salzburg: Peter Lang, 2013).

14. See: Simone Goyard-Fabre, "L'inspiration kantienne de Hans Kelsen," *Reveu de Métaphisyque et de Morale* 83, no. 2 (1978): 204–33; Michel Troper, "Hans Kelsen et la jurisprudence," *Archives de philosophie du droit* 30 (1985): 83–94.

15. Olivier Beaud et Pasquale Pasquino sous la direction de, *La controverse sur 'le gardien de la constitution' et la justice constitutionelle. Kelsen contre Schmitt* (Paris: Éditions Panthéon Assas, 2007).

16. See: Horst Dreier, *Kelsen in Kontext. Beiträge zum Werk Hans Kelsens und geistesverwandter Autoren*, hrsg., Matthias Jestaedt und Stanley L. Paulson (Tübingen: Mohr Siebeck, 2019).

17. See: Lars Vinx, *Hans Kelsen's Pure Theory of Law: Legality and Legitimacy* (Oxford: Oxford University Press, 2007); Lars Vinx ed., *The Guardian of the Constitution: Hans Kelsen and Carl Schmitt on the Limits of Constitutional Law* (Cambridge: Cambridge University Press, 2015).

18. Ian Bryan, Peter Langford, and John McGarry eds., *The Foundation of the Juridico-Political Order* (London: Routledge, 2015); Ian Bryan, Peter Langford, and John McGarry eds., *Hans Kelsen and the Natural Law Tradition* (Leiden: Brill, 2019).

19. See: Jeremy Telman, *Hans Kelsen in America—Selective Affinities and the Miysteries of Academic Influence* (Netherlands: Springer, 2016).

20. See in particular: Alberto Calsamiglia, *Contribución a un estudio crítico de la teoria kelseniana* (Madrid: Servicio de Publicaciones, 1979); Juan Antonio García Amado, *Hans Kelsen y la norma fundamental* (Madrid: Pons, 1996).

21. See: Mario Alberto Montoya-Brand y Nataly Restrepo Montoya editors y compiladores, *Hans Kelsen. El reto contemporáneo de sus ideas politicas* (Medellin: EAFIT, 2011).

22. See in particular: José Lamego, *A Teoria pura do dereito de Kelsen* (Lisboa: AAFDL Editora, 2019).

23. See: Robert C. Van Ooyen, *Der Staat der Moderne: Hans Kelsens Pluralismustheorie* (Berlin: Duncker & Humblot, 2003); Robert C. Van Ooyen, *Hans Kelsen und die offene Gesellschaft* (Berlin: Duncker & Humblot, 2010).

24. See: Tamara Ehs, *Hans Kelsen: eine politikwissenschaftliche Einführung* (Baden-Baden: Nomos Verlag, 2009).

25. See: Marco Caserta, *La forma e l'identità. Democrazia e costituzione in Hans Kelsen* (Torino: Giappichelli, 2005); Raimondo De Capua, *Hans Kelsen e il problema della democrazia* (Roma: Carocci, 2003); Gaetano Pecora, *La democrazia di Hans Kelsen. Un'analisi critica* (Torino: UTET, 1995).

26. See: Carlos G. Herrera sous la direction de, *Le droit, le politique. Autor de Max Weber, Hans Kelsen, Carl Schmitt* (Paris: L'Harmattan, 1995); Sandrine Baume, *Hans Kelsen. The Case for Democracy* (Bruxelles: ECPR, 2012).

27. See: Pasquale Pasquino, "Penser la démocratie: Kelsen en Weimar," in *Le droit, le politique. Autor de Max Weber, Hans Kelsen, Carl Schmitt*, 119–31.

28. See: Carlo Invernizzi-Accetti, "Reconciling Legal Positivism and Human Rights: Hans Kelsen's Argument from Relativism," *Journal of Human Rights* 17, no. 2 (2018): 215–28; David Ragazzoni, *Il Leviatano democratico. Parlamento, partiti e capi tra Weber e Kelsen* (Roma: Edizioni di Storia e Letteratura, 2016); David

Ragazzoni, "An Overlooked Puzzle in Kelsen's Democratic Theory," in *Compromise and Disagreement in Contemporary Political Theory* (New York: Routledge, 2017), 96–118; Nadia Urbinati, "Editor's Preface," in Hans Kelsen, *The Essence and Value of Democracy*, ed. Nadia Urbinati and Carlo Invernizzi-Accetti (Lanham, MD: Rowman & Littlefield Pub. Inc, 2013), 1–25.

29. On this issue, see in particular: chapters 1 and 4.

30. On this issue, see in particular: chapters 3 and 4.

31. On this issue, see in particular: chapter 1.

32. On this issue, see in particular: chapter 2.

33. Steven Wall, "Introduction," in Steven Wall ed., *The Cambridge Companion to Liberalism* (Cambridge: Cambridge University Press, 2015), 1–19.

34. See: John Gray, *Liberalism* (New York: Routledge, 1986) and also: Massimo L. Salvadori ed., *European Liberalism* (New York: John Wiley and Sons Ltd., 1972), 92 ff.

35. See: Alexis de Tocqueville, *Democracy in America*, vol. 1 and 2 (London: Forgotten Books, 2012).

36. See: John S. Mill, *Principles of Political Economy* (Amherst: Prometheus Books, 2004) and Leonard T. Hobhouse, *The Elements of Social Justice* (Chicago: Hardpress Publishing, 2009).

37. See: Wall, *The Cambridge Companion to Liberalism*, 2015.

38. See: Max Weber, "Parlament und Regierung in neugeordneten Deutschland," in *Gesammelte Schriften*, hrsg. Johannes Winckelmann (Tübingen: Mohr Siebeck, 1988).

39. See: Albert S. Lindemann, *A History of European Socialism* (New Haven: Yale University Press, 1983).

40. See: Wall, *The Cambridge Companion to Liberalism*, 2015.

Chapter 1

Democracy and Pluralism

THE LEGAL PRECONDITIONS TO
KELSEN'S DEMOCRATIC THEORY

At the beginning of the twentieth century, Hans Kelsen was a young, promising jurist who had intellectually developed in Austria by studying law at the University of Vienna. His mentor had been Edmund Bernatzik,[1] professor of public and constitutional law, who gave Kelsen the opportunity to spend one semester at the University of Heidelberg, where Georg Jellinek—one of the most prominent jurists of that time and representative of German legal positivism—taught.

His stay in the German city was not particularly fruitful: Kelsen did not find Jellinek's lessons stimulating and, as Kelsen's official biographer Rudolf A. Métall noticed, Kelsen did not make a positive impression on Jellinek.[2] After his return to Vienna from Heidelberg, Kelsen began his academic and scientific career, while developing his systematic reflection on the meaning of "legal science." This was the first step toward a complex re-definition of the concept of State and sovereignty through works such as *Die Hauptprobleme der Staatsrechtslehre (Main Problems in the Theory of Public Law)* (1911)[3] and *Das Problem der Souveränität (The Problem of Sovereignty)* (1920)—a re-definition, which brought Kelsen to break with late-nineteenth-century German legal positivism and more precisely with a series of thinkers who embodied that particular tradition of legal thought, such as Carl Friederich Von Gerber, Paul Laband, and Georg Jellinek himself.[4] At the end of the Preface of the *Hauptprobleme der Staatsrechts lehre* Kelsen recognized the great role played by Jellinek within German-language legal science, and the relevance of his work. Yet, beyond his homage to Jellinek's reputation, the *Hauptprobleme der Staatsrechtslehre* could be considered as

Kelsen's serious attempt to take a radical distance from that past tradition of thought, while remaining a legal positivist.[5] In the *Hauptprobleme der Staatsrechtslehre*, Kelsen concentrated upon the meaning of legal science: critically discussing the latter implied for him to re-formulate the meaning of State and sovereignty against late-nineteenth-century legal positivism. The latter was characterized by two distinctive aspects: first, the idea of a coherent "legal method," scientifically consistent, to be applied to public law by jurists who had to stay above political disputes and prevent legal science from being contaminated by politics; second, the definition of the State as "a legal person" equipped with a "will" and as the only and true "sovereign subject." In this sense, neither the People nor the King were the sovereign, only the State.[6]

There was an evident mistrust toward political dynamics, as a potential source of chaos and conflicts, as well as a similar mistrust toward the concept of people's sovereignty. Such view reflected, in first instance, the conservative spirit of the German bourgeoisie, which—after the turmoils of 1848 Revolution—opted for stability and cooperated with the Hohenzollern Monarchy.[7] Yet, there was a substantial difference between major late-nineteenth-century legal positivists: unlike Gerber and Laband, Jellinek did not define individual rights as a mere "reflection" of the State power. They were rather the effect of an act of "self-limitation" (*Selbstbeschränckung*) made by the State toward civil society[8]: This particular way of interpreting the relationship between the State and individuals differed from Gerber's and Laband's not only for its clear liberal implication but chiefly because it assumed a twofold theory of the State.[9] Jellinek identified in fact two different perspectives to consider the State from, which corresponded to two different types of knowledge: legal and sociological.[10]

Legally, the State was a "person," a "sovereign subject." Sociologically, it was an entity which limited itself with respect to individuals and, doing so, granted them rights.[11] Kelsen blamed legal positivists for having been un-coherent with their methodological premises: in his opinion, they had not been able to develop a true "legal science." Their definition of the State as a "person" with a "will" or Jellinek's recall to a sociological concept of the State were all examples—for Kelsen—of a persisting contamination of legal science with extra-legal elements, which he wanted to remove, in order to make legal science truly scientific. Kelsen admitted only one kind of law, that is, positive law, and like all positivist jurists he considered law as a human product. In this sense, there was no divergence between him and his predecessors.[12] The true point of rupture was represented rather in Kelsen's will to transform the theory of law into a true science which—like all sciences—had to find the reasons of its own legitimacy, unity, and autonomy, in itself.[13]

For Kelsen, the major challenge for a positivist legal scientist of his time was thus to theorize the purity of legal theory, which meant to define the latter as the "pure theory of positive law."[14] In his opinion, this implied two chief elements: positive law had to be conceived as the "autonomous object of legal science" and in order to accomplish this goal, it was likewise necessary to believe legal science as epistemologically and methodologically separate from other disciplines, such as sociology or political science. In both respects, law had to be "purified": it had to be considered as a "pure norm," and the theory of law had to coherently become a "normative science," detached from "political-ideological" components.[15]

As we can read in the *Vorrede* (*Preface*) to the second edition of the *Hauptprobleme der Staatsrechtslehre* (1923), Kelsen's reflection on the status of legal science and on the meaning of law was strongly influenced by neo-Kantianism and more exactly by the person of Hermann Cohen, the founder of the neo-Kantian School of Marburg.[16] The centrality of the episte-mological issue can be in fact traced to Cohen, from whom Kelsen learned the relevance of the knowledge process for determining what counts for an object to us and the intrinsic unitary essence of the knowledge process determining the unitary essence of the known object too.[17]

From other neo-Kantians (such as Wilhelm Windelband and Heinrich Rickert, who belonged to the German Southwestern neo-Kantian school), Kelsen internalized the separation between natural sciences and the science of mind.[18] On the basis of both lessons, Kelsen identified the science of mind with legal science, while interpreting legal science as purely normative, that is, concerning the realm of positive norms and therefore with the dimension of the "ought," which he frontally opposed to the dimension of the "is."[19] The latter—differently from the "ought"—concerned "material facts" which could be understood only through their specific cause-effect relations.[20]

Having re-interpreted law and legal theory in terms of normative purity, the next step was, for Kelsen, to rethink the concept of State and sovereignty. Kelsen blamed old legal positivists for mixing the dimensions of natural science and legal science, which for him were separated, and therefore for mixing, to his opinion, two radically different forms of knowledge.[21] Since, according to Cohen's philosophy, the knowledge process determined the object itself of one's knowledge, Kelsen argued that old legal positivists' inability to maintain natural science knowledge separate from science of mind knowledge determined a totally wrong way of conceiving the State and sovereignty.[22]

More exactly, in the *Hauptprobleme der Staatsrechtslehre*, Kelsen criticized legal positivists (and mainly Jellinek) for considering the State as a "person" having and expressing a "will." To Kelsen, their mistake was to look at the State through the lens of natural sciences and thus to formulate a theory of the State as belonging to the realm of natural facts rather than to that of norms.[23]

Kelsen drew the radical consequences of his critique to late-nineteenth-century legal positivism in *Das Problem der Souveränität* (1920). As an object of legal knowledge, the State had to be considered and defined only in a strictly normative sense, that is, as an order of positive norms: State and Law perfectly coincided.[24]

Within this normative concept of the State, sovereignty simply became the "quality" of the State as "legal order."[25] This process of State de-personification immediately provoked many strong and thorough reactions. Kelsen became the target of legal theorists' and sociologists' critiques, who contested his legal theory and his very concept of law and State, sometimes in very harsh tones. Between 1913 and 1916 Kelsen was involved, for example, in a dispute with Eugen Ehrlich—one of the pioneers of the sociology of law, along with Max Weber and Emile Durkheim—on the meaning and epistemological status of the sociology of law. Ehrlich proposed considering legal science as an integrative part of social sciences. Kelsen replied by underlining the differences between sociology and legal science. Ehrlich's critical remarks were very similar to those of another prominent intellectual of that time, Hermann Kantorowicz who advocated the necessity to connect legal science to social reality against any form of normativism and normative purity.[26]

It was a dialogue where nobody was listening, which showed one important fact: Kelsen's work ended up nurturing a powerful reaction from those intellectuals who, against him, professed the vital connection between legal science and sociology, between Law and social facts.[27] Ehrlich and Kantorowicz were obviously not the only ones: the name of the legal theorist and sociologist Hermann Heller[28] was of great relevance among Kelsen's opponents. Heller saw Kelsen's legal theory as the most radical effect of nineteenth-century legal positivism, which—for Heller—played a crucial role in separating legal science from social and political sciences.[29] To Heller, Kelsen de-substantialized the concept of State and sovereignty by removing what he considered the true and most profound meaning of sovereignty, that is, the power of making decisions within a territory, which presupposed the existence of the State, as a concrete subject, historically determined.[30]

Heller's legal vision was intertwined with his role as a political thinker: looking at the early postwar period, he denounced the widespread crisis of many European democracies. For him, a necessary step to face that problem was to critically understand the (political and legal) significance of democratic sovereignty. He thought that the only way was to recover—against Kelsen's legal theory—the more concrete meaning of State and sovereignty by focusing on the ties between society and Law, between politics and Law.[31]

Yet, what Heller identified as the Kelsenian legal theory's major fault could be seen from a totally different point of view. As observed by scholars,

Kelsen's de-personalized concept of sovereignty and State might have been motivated by the necessity to detach the "validity of the law" from the "action of a person" and thus to propose "the normative idea of the rule of the law as opposed to the rule of the men."[32] Assuming this perspective as valid, we could situate Kelsen's theory within the broader context of European legal and political reflection on how to protect people and their rights from an arbitrary political power—how to impede rulers from imposing their arbitrary and discretional will. This very problem was at the center of the "Rechtsstaat" tradition as well as of the "rule of law" tradition. Regardless of the fact that, historically speaking, the concepts of "Rechtstaat" and the "rule of law" belong to "two different constitutional traditions" (the first, German and continental; the second, Anglo-American), both share one core concept: how to pose legal restraints to the State, in order to grant liberty and security.[33]

With his theory, Kelsen went much further: he went beyond the duality between State and Law, by stating that State and Law were the same.[34] One could reply—as Stephen Holmes did some years ago—that Kelsen's identification of State and law ended up defining as legal any form of State, including the nazi one.[35] This kind of critique seemed to recall the widespread anti-positivist literature, according to which legal positivism would be one of the sources of modern totalitarianism because of its rejection of a natural law superior to human laws, and can be counter-replied by following three types of argumentation.[36] Regarding the first argumentation, it might be useful to be reminded that Kelsen elaborated on his *Hauptprobleme der Staatsrechtslehre* and a "pure" theory of Law and State in the early twentieth century. This meant he was living within a very peculiar and complex historical and political context, that is, the Dual Austro-Hungarian Empire, which was a puzzle of different nationalities and religious denominations.[37] Also, since the mid-nineteenth century it had been involved in huge conflicts among non-German and Austro-German nationalities.[38] It is very likely that the multinational and complex nature of the Empire stimulated Kelsen to conceive a legal positivism, which wanted to be "pure," independent from "national and religious ideologies," and from particular political, national, or ideological forces. In this sense—as suggested by scholars—the purity of legal science, the de-personification of State and sovereignty could be inspired by the necessity to manage and consider the complexity of the Austrian reality. In such a context, made up of a variety of different nationalities which were often in reciprocal contrasts, it became in fact vital to theorize the "normative rule of the law," in the strongest way possible, and the identification between State and Law could be a significant move in this direction.[39]

The second kind of argumentation brings us into Kelsen's legal theory and more precisely his *Reine Rechtslehre*, which was published for the first time in 1934. In this work, which was a systemization of his legal normativism,

Kelsen openly identified the elements characterizing the "Rechtsstaat" in its more political implications: administration and jurisdiction were bound by legal norms, which were created by the Parliament; the latter was elected by the people; the courts had to be independent; citizens were provided with civil and political rights, etc. Kelsen was thus well aware of the traditional meaning of "Rechtsstaat" and—as we are going to see—his theory of democracy assumed it, in many respects.[40]

The third argumentation is directly related to the complexity of Kelsen's intellectual production as a whole. Kelsen did not limit himself to elaborating only and exclusively on the conditions of pure legal science. He left us a theory of democracy: in particular, just the identification between State and Law—which can be seen as functional to the ideal of the "rule of the law"—never implied Kelsen's indifference toward the concrete process leading to the creation of laws. Already in his *Hauptprobleme der Staatsrechtslehre*, he faced the problem of who concretely created the (political) content of the laws and therefore he faced the problem of how materially the legislative process worked. I will argue that the particular way Kelsen identified and discussed both issues in his 1911 monographic study had strong and relevant implications, which we must take into account to comprehend his democratic theory and the relationship between democracy and pluralism within his political reflection.

BRINGING THE VITALITY OF SOCIETY INTO THE REALM OF LAW: FROM THE *HAUPTPROBLEME DER STAATSRECHTSLEHRE* TO THE BIRTH OF THE AUSTRIAN REPUBLIC

According to nineteenth-century legal positivism the State was that "legal person," who—equipped with "will"—created the law. Within this conceptual framework, which obviously rejected jusnaturalism and any idea of natural law being superior to positive law, legal positivists defined the Parliament as the "organ" of the State. This meant that the legislative process reflected the "will of the State," the deputies were all "State functionaries," and the act of voting was itself a "function of the State."[41] This particular definition of the Parliament and its relationship with the State was an elegant and sophisticated way to legitimize the State as the true sovereign. Moreover, it was a way to neutralize the principle of people's sovereignty, whose image still evoked the "ghost" of the French Revolution and the Jacobin democracy in many nineteenth-century European legal and political theorists with conservative tendencies.[42]

Unless we take into account this specific aspect of the nineteenth-century legal positivist tradition of thought, it becomes harder, in my opinion, to grasp the ultimate sense of Kelsen's definition of the Parliament in his *Hauptprobleme der Staatsrechtslehre*. We have seen that Kelsen clearly rejected any personification of the State, the idea that the State had a "will," that it could be identified with a "person," and so forth. He thus elaborated on a different concept of the "will of the State," which became a "center of legal imputation" ("Zurechnung") of a series of actions that had to be considered as "actions of the State": such actions were "imputed" to the State by the application of rules. For Kelsen this was the only valid way of interpreting the concept of the "will of the state."[43] The de-personalization of the "will of the State" thus implied a re-definition of the meaning of the Parliament and the legislative process itself. Parliament could no more be considered the "organ" of the State and the State could no more be considered as the main actor of the legislative process. The latter was "legally imputed" to the State, but its political content was entirely determined by the legislative body, which Kelsen defined as "the organ of the society."[44] Against late-nineteenth-century legal positivism, Kelsen did something innovative in legal and in political terms: he theorized and stressed the connection between the legislative moment and the social body. The key premises to this were, in my opinion, the de-personalization of the State and the formulation of the "legal imputation" concept. It was by means of the Parliament that the vitality and pluralism of the society could penetrate into the State, determining the (political) content of the law, according to specific rules.[45] Some years before, and more exactly in a brief essay entitled "Wählerlisten und Reklamationsrecht" published in 1907, Kelsen had somehow anticipated this concept by stating—differently, for example, from Georg Jellinek's *Staatslehre*—that the right to vote was the right to make one's interests represented, because "the deputy is not only part of a collective boy but also someone who represents social interests."[46]

It is important to notice that in 1907 the Austrian Empire was involved in a massive electoral reform enlarging the right to vote in favor of popular masses.[47] Kelsen finally stated the connection between the legislative body and society in his *Hauptprobleme der Staatsrechtslehre*, where we can read:

> There must necessarily be a point—writes Kelsen—in which the current of social life enters the State body again, a place of passage where the amorphous elements of society penetrate into the fixed forms of State and Law. It is the place where customs and morals, where economic interests and religious interests become legal propositions (i.e. norms), content of the State will: the legislative act. Thus the process of forming the State's will is, so to speak, the umbilical cord that durably binds the form of the State to the material womb of society.[48]

As we can argue from the aforementioned passage, Kelsen looked at society as a plural entity: in the next pages, we are going to examine the pluralistic connotation of Kelsen's theory of democracy (social, ideal, political pluralism). For now, I would like to recall the reader's attention to the fact that already in the *Hauptprobleme der Staatsrechtslehre*, Kelsen depicted an image of society that was everything but a monolithic subject supposed to be perfectly homogeneous. This aspect of Kelsen's reasoning is worth highlighting because it can be considered as strictly related to his likewise particular idea of the people. In the *Hauptprobleme der Staatsrechtslehre* and then in his essays on *Vom Wesen und Wert der Demokratie*, Kelsen defined the people as a complex, articulated, pluralistic reality.[49] He thus opposed thinkers such as Gerber and Laband, who looked at the people as a single, monolithic entity, as well as the Rousseauian concept of the people demonizing pluralism and the dialectic between the majority and the minority, which pluralism inevitably implies.[50]

Kelsen's legal theory, as it took shape between 1911 and 1920, ended up re-valuating the role of society within the political process and recognizing the central role played by Parliament, as an "organ of the society," in the making of political decisions. With his *Hauptprobleme der Staatsrechtslehre* Kelsen situated the legislative process as a whole within society.[51]

In fact, in a further passage of his work, Kelsen clarified that "a naïve turn of phrase attributes all acts that are part of legislation to the single human beings and groups that carry out these acts and not to the State [. . .] and that naïve turn of phrase surely hits the mark!"[52]

His idea of a vital connection between Parliament and society might have played a role in stimulating Kelsen's interest for the major political events occurring on the Austrian soil in the early twentieth century. The years following the first edition of *Hauptprobleme der Staatsrechtslehre* were rich of events and changes for Kelsen, his country, and Europe itself. The outbreak of World War I was a turning point for Austria: the multinational and multilinguistic Habsburg Empire—which might have influenced Kelsen's attention to the issue of pluralism—came to an end between 1918 and 1919. In 1919 a Constitutional Assembly, including the major political forces of the country (Social Democrats, Christian Socials, and Nationalists) gathered together to establish a constitution and new institutions which had to be republican and democratic. The articulated and heated debate within the Assembly showed the political relevance of Kelsen's intuition about pluralism. The Assembly hosted a plurality of political actors embodying a variety of different ideas, projects, and interests.[53] For now, I would stress one core element showing us how far Kelsen's reflection on the meaning of Parliament and the legislative process, with its pluralistic implication, from his point of view were relevant beyond his work on legal theory. Within the particular historical and political context following to the collapse of the Empire, one of the many issues debated by Austrian parties was the kind of voting system to adopt for the election of the Constitutional Assembly. Kelsen decided to give his personal contribution to such debate by publishing a series of articles—entitled *Das Proportionalwahlsystem* (*Proportional Voting System*), *Der Proporz im Wahlordnungsentwurf* (*Proportional in the Voting System Project*), and *Ein einfaches Proportionalwahlsystem* (*An Easy Proportional Voting System*)—in two of the major newspapers of his country, *Arbeiter Zeitung* and *Österreichicher Volkswirt*. It is quite interesting to observe that just these articles contained a series of argumentations, which Kelsen was going to develop in his popular works on *Vom Wesen und Wert der Demokratie*. These were related to the concept of political representation and to that of the best voting system to enhance within a democratic government.[54]

Kelsen immediately took a clear distance from the past Habsburg electoral system, which—in his opinion—was based on an internal contradiction between universal suffrage—introduced in 1907—and the division of the electoral body into constituencies according to "arbitrary" territorial criteria.[55] For Kelsen, such division had perverted the ultimate sense of political representation by creating an artificial separation between "urban and rural constituencies," while paradoxically providing the minority of voters with the majority of seats within the legislative assembly. In this way, the relationship between electors and who they voted had been falsified and altered. In his opinion, consciousness of such unjust mechanism had to become the guiding light of the post-Habsburg political forces. If the ultimate goal was to establish a true parliamentary democracy, a true "Volksvertretung" ("representation of the people") had to be carried out. In order to do that, no artificial divisions of the electorate had to be accepted.[56] The "Wahlkörper" ("the electing body") was a "unity" and thus the whole country ("Staatsgebiet")—in Kelsen's opinion—had to be considered as one, single constituency.[57]

In my opinion, the unitary connotation of the electoral body did not contradict Kelsen's idea of pluralism as a blueprint of society: it was simply a way to stress that the electoral body consisted of subjects having all the same political rights and the same right to express their political preference in any part of the country. The intimate connection between pluralism and the unity of the "electing body" emerged from Kelsen's open defense of the proportional system, which was, for him, the only mechanism capable of giving voice to the minorities and to a pluralism of ideas and interests. Each political force—Kelsen underscored—deserved to be "represented in proportion to its numerical strength," that is, according to the "Personalitätsprinzip" ("personality principle") which had to replace the traditional "Territorialprinzip" ("territorial principle"), dating back to the Habsburg period, and based on the majority voting system.[58]

Kelsen's critique of the Habsburg electoral mechanism followed, in my opinion, two objectives: on the one hand, he seemed to push for a concrete

and effective break with the past, and on the other, he seemed to use that critique precisely to express his idea of democracy. Kelsen's reasoning as developed in his articles already contained a large part of his political vision. This
clearly emerged when Kelsen identified the more stringent reasons that made
the proportional voting mechanism preferable to the majoritarian one. The
latter changed political competition into a "race," in which the "winner" took
it all, to the detriment of the "loser." The electoral contraposition became
thus a "battle" which inevitably was doomed to exacerbate the relationships
between the majority and the minority.[59]

If all citizens were provided with political rights and if—inevitably—there
was a pluralism of interests and ideas characterizing the legislative body,
the body could not represent only and exclusively those having the majority of votes. The minority deserved to be adequately represented because,
for Kelsen, a true democratic legislative process could never be the result
of a majority unilaterally imposing its will on the minority. Bills had to
be rather the outcome of a "compromise" between the majority and the
minority within the Parliament.[60] The true function of the minority was not
so much—as stated by a large part of nineteenth-century European liberalism—to control the majority, as to influence the majority political decisions,
which meant the political content of the law. This was feasible only if the
minority was given a broad representation within the Parliament.[61] Yet, the
concept of compromise—which plays a crucial role in all Kelsen's writings
on democratic theory—should be situated within a broader reflection on the
meaning of democracy, which already at that time, showed the importance
of Jean Jacques Rousseau's thought for Kelsen. I will focus on this particular aspect in the next pages, when discussing about the two editions of *Vom
Wesen und Wert der Demokratie* but I think that it is quite relevant to observe
that the first declared "encounter" between Kelsen and Rousseau dates
back to his 1918 articles. In the incipit of "Das Proportionalsystem" Kelsen
acknowledged Rousseau's merit in giving a convincing and robust definition of democracy as "self-determination," which meant that citizens were
free because they obeyed laws, which they directly made. In other words,
for Kelsen, Rousseau had perfectly realized that, politically speaking, a full
democratic freedom implied the coincidence between the rulers and the ruled.
Although Kelsen rejected direct democracy as merely unfeasible, he thought
that it was possible, at precise conditions, to approach "self-determination."
One of these conditions was just the enhancement of the proportional system.
A widespread political representation of the minorities would prevent the
majority from making "diktats" and this would soften the minorities' sensa-
tion of being merely subject to the will of the "winners." In other words, for
Kelsen, it would soften the dichotomy between the rulers and the ruled.[62]
Kelsen ended up providing us with a democratic justification of the minority

representation. He would re-propose a strongly similar kind of argumentation in both of his essays on *Vom Wesen und Wert der Demokratie*.

In 1918 Kelsen sketched a political reflection which was critical toward the past Habsburg electoral logic and supportive of a parliamentary democracy based a strong representation of the minority and compromise. The collapse of the Empire, the political debate among the major parties of his country, the necessity to elect a Constitutional Assembly, and his role of intellectual and academic of public prestige were all key factors pushing Kelsen to express his opinion on the challenges which, according to him, his country had to face to establish a functioning democracy. But what was the meaning of democracy? And how did a democratic government work? Kelsen tried to answer this question in 1920, with the first edition of *Vom Wesen und Wert der Demokratie*.

THE ENEMY OUTSIDE: DEMOCRACY AND PLURALISM IN THE FACE OF THE SOVIET REGIME

Historical events and changes matter. If it is true that there is a direct connection between Kelsen's articles on the proportional voting system and his time, it is likewise true that trying to analyze the first edition of *Vom Wesen und Wert der Demokratie* and all his political writings regardless of the political and historical dimension would give a partial view of his democratic theory. Yet, it would be no less partial if we looked at such writings merely as Kelsen's particular and contingent response to contingent problems. I will seek to show how concrete historical-political events and political ideals, such as a particular way of conceiving democracy, intertwined in his works. The text of the first edition of *Vom Wesen und Wert der Demokratie* was initially considered by Kelsen as a *Vortrag* (paper), which he read in 1919 for the "Wiener Juristische Gesellschaft" (Wien Legal Society). One year later, with no substantial changes, Kelsen published the paper as an autonomous essay. It was a complex and delicate time for Austria: the country was moving toward a democratic republic, within a European context characterized by similarly relevant political and institutional transformations. In 1919 the German democratic constitution (the Weimar constitution) was officially promulgated, while the echo of the Russian Revolution of 1917 still resounded powerfully in many parts of the Continent. The end of World War I was in fact hallmarked by the blooming of Workers and Soldiers' Councils in Germany and Austria, which took inspiration from the soviet ones.[63] The weight of history emerged from the first pages of *Vom Wesen und Wert der Demokratie*, when Kelsen reminded that in the early twentieth century the meaning of democracy was violently attacked by those radical forces, namely Bolsheviks, who opposed "false democracy"—based on civil and political rights but not on a perfect social equality—with the "true democracy." The latter would have been carried out through—as Marx taught in the *Manifesto of the Communist Party*—the "dictatorship of the proletariat." In particular, Kelsen was referring to the bolshevik claim to replace the Czarist Empire with a true, just democracy. To him, such claim was groundless: most importantly the political impact of the bolshevik Revolution was such that it became necessary to define the correct meaning of democracy.[64] His writing of 1920 could be interpreted in first instance as his personal opposition to Bolshevism and the soviet Revolution.[65]

The soviet Revolution posed a serious challenge to parliamentary democracy and Kelsen wanted to respond to it by investigating the meaning of democracy. This implied, for him, to make a fundamental distinction between "real" and "ideal" democracy.[66] The term "ideal" coincided sometimes with "ideological" which—at least in his political writings—was a synonymous of "masquerade."[67]

I will argue how—despite his claims to analyze democracy in a rigorous scientific way which was thus anti-ideological—Kelsen used precisely the distinction between "real" and "ideal" to defend a specific kind of democracy—parliamentary, representative, and pluralist—in opposition to the just-born soviet regime and in support of the principle of pluralism. Investigating and defining the *essence* of democracy evidently implied to defend it against its opponents.[68]

From a perspective of the history of political thought, the aforementioned distinction between "real" and "ideal" might relate to that European tradition of political thought, which from Machiavelli formerly wanted to define and highlight the gap between reality and ideal in politics.[69] In particular, between the late nineteenth century and the early twentieth centuries, Italian Elitists such as Gaetano Mosca, Vilfredo Pareto, and the German but Italian-naturalized Robert Michels followed precisely in the wake of that tradition. Italian Elitists insisted on the hiatus between the ideal meaning of democracy—people's sovereignty—and its reality characterized by the (unavoidable) existence of an élite ruling over the mass.[70] Kelsen aimed at a realistic reflection on democracy and, similarly to Italian Elitists—although he was very far politically from their conservative tendencies[71]—he underscored the inevitable split between the rulers and the ruled within a democratic system.[72]

Kelsen's search for a realistic understanding of democracy started from a critical analysis of Rousseau as "the major democratic theorist."[73] Like in his 1918 articles, he thought in fact that the Geneva philosopher had expressed the ideal meaning of democracy, in the most effective way, as that form of government based on the principle of "self-determination," that is, on the identification between the rulers and the ruled.[74] Only in this case, laws would no more have been the expression of an oppressive and heteronomous power but rather the expression of the *volontè general*.[75] Kelsen depicted Rousseau as the theorist of direct democracy and therefore substantially hostile to representative government, which, for the author of the *Contract social* (*Social Contract*) was a remarkable limitation to the principle of "self-determination."[76]

The Rousseauian ideal of democracy was, to Kelsen's eyes, far from the reality of democracy, because in the latter the separation between the rulers and the ruled was ineradicable. Perfect "self-determination" was unfeasible for Kelsen: within real democracy social order as "heteronomy"[77] was inevitable and two of the most effective examples of this were the "fiction" (*Finktion*)[78] of parliamentary representation and the majority principle.[79]

In a footnote, Kelsen highlighted two relevant aspects: first, the Parliament was the "organ of the State," rather than the "organ of the People," and second, political representation was really a "fiction" because the Parliament did not represent the "will of the people," as the "will of the State."[80] The discrepancy with the definition of the Parliament as an "organ of the society," which we find in *Hauptprobleme der Staatsrechtslehre*, was evident. Kelsen was straightforward: "the fiction of the people's representation by means of the Parliament has a political bias. The dogma of the people's sovereignty ascribes the legislative power to the people. The fiction of the representation preserves this dogma, although the division of labor delegated legislative power to a special body."[81]

In the first edition of *Vom Wesen und Wert der demokratie* a relevant change of perspective thus took shape. How should this be interpreted? The definition of the people's representation as a "fiction" evokes the previously mentioned Italian Elitist critique of the people's sovereignty. It is reasonable to suppose that Kelsen could have some kind of familiarity with this literature, not only because these thinkers were quite popular during the first half of the twentieth century but also because he mentioned the works of Vilfredo Pareto and Robert Michels in the second edition of *Vom Wesen und Wert der demokratie*.[82] Another interpretation might be the direct connection that Kelsen established in the aforementioned passage between "the division of labor" and the idea of the parliamentary representation as a "fiction." Already during the French Revolution, one of its leading theorists, Emmanuel Joseph Sieyès, related the division of labor to political representation. In his opinion, since citizens were much more focused on economic activities, they were less inclined to directly participate in public affairs. Some years later, the Geneva political philosopher and constitutionalist Benjamin Constant—one of the spiritual fathers of early European liberalism—identified the political representation as the blueprint of "modern liberty" (in opposition to the "ancient liberty"). In his *De la Libertè des Anciens comparée a celle des Modernes* (*The Liberty of Ancients Compared with That of Moderns*) (1819), Constant argued—similarly to Sieyès—that the complexity of social organization and the involvement of citizens in commercial activities made political representation the best and the only plausible mechanism to take political decisions and thus to rule.[83]

In the late nineteenth century Max Weber returned on this concept by connecting the aftermath of a representative and indirect democracy with the development of a more and more complex social system forcing delegation of political decisions. Behind that term "division of labor," there was thus a long-term tradition of political thought, which somehow might have reached Kelsen. For sure, Kelsen knew Weber's work: in the first edition of *Vom Wesen und Wert der Demokratie* the Austrian legal theorist quoted Weber's *Parlament und Regierung im neugeordneten Deutschland* (*Parliament and Government in Germany*) (1918). I think that Kelsen was influenced by the German sociologist, while defining the Parliament as an "organ of the State" and denouncing the parliamentary representation as a "fiction."[84]

At the same time, the use of this specific term "fiction" might have been influenced by the philosopher Hans Vaihinger: in 1919 Kelsen published an essay, in which he devoted particular attention to Vaihinger's theory of "als ob" ("as if"). Starting from the Kantian premise, according to which knowledge could not reach phenomena *in se*, Vaihinger elaborated on humans' ability to create "fictional explanations" to understand and manage reality.[85] Kelsen might be indebted to Vaihinger for his idea of political representation as a "fiction."[86]

Yet, my argumentation so far does not explain one core element. Kelsen openly defined the Parliament as an "organ of the State" in the first edition of 1920, why just in that work? In my opinion, we should take into account the impact of historical context and more precisely Kelsen's anti-bolshevik declaration of intents. In *Vom Wesen und Wert der Demokratie*, Kelsen devoted special attention to the soviet system and to Lenin's political doctrine as developed in *State and Revolution* (1917). Kelsen connected Lenin's *State and Revolution*, the soviet experience and Karl Marx: he stressed how radical Lenin's attack on parliamentarism and representative democracy was and how the bolshevik leader invoked "pure democracy" against indirect, parliamentary democracy. In such a claim, Kelsen saw a direct reference to Marx's *The Civil War in France* (1871), where the Paris Commune—established after the French defeat in the French-Prussian war—had been seen by the German-Jewish philosopher as the realization of a true proletarian, direct democracy.[87]

Kelsen's critical interpretation of Marx and Lenin should be situated within a broader context of reflection. In 1920 Kelsen published a long essay entitled *Sozialismus und Staat* (*Socialism and State*), in which he systematically criticized marxist political and economic ideology, by arguing that Marx ended up sketching a fundamentally anarchic kind of future, communist democracy: a society without a State. Most importantly, in this work Kelsen identified in marxism a direct connection between the anarchic component and the tendency toward direct democracy within.[88] Similarly to *Sozialismus und Staat*, in *Vom Wesen und Wert der Demokratie*, Kelsen wanted to show first of all how Marx's and Lenin's work shared the same, ferocious critique of parliamentarism and indirect democracy. It was in the light of such idealism that—according to Kelsen—the soviet system had been interpreted by Lenin and his followers as an extraordinary experiment of "true democracy," "direct democracy," capable of subverting the rules and the limits of the traditional representative institutions.[89]

Against the bolshevik claims, Kelsen replied that the Soviets were themselves nothing but "small parliaments." For him, the Bolsheviks had replaced the Czarist regime with a plethora of micro-parliaments, generating the exact opposite of what Lenin dreamed in *State and Revolution*, that is, an "hypertrophy of parliamentarism." The latter became inevitable for Kelsen when trying to carry out the principle of direct democracy within a context of social complexity and diversification: Kelsen had learned Weber's lesson very well.[90]

Here, in my opinion, Kelsen's definition of the parliamentary representation as a "fiction" acquired and showed all its political significance. In front of the "dogma" of the people's sovereignty and the belief that only the people were the true subject of the legislative process, Kelsen stated that the legislative process was in the hands of the Parliament as an "organ of the State," that is, that real democracy was necessarily indirect. Looking at soviet Russia and Lenin's claims of creating a "pure," direct democracy, Kelsen replied that this was unfeasible because the Soviet themselves acted like small parliaments. The representative mechanism could not be overcome, not even in Russia. For Kelsen, what made the soviet regime profoundly different from any democratic government was rather the fact that the former unlike the latter did not recognize equal civil and political rights.[91] He mentioned the constitution of 1920 adopting a voting system, which discriminated the bourgeoisie and thus provided the right to vote according to a criterion of socio-economic belonging. In this, Kelsen saw the rejection of one of the key components of a real democracy: the universality of political rights. Similarly to his 1918 articles, in *Vom Wesen und Wert der Demokratie*, Kelsen argued that a democratic government was based on a "Wahlkörper" made up of citizens all provided with full political rights, regardless of the place where they lived, the class they belonged to, and so on. In this sense, for Kelsen, there was no substantial difference between the voting system of the Habsburg Empire and that of soviet Russia: both were not fully democratic.[92]

I think that the soviet experience greatly influenced Kelsen's reflection on democracy in the early twentieth century and I think also that it played a crucial role in his formulation of the parliamentary representation as a "fiction."[93]

Once real democracy is identified as indirect and representative, one big issue remained open: how were political decisions concretely taken within the legislative assembly? Kelsen was extremely clear on this point: the decision-making process followed the majority principle. The latter was evidently one of the core differences between real and ideal democracy. The full principle of "self-determination"—that is, the coincidence between the rulers and the ruled—could not admit that decisions were taken according to the majority criteria: only those belonging to the "majority" would be technically free in the Rousseauian sense of the term, because only the majority would obey laws, which would perfectly reflect its will. In his *Contract Social*, Rousseau conceptually neutralized the problem of the minority, by stating that laws entailed the general will and therefore "each time an opinion contrary to mine prevailed, it simply meant that I made a mistake." Dissent and the concept of minority itself ended up by losing their validity and raison d'etre. They had to be considered as the effect of one's inability to comprehend general will, which could never be mistaken because it pursued the "common good."[94]

Kelsen could not follow Rousseau's direction,[95] nor could he admit unanimity, which was materially unfeasible within a context of pluralism (of ideals, of values, both social and political). He had to develop a justification of the majority principle, which provided the recognition of the minorities and pluralism. More concretely, for Kelsen this implied understanding how to soften that heteronomous connotation of decisions taken according to majority principle. The latter could not be eliminated, but the adoption of a particular voting system capable of providing wide and articulated representation within the Parliament would enable the minority to influence the majority and prevent the laws from being the simple majority diktat. This voting system was proportional: using it, the minority would count on a strong representation in the Parliament, and although decisions would be taken according to the majority criteria, the minority would have the opportunity to make its voice resound. More specifically, a visible and structured parliamentary representation of the minority was to be assumed to render political "compromises" feasible, which were the specific form of the influence of the minority over the majority.[96] Similarly to his 1918 articles, Kelsen formulated a democratic defense of the minority and of the proportional system. The virtuous political process carried out through the proportional voting system—assuming full civil and political rights for all citizens—would, in Kelsen's view, soften the division between the rulers and the ruled, between the majority and the minority. As a result of this, a truly modern and civilized political debate and life would take shape instead of a frontal struggle.[97]

In other words, for Kelsen, it was impossible to eliminate the split between the rulers and the ruled; that is, it was impossible to erase the fundamentally heteronomous component of political decisions taken according to majority mechanism, but it was possible to reduce it. His stance in favor of this particular voting system was original for that time in Europe: historically speaking, the proportional mechanism was adopted for the first time in Europe after World War I.[98]

A sort of hidden tendency toward the principle of unanimity has been seen by some scholars behind Kelsen's defense of the minority: that defense is presumed to work in its best insomuch as the distance between the majority and the minority is softened, through the proportional system. It would seem—quite paradoxically—that Kelsen, searching for a realistic definition of democracy, ended up being closer to Rousseau's allegedly ideal democracy than he would have admitted.[99]

I maintain that this kind of reasoning does not consider two points, which are particularly relevant from my perspective. First, ideal democracy had, in Kelsen's thought, two implications: on the one hand, it represented the opposite pole of real democracy within a political reflection aiming at a realistic definition of democracy. On the other, it represented a sort of goal, which could never been completely achieved, while remaining a point of reference, a permanent stimulus for real democracy: in Kelsen, the realistic attitude co-existed with a sort of *tension* toward the ideal. What is interpreted as an inner contradiction or a point of weakness within his democratic theory is rather, in my opinion, the expression of its complexity and of the complex relationship between Kelsen and Rousseau, which cannot be reduced to a mere refusal of the former toward the latter. Second, the objections previously mentioned do not take into account that Kelsen' s defense of the minority and of the proportional system as the best option did not have only a democratic connotation, but also a liberal one. The latter allows me to show how the alleged danger of a tendency toward unanimity is more apparent than substantial.

If it is true that, historically speaking, European liberalism (both British and Continental) has developed and changed over centuries, there are some core concepts and principles which have remained unchanged. As correctly observed, liberalism as a political theory is based on "a view of power as limited in order to protect individuals' freedom," on "society dynamism," and on a "fear towards conformism."[100] The works of all major European liberal intellectuals seem to share these principles: from John Locke to John Stuart Mill, from Immanuel Kant to Alexis de Tocqueville, and from Isaiah Berlin to Raymond Aron and Luigi Einaudi, to mention some iconic figures. In particular, one of the conditions identified to grant "power as limited" was to combat the "tyranny of the majority." The latter has been interpreted, for example, as the tyranny of public opinion or as the tyranny of the majority against the minority within the Parliament. Tocqueville with his *Démocratie en Amérique* gave a unique contribution to the theorization of this concept.[101]

In 1920 *Vom Wesen und Wert der Demokratie* Kelsen openly spoke about the "power abuses" committed by the majority, which he defined slightly ironically "the Queen of democracy." He warned against the majority and the dangers of its tyranny, which—as he stressed—were "not less fearsome than that of an absolute monarch."[102] His words echoed, in my opinion, Alexis de Tocqueville's lesson. The fact that Kelsen did not openly refer to such thinker or that in his political writings the footnotes apparatus was almost absent does not imply that there was no connection between his political theory and the rich tradition of European political thought. In my opinion, his definition of "fundamental rights" as "a bulwark" against the majority abuses can be traced back to the heritage of European liberalism.[103]

I have been focusing on the issue of the "tyranny of the majority" because such a concept proves particularly interesting for a more articulated under-standing of Kelsen's defense of the proportional system: "within representa-tive democracy—Kelsen stated—the protection of the minority found its most perfect expression in the proportional principle."[104] Kelsen identified the latter with a means to defend the minority against the potentially dangerous majority. It is true that from this point onwards, Kelsen stressed that such protection was functional to a greater proximity to ideal democracy while remaining within the real and representative one. Yet, he seemed also to pro-mote a consistent liberal argumentation in favor of the proportional. In fact, in the history of European political thought, the very idea of protection of the minority being necessary, the consciousness that the majority could act like a tyrant, the recall to fundamental rights as an instrument to protect the minor-ity, all belong to the tradition of liberalism and—since the late nineteenth century—to that of liberal-democratic thought.[105]

With regard to this specific point, there was, in my opinion, another rel-evant aspect joining Kelsen's democratic theory to liberalism: the democratic and liberal defense of the proportional system assumed one fundamental condition, that is, the existence of social and political pluralism of values, of ideals.[106] In Kelsen, the very dichotomy between majority and minority existed because of such pluralism. To this effect—although the Parliament was now defined by Kelsen as an "the organ of the State"—there was a sub-stantial continuity between the *Hauptprobleme der Staatsrechtslehre* and the first edition of *Vom Wesen und Wert der demokratie*. The issue of pluralism was crucial in the second edition of his writing on democracy too. In his

1929 work, the dichotomy between real and ideal democracy persisted as well as the issue of political representation and the central role played by the proportional system. Yet, in my opinion, Kelsen concentrated much more on the parliamentary mechanism, whereas parliamentarism and parliamentary democracy were both the object of ferocious attacks from many European radical forces: both from extreme left and from extreme right.

THE ENEMY INSIDE: DEMOCRACY AND PLURALISM IN THE FACE OF RISING REACTIONARY FORCES

Like for the first edition, the second one has to be situated within its own historical and political context. The second and enriched *Vom Wesen und Wert der Demokratie* is still today Kelsen's most iconic and popular political writing.[107] It represents a deepening of ideas and intuitions already elaborated by Kelsen nine years earlier, while containing some aspects of diversity and further complexity. In the second edition, Kelsen analyzed the concept of the people and the parliamentary system much more in depth, by inserting in the book a series of reflections, which he had already developed some years earlier in *Das Problem des Parlamentarismus* (*The Problem of Parliamentarism*) (1925), the issue of political representation versus corporatist representation and the majority principle. Between 1920 and 1929 there was a shift in Kelsen's focus, which—in my opinion—had a direct connection with the historical context and even some events concerning his personal life.

During the 1920s, Europe appeared to external eyes as a crucible of intellectual and scientific greatness, instability and contradictions. Yet, political radicalization was increasing: parliamentary democracy was criticized for not being able to grant stability and prosperity.[108] Communists looked at soviet Russia and claimed to replace "formal" democracy with a "true" democracy based on social equality, whereas extreme-right forces of nationalist inspiration looked at Mussolini's Italy as a fruitful and successful experiment. After World War I most of European countries (chiefly in the Western part of the Continent) had opted for democratic and parliamentary institutions. In Germany, for example, a democratic and socially progressive Republic was established in 1919 and—as we have already seen—Austria had chosen democracy too. Yet, German Republic (the Weimar Republic) was characterized more and more by political paralysis with a government made up of parties much more interested in endless disputes than in ruling.[109] In Kelsen's country the situation was not much better: despite the ambition to found a progressive democracy and an apparently satisfactory compromise between the Socialist Democrats and the conservative forces, since the mid-1920s it became more and more evident that the intention of right wing parties (Christian Socials and Nationalists) was to concentrate the political control into their hands.[110]

A turning point was the 1929 financial crisis, which contributed to the rise of the Nazis in Germany (1933) and that of Clerical Fascists in Austria (1934). During the 1920s Kelsen was Professor of law in Vienna and a prominent public figure. He was also a member of the Austrian Constitutional Court, which—as we are going to see in the next chapter—he contributed to create.[111] He occupied prestigious roles, which enabled him to have a privileged viewpoint on what was happening in his country. Throughout the 1920s, Kelsen continued to have a clear interest in politics and in democratic theory, which seemed to be reinforced due to the growing problems of Austrian and European democratic governments.

Faced with radical and anti-system forces claiming a revolutionary overthrow of democratic and parliamentary institutions, Kelsen published in 1926 an essay entitled *Soziologie der Demokratie* (*Sociology of Democracy*). The analogy with the anti-soviet and anti-marxist connotation of the first edition of *Vom Wesen und Wert der demokratie* clearly emerged. Kelsen's true aim was to use the anti-marxist critique to re-state his political view in opposition to those forces attacking democratic institutions. He criticized Marx's theory of the "proletarian revolution" and "class violence"[112] as a means to establish a new society of equal and free people the democratic principle.[113] In Kelsen's opinion the "class conflict" could only be peacefully fixed only within a democratic system, because the latter was essentially based in its essence on the dialectic between the majority and the minority, that is, on a compromise-oriented logic.[114]

The absolute centrality of the latter within Kelsen's thought is also proved by the fact that just one year earlier—in his *Allgemeine Theorie der Normen* (*General Theory of Norms*)—he identified five aspects characterizing the compromise, among which three of the most relevant, politically speaking, were (1) compromise as a means to connect instead of dividing; (2) compromise as a means of integration; and (3) compromise as functional to the shaping of the majority itself. I will illustrate that each of these three principles—which were somehow already present in 1920 *Vom Wesen und Wert der Demokratie* and in 1918 articles—were systematically re-proposed and deepened by Kelsen in his work of 1929.[115] We have seen that *Soziologie der Demokratie* was underpinned by Kelsen's personal and intellectual urgency to take a stance in favor of parliamentary democracy. The same kind of urgency again emerged from the second edition of *Vom Wesen und Wert der demokratie*.

1929 was not only the year of the financial debacle in the United States and in Europe; it was a year full of relevant political events for Austria itself and for Kelsen, personally as well. The Austrian constitution was reformed: there was a shift in the balance of power in favor of executive power, to the detriment of the legislative one. That reform was used by the Christian Socials to prevail over the Social Democrats and make the Austrian Republic an authoritarian regime.[116] Within this complex context, Kelsen again investigated the meaning and the implications of parliamentary democracy in a time of crisis. For Kelsen, in the late 1920s the real and most dangerous threat to democratic institutions came from reactionary forces, which were impressively growing in most of Europe, including in his country. In particular, all these forces attacked political representation and parliamentarism as ineffective and incapable of fixing the most urgent problems of the time.[117]

Kelsen realized that the true target of these critiques and attacks were political party pluralism seen as a source of fragmentation and chaos. Corporatist representation was opposed to purely political representation whose actors—as Kelsen himself reminded us—were political parties and the alleged unity of the people was opposed to pluralism, be it social, value, political, or ideal. Not only political forces were involved in these attacks: we can observe that some of the most prominent intellectuals considered pluralism and party pluralism as a curse for the Continent, as the ultimate reason for instability, and as a threat to the unity of the State and the people. Focusing on the German-speaking context, we could mention Ignaz Seipel, Heinrich Triepel, and Carl Schmitt.[118]

Kelsen's 1929 writing was based on an adamant intuition: whoever wanted to reflect on the meaning of democracy at that time, while defending it from its enemies had to face two core issues—reciprocally intertwined—pluralism (notably party pluralism) and the political representation mechanism. Like in the first edition, Kelsen commenced from the Rousseauian definition of ideal democracy and the distinction between ideal and real democracy.[119]

In ideal democracy, the people were assumed as a perfect unity, because—as Kelsen stressed—only conceiving them as a unity allowed us to think it as a truly "subject of power": Rousseau's echo was evident. Yet, in real democracy, the people were nothing but a "plural entity": "the people emerges as divided by religious, national and economic contrasts—Kelsen wrote—to the eyes of a sociologist, the people appear as a multiplicity of separate groups."[120]

The only conceivable unity for Kelsen was "normative" and thus "legal": the people was a unity only because it was subject to the unitary legal order, which was the State. Only as an "element of the State" the people represented a "unity." In this case—Kelsen argued—the people is the "object of the power."[121] Yet, one main issue remained to explore: how and to what extent could the people—which, sociologically speaking, were a plurality—participate in the making of political process? In other words, how were the people a "subject of power" within a real democracy? Kelsen's purpose here was, in my opinion, twofold. On the one hand, he wanted to identify the real role played by the people within a real democratic system, and on the other, he argued that the pluralistic identity of the people was perfectly compatible with the functioning of real democracy and furthermore: it was an integrative part of it. By stating this, he took a position diverging from most contemporary intellectuals.[122]

In political terms, the people's participation in decision-making process developed, according to Kelsen, on two levels: within the people, he identified those having political rights. Yet, within this group, it was necessary to make a fundamental distinction between those having such rights and those actually exercising them. With regard to the latter aspect, Kelsen introduced a further separation: that between those who exercised their political rights by following the influence of a specific person or group of persons and those exercising their rights in an active way, that is, by influencing their fellow citizens' vote.[123] Those capable of practicing such influence gathered in political parties, which were, for Kelsen, "one of the most important elements of democracy" because they put together individuals sharing the same opinion to grant them the opportunity to have an impact on public life."[124]

In open opposition to those intellectuals blaming political parties and pluralism for being the source of fragmentation and political instability, Kelsen reminded that the people had a pluralistic essence and that the people (at least a part of it) could participate in political life and take political decisions through political parties. With his second edition of *Vom Wesen und Wert der Demokratie* he actually contributed to the "rehabilitation of political parties" in a time in which they were often an object of ferocious denigration.[125]

For Kelsen: "modern democracy was based on political parties" and the full realization of the "democratic principle" relied on the existence of political parties and pluralism itself. In the light of this principle, Kelsen opposed to Heinrich Triepel and his idea of a fundamental incompatibility between the intrinsic unity of State and political parties. The latter would promote "egoistic" and "particularist" interest, which were, for Triepel, in open opposition to the "organic" nature of the State. In early postwar Europe, Triepel reproposed a concept of the State, which can be traced back to a long tradition of European organicist thought, which included jurists such as Johann Caspar Bluntschli and Otto Von Gierke.[126] In his *Staatsverfassung und die politische Parteien* (1927) (*State-constitution and Political Parties*), Triepel opposed political parties (and generally political party pluralism) as an expression of "atomistic-individualistic" tendencies with the State, seen as a social organism, which embodied the good for collectivity. Political parties were a dangerous breach in the life of the State because they threatened its unity.[127]

Triepel dreamed of a State above the parties during a historical and political period which was characterized by a "multi-party State based on masses" and therefore by the ultimate sunset of the late-nineteenth-century liberal parliamentarism.[128] Kelsen refused Triepel's argumentation by following two lines of reasoning: he stated that Triepel's invective against political parties was a threat to the unity of the State, because they would be imbued with "egoism," and had nothing scientific. It had to simply be considered as the expression of Triepel's own ideological view. For Kelsen, if looking at reality we had to admit that political parties were integrative parts of the State and that over time they succeeded as means for the formation of the political will of the State.[129]

Yet, Kelsen did not counter-reply to Triepel by portraying a defense of political parties as the supposed embodiment of "a solidaristic" and common "general interests." He stressed that political parties did nothing but organize individuals with same opinions, ideas, interests. This was precisely the aspect that made political parties so vital to real democracy. They gave voice, by means of a functioning organization, to a plurality of ideas, interests, and beliefs. By doing so, they made political "compromises" within Parliament feasible and therefore they contributed to the creation of political will, which could not express only "the interests of one single group."[130]

The people as a political entity and force capable of participating— although indirectly to political and public life—did exist, for Kelsen, by means of political parties because only the latter could change that plurality in structured and organized political forces. In the light of such a principle— which was not only a defense of political parties but also more deeply a defense of pluralism—Kelsen argued that the "hostility" to political parties "served to those political forces aiming at the supremacy of one single group of interests"[131]—a hostility which was profoundly anti-democratic. Here Kelsen identified a line connecting political parties, pluralism, and real democracy. That was the main reason, in my opinion, why Kelsen proposed to provide political parties, with a foundation within the constitution.[132] By this way, political parties could be officially recognized as having the role of creating the (content) of the State political will. At the same time, Kelsen thought that the transformation of political parties into "constitutional organs of the State" would promote inside them the development and strengthening of a truly democratic dynamics inside them. Kelsen was realistic enough to realize—as the Elitist Robert Michels showed in 1911 with his book *Die Soziologie der politischen Parteien* (*Sociology of Political Parties*)—that the internal structure of modern parties, including those professing ultra-democratic ideals, tended to be "aristo-autocratic."[133]

All Kelsen's reasoning on the (real) meaning of the people and political parties was functional, in my opinion, to analyze in depth the political role of the Parliament in depth. More than in the first edition of *Vom Wesen und Wert der demokratie*, Kelsen devoted a great attention to the legislative body, to its components, to its intrinsic logic, to political representation and the

representation mechanism. I am going to argue that precisely this aspect can
be seen in part as Kelsen's personal reply to those political forces, largely
spread around in his country at that time, which were pushing to replace
political representation with a corporatist representation.

Kelsen reminded in fact how Parliaments and parliamentarism had fallen
into disrepute across Europe: at his time, both were attacked almost daily by
the radical left and radical right. Communists continued to invoke a proletarian dictatorship, while reactionary movements pushed to establish a corporatist kind of representation.[134]

Again recalling the distinction between "real" and "ideal," Kelsen
observed that parliamentarism represented a strong blow to the (Rousseauian)
concept of ideal democracy as perfect self-determination. Kelsen wrote,
"Parliamentarism is the formation of the directive will of the State by means
of a collegial organ elected by the people on the basis of universal and equal
suffrage, i.e. democratic, according to the majority principle."[135] Similarly
to the first edition of *Vom Wesen und Wert der Demokratie*, Kelsen established that political representation was a "fiction" that was necessary for
maintaining the principle of people's sovereignty when, in reality, it was the
Parliament and not the People that made the laws. The fictionist connotation
of representation was sanctioned by the "free mandate" which did not bind
the elected to the wishes or "mandatory instructions" of the electors. In the
light of Weber's lesson, Kelsen again explained the infeasibility of direct
democracy and thus the creation of the Parliament as the historical result
of the extreme social complexity and diversification preventing citizens'
direct participation in political decisions.[136] Ideologically, Parliament and
parliamentarism had been justified in the name of the people's sovereignty.
Yet, in real terms, both were considered by Kelsen as the "compromise"
between the principle of people's sovereignty and the principle of "division of labor."[137] Faced with the early postwar democratic crisis—which in
1929 was extremely visible—Kelsen recalled that some actions aimed at
"reforming parliamentarism" would be however beneficial. These reforms
had to strengthen and implement the relationship between the rulers and
the ruled and soften the (inevitable) split between the two, to combat the
sense of disorientation and mistrust that many citizens in Europe seemed
to feel. He was surely thinking about the Weimar crisis, the slow but progressive conservative involution of his own country, and about the fact that
since 1922 Italy had been ruled by Fascists. In particular, Kelsen proposed
popular referendum and even to abolish the irresponsibility of the elected,
which—in his opinion—had turned into one of the main motives of disaf-
fection toward parliamentary democracy. If an imperative mandate was not
an option, such measures might have given citizens a stronger influence on
political decisions.[138]

I think that Kelsen's proposals once again entailed a fundamental tension between ideal and real democracy, similarly to the first edition of *Vom Wesen und Wert der Demokratie*. The former was unfeasible, but one could elaborate on the methods and means to get as close as possible to it: this was, in his opinion, one of the possible solutions to the crisis of democracy in his time.

Kelsen's argumentation also shows again how it would be simplistic to label him as anti-Rousseauian. As I have in fact sought to argue, in both editions of *Vom Wesen und Wert der Demokratie* Kelsen's defense of parliamentarism and representative democracy was related to the belief that there was an ideal democracy—never reachable—but necessary to consider as an ideal point of reference. Yet, Kelsen had still to identify the aspects, which made parliamentarism functional to real democracy and most importantly which made political representation preferable to corporatist representation. I maintain that his defense of political representation specifically targeted the filo-fascist and reactionary groups rising in his country. The latter were pushing—as Kelsen observed—to replace political and parliamentary representation with the corporatist-professional representation.[139] They stated that political representation was obsolete and incapable of giving voice to the true interests of society: with corporatist representation every professional group would have been given the right to participate in political decisions, on the basis of its relevance within society.[140]

Kelsen critically elaborated professional representation following two lines of reasoning: the first, professional representation was, for him, totally incapable of creating a political will, because it tended to a maximize diversification and divisions: "the corporatist idea can become true only if the professional group is based on a perfect community of interests." Kelsen argued that among professional groups "did not exist community, rather conflict of interests."[141]

Also, due to their intrinsic nature such groups would take only issues having a direct relation to their own interests into account. For Kelsen, when dealing with politics, there were always problems to fix and decisions to take, which went beyond the particularity of specific interests and which might be the source of contrasts precisely among the various professional groups. Kelsen portrayed professional representation as the source of a "huge differentiation," which would end up making political decisions simply chaotic, extremely difficult, or simply unfeasible. In addition, the realization of such a representation mechanism would never mean the creation of direct democracy: professional groups would merely replace political parties.[142]

Politically speaking, professional representation could not be applied to a democratic system: its inability to create a true dialogue among the groups in order to find common ground was undemocratic. It was undemocratic because it did not generate compromises, which—as we have already seen—were,

for Kelsen, the core of parliamentary democracy. He was against corporatist representation because it was a source of divisions, because it separated
people rather than connecting them: the defense of democracy and political
representation coincided with a clear-cut stance in favor of compromise.[143]

The relevance of anti-professional representation critique emerged also
from another Kelsenian essay—*Der Drang zur Verfassungsreform* (*The
Push of the Constitutional Reform*) (1929). Here, the Austrian legal theorist
critically examined the Christian Social proposal of a constitutional reform
including the creation of a "corporatist Chamber"—that is, a chamber with
a professional representation. The true purpose behind that proposal was,
for Kelsen, to destroy both parliamentarism and the parliamentary government because, in the late 1920s, the Social Democrats were the major force
precisely within the Austrian legislative assembly. Behind the conservatives'
plan for large-scale professional representation Kelsen was seeing a political
project aiming to dismantle political pluralism.[144]

I believe that Kelsen thus made a distinction between two types of pluralism—that embodied by professional groups, generating "conflicts of
interests," and that embodied by political parties generating "compromises."
In other words, only the latter was capable of creating a true "integration"
regardless of which, for him, no political and democratic will could take
shape.[145] How could political parties accomplish such an objective? Through
parliamentarism and the parliamentary system. In this sense, Kelsen was
replying to all those anti-democratic forces (notably, the reactionary ones
supporting the corporatist representation), which were gaining ground in his
time, and above he was elaborating a clear defense of pluralism.

More precisely, Kelsen focused on two levels of "integration." In the first
instance, he identified the majority principle as one of the key components of
real democracy, while distinguishing between its real and ideal significance.
In ideal terms, such principle would mean that the majority will (the will of
the larger number of people) prevail over the minority will. Yet—Kelsen
argued—if considering "social reality," such principle referred rather to the
fact that people organized themselves in two groups: majority and minority.
It is quite clear how Kelsen's argumentation aimed at neutralizing any con-
flictual connotation in the majority criteria.

Majority and minority seemed to be intimately connected with each other,
precisely because both were, for Kelsen, a form of rational organization by
means of which the huge variety of ideas and interests found a first level of
"integration" into a majority and a minority.[146]

The second level of integration, maybe the most important one, took place
through the parliamentary dialectic made by peaceful dialogue and discussion
among political parties. As a result of this, decisions taken according to the
majority principle would never be the "diktat" of the majority at detriment

of the minority but rather a result of compromises. Within the parliamentary system, pluralism could generate "integration," through the determining vehicle of political parties. Yet, parliamentarism needed some specific preconditions to properly work: civil and political rights for everyone and, again, a proportional voting system, which Kelsen justified exactly as he had nine years ago, that is, on the basis of its alleged ability to soften the separation between the rulers and the rules. Against anti-democratic forces and chiefly against those reactionaries in Austria who were preparing an authoritarian turn, Kelsen stated that (1) parliamentarism and political representation were the only means to effectively take political decisions within complex societies; (2) both presupposed pluralism and the majority principle; (3) the latter served as a first level of "integration" which was necessary to the decision-making process; (4) the second level of "integration" was identical to the special nature of parliamentary debate and dialectic, resulting in compromises and thus in the creation of a democratic political will.[147]

Those attacking political representation and parliamentarism as ineffective or obsolete were in reality trying to destroy democracy, because, according to Kelsen, they fundamentally refused pluralism and the possibility of finding a true social and political "integration." In the late 1920s concepts and terms such as "pluralism" and "integration" were far from being widespread and popular in Europe: Carl Schmitt, for example, blamed party pluralism for being one of the sources of radical divisions and thus of the Weimar collapse itself.[148] Kelsen was one of the few voices who stood out from the crowd, along with—for example—the legal theorist and sociologist Hermann Heller. It is a little ironic to observe that Heller, who was such as profoundly adverse to Kelsen's legal theory, shared with him precisely the idea that only political and parliamentary representation could contribute to achieve an effective political integration, as opposed to the corporatist "integration."[149]

It is true that—differently from Kelsen—for Heller, that integration could successfully take the place only if the working class was effectively integrated into the body politics and thus only if there was a true "social homogeneity," which needed a likewise true "social justice."[150] Yet, it is without doubt that Kelsen and Heller were two convinced supporters of political representation and parliamentarism, when both were the object of continuous attacks.

Kelsen's focus on parliamentarism and his defense of it were both much more marked in the second edition of *Vom Wesen und Wert der Demokratie*, than in the first one—maybe because the first edition dated back to a period which was still full of promises and hopes for the democratic future of Austria. In 1920 the "enemy" was physically far away—it was soviet Russia— whereas in 1929 the "enemy" was inside the Austrian borders: it was a group of reactionary political forces aiming to dismantle the democratic constitution and institutions. In 1929, Kelsen's attention was much more oriented toward the problem of rationally and credibly justifying political representation and parliamentarism, which were—more than nine years before—under a concentric attack. The weight of historical context and political reflection on the *essence* of democracy appeared profoundly intertwined.

NOTES

1. Edmund Bernatzik (1854–1919) was a professor of public law, with a profound interest in politics and Austrian constitutional development, as we can see from his work on the Austrian constitutional laws. It was thanks to Bernatzik that Kelsen could publish his degree thesis on *Die Staatslehre des Dante Alighieri* (*Dante Alighieri's theory of State*) on the prestigious review *Wiener Staatswissenschaftlichen Studien* in 1905; Felix Czeike, *Historische Lexikon* (Wien: Kreymar und Sherian, 1994), 103; Rudolf Adalar Métall, *Hans Kelsen. Leben und Werk* (Wien: Deuticke, 1969), 10. On Kelsen and Dante see: Oliver Lepsius, "Hans Kelsen's on Dante Alighieri's Political Thought," *European Journal of International Law* 27, no. 4 (November 1, 2016): 1155–1167.

2. Métall, *Hans Kelsen. Leben und Werk*, 2–10. Georg Jellinek (1851–1911) was one of the leading nineteenth-century German legal theorists. He was a legal positivist with a strong interest in the public law theory, international law and constitutional justice, although he was also a passionate scholar of the history of ideas and even history of religion. From 1883 to 1889 he taught at the University of Vienna, and then in 1891 he was awarded the chair of public law and international law at the University of Heidelberg. Jens Kersten, *Georg Jellinek und die klassische Staatslehre* (Tübingen: Mohr Siebeck, 2000), 17.

3. The *Hauptprobleme der Staatsrechtslehre* was originally Kelsen's doctoral dissertation, which was discussed in 1910. Kelsen had to defend his dissertation in front of a commission consisting of Edmund Bernatzik and Adolf Menzel, chair of constitutional law. Métall, *Hans Kelsen. Leben und Werk*, 10–15.

4. See: Carl Friedrich Von Gerber, *System des deutschen Privatesrechts* (Jena: F. Mauke, 1850); Paul Laband, *Deutsches Reichsstaatsrecht* (Tübingen: Mohr Siebeck, 1907).

5. Hans Kelsen, "Vorrede zur 1. Auflage," in Hans Kelsen, *Die Hauptprobleme der Staatsrechtslehre entwickelt aus der Lehre vom Rechtssatze* (Tübingen: Mohr Siebeck, 1923), III–XIII; Hans Kelsen, *Die Hauptprobleme der Staatsrechtslehre entwickelt aus der Lehre vom Rechtssatze*, (Tübingen: Mohr Siebeck, 1911), 97 ff. See on this point: Thomas Olechowski, "Kelsens Rechtslehre im Überblick," in *Hans Kelsen. Eine politikwissenschaftliche Einführung* (Wien: Manz, 2009), 47–62.

6. Michael Stolleis, *Geschichte des öffentlichen Rechts in Deutschland. Staatsrechhtslehre und Verwltungswissenschaft 1800–1914*, Bd. 2 (München: Verlag C. B. Beck, 1992), 330–455. See also: Losano, *Forma e realtà in Kelsen*, 28 ff.

7. Peter Caldwell, *Popular Sovereignty and the Crisis of German Constitutional Law: The Theory and Practice of Weimar Constitutionalism* (Durham North Carolina: Duke University Press, 1997), 15 ff. See also: Michael Stolleis, *Geschichte des*

öffentlichen Rechts in Deutschland. Staatsrechhtslehre und Verwltungswissenschaft 1914–1945, Bd. 3 (München: Verlag C. B. Beck, 1993), 42–44.

8. Georg Jellinek, *Das system der öffentlichen subjektiven Rechte* (Freiburg: Akademische Verlagsbuchhandlung, 1892).

9. Duncan Kelly, "Revisiting the Rights of Man: Georg Jellinek on Rights and the State," *Law and History Review* 22, no. 3 (Autumn 2004): 493–529.

10. Max Weber's influence might be behind the idea of a sociological understanding of the State. It is important to notice that Weber and Jellinek were good friends and colleagues at the University of Heidelberg, where both were members of the Eranos Circle, gathering intellectuals of different scientific disciplines who investigated the relationships between religion and economics, religion and politics, religion and society. Stefan Breuer, *Georg Jellinek und Max Weber. Von der soziale zur soziologischen Staatslehre* (Baden-Baden: Nomos Verlag, 1999), 56–57. On Jellinek's life, see: Kersten, *Georg Jellinek und die klassische Staatslehre*, 59–68.

11. Jellinek, *Das system der öffentlichen subjektiven Rechte*, 1892 and his *Allgemeine Staatslehre* (Berlin: Verlag von O. Häring, 1914).

12. Jellinek had devoted much effort, for example, to de-legitimize jusnaturalist theories and the concept itself of natural law as nothing but a philosophical invention or Weltanschauung. See: Jellinek, *Die Erklärungen der Bürger und Menschenrechte*, 2006. On Jellinek's legal theory, see: Wilhelm Hebeisen, *Die Souveränität in Frage gestellt: Die Souveränitätslehre von Hans Kelsen, Carl Schmitt und Hermann Heller im Vergleich.*

13. Kelsen, *Die Hauptprobleme der Staatsrechtslehre entwickelt aus der Lehre vom Rechtssatze* (1st ed.), 3–94; 189 ff. On this point, see: Baume, *Hans Kelsen and the Case for Democracy*, 7–8.

14. On Kelsen's idea of positive law, see: Kazimierz Opalek, "Kelsens Kritik der Naturrechtslehre," in *Ideologiekritik und Demokratietheorie bei Hans Kelsen*, 73.

15. Kelsen, *Die Hauptprobleme der Staatsrechtslehre entwickelt aus der Lehre vom Rechtssatze* (1st ed.), 33 ff.

16. See: Frederick H. Beiser, *Hermann Cohen. An Intellectual Biography* (Oxford: Oxford University Press, 2018); Dreier, *Rechtslehre, Staatssoziologie und Demokratiethorie bei Hans Kelsen*, 76–78. See also: Mario Garcìa Berger, "The Legal Norm as a Function: The Influence of Ernst Cassirer and the Marburg Neo-Kantians on Hans Kelsen," *Problema anuario de filosofía y teoría del derecho* (online) 12 (2018): 255–261; see: Paulson, *Die Rolle des Neukantianismus in der Reine Rechtslehre: eine Debatte zwischen Sander und Kelsen*. For a general introduction to Kelsen and neo-Kantianism, see: Peter Langford and Ian Bryan, "Introduction: The Kelsenian Critique of Natural Law," in *Hans Kelsen and the Natural Law Tradition*, in particular 18–35.

17. Hans Kelsen, "Vorrede zur 2. Auflage," in *Die Hauptprobleme der Staatsrechtslehre entwickelt aus der Lehre vom Rechtssatze* (2nd ed.), III–XXIII, in particular XVI–XXII.

18. Iain Stewart, "The Critical Science of Hans Kelsen," *Journal of Law and Society* 17, no. 3 (January 1991): 275–277.

19. Riccobono, *Antikelsenismo italiano*, 93.

20. Stewart, "The Critical Science of Hans Kelsen," 276. On the difference between "ought to and is" see also: Vinx, *Hans Kelsen's Pure Theory of Law. Legality and Legitimacy*, 39 ff.

21. Kelsen, *Die Hauptprobleme der Staatsrechtslehre entiwickelt aus der Lehre vom Rechtssatze* (1st ed.), 97 ff; 162–188; see also: 395–412.

22. Ibid., 97 ff. On Kelsen against Gerber, Laband and Jellinek, 450–655.

23. Ibid., 97–188; 450 ff.

24. Hans Kelsen, *Das Problem der Souveränität und die Theorie des Völkerrechts. Beitrag einer Reinen Rechtslehre* (Tübingen: Mohr Siebeck, 1920), III–VII; 9–47. Here, Kelsen founded the unity of the legal order on a "Ursprungnorm" which later—in his *Reine Rechtselehre* (Pure Theory of Law)—would become the "Grundnorm." Andreas Kalvyas, "The Basic Norm and Democracy in Hans Kelsen's Legal and Political Philosophy," *Philosophy and Social Criticism* 32, no. 5 (July 2006): 577.

25. Kelsen, *Das Problem der Souveränität*, 102 ff. The subtitle of *Das Problem der Souveränität* was *Die Theorie des Völkerrechts* (Theory of international law): in this book, the identification between State and Law became the first condition to found the primacy of international Law over the law of nation states. From Cohen, Kelsen had learned that the knowledge process determined the knowledge object. Since the legal knowledge was intrinsically unitary, its object—the law—would be the same too. From such premises, Kelsen argued that there was no split between international and national Law, that the latter was part of the first, which encompassed all national legal orders. Kelsen's approach to international law was original and innovative. Moreover, it would become functional to his pacifist theory, as he expressed it in his *Peace through Law*, which he published in 1944 when he was already in the United States. Here he stated that the primacy of the international law was the first condition to develop after the war an international cooperation (the "Permanent League for the Maintenance of Peace"), which would be the first step toward the building of an international federation, granting peace and stability on a global level. It is quite evident how Kelsen's pacifist project was similar to Kant's *For Perpetual Peace* and also to Christian Wolff's *civitas maxima* ideal. Hans Kelsen, *Peace through Law* (Chapel Hill: The University of North Carolina Press, 1944); see also: François Rigaux, "Hans Kelsen on International Law," *European Journal of International Law* 9, no. 2 (1998): 325–331.

26. See: Eugen Ehrlich, *Grundlegung der Soziologie des Rechts* (München und Leipzig: Duncker & Humblot, 1913–1914); Kelsen, *Eine Grundlegung der Rechtssoziologie*, 1915. Ehrlich counter-responded to Kelsen's reply, triggering a long dispute, which lasted until 1916. See: Renato Treves, "Sociologia del diritto e sociologia dell'idea di giustizia nel pensiero di Kelsen," *Sociologia del diritto* 3 (1981): 164–165.

27. Stolleis, *Geschichte des öffentlichen Rechts in Deutschland. Staatsrechhtslehre und Verwaltungswissenschaft 1914–1945*, Bd. 3, 166–186.

28. Hermann Heller (1891–1933) was one of the leading intellectuals of the Weimar Republic. Like Kelsen, he was Jewish and was born in the Austrian Empire

and studied law at the University of Vienna. He was a militant of the German social democratic Party. He left Germany after the nazi rise to power. On Heller as jurist and political thinker in comparison with Kelsen: See: Stolleis, *Geschichte des öffentlichen Rechts in Deutschland. Staatsrechhtslehre und Verwaltungswissenschaft 1914–1945*, Bd. 3, 190–194; see also in general: David Dyzenhaus, *Legality and Legitimacy. Carl Schmitt, Hermann Heller and Hans Kelsen* (Oxford: Oxford University Press, 2003).

29. Hermann Heller, "Souveränität. Ein Beitrag zur Theorie des Staats-und Völkerrechts," in Hermann Heller *Gesammelte Schriften*, Bd. 2, hrsg. Christoph Müller (Leiden: A. W. Sijthoff, 1971), 39 ff.

30. Ibid., 68–92.

31. Ibid., 97.

32. Petra Gümplova, "Hans Kelsen's Critique of Sovereignty," in *Jurisprudence and Political Philosophy in the 21st Century*, vol. 2, ed. Miograd A. Jovanovič and Bojan Spaič (Frankfurt am Main: Peter Lang, 2012), chiefly 106 ff.

33. Gustavo Gozzi, "Rechtsstaat and Individual Rights in German Constitutional History," in *The Rule of Law. History, Theory and Criticism*, ed. Pietro Costa and Danilo Zolo (Berlin: Springer Verlag, 2007), 237–239.

34. Theo Öhlinger, "Represäntative, direkte und parlamentarische Demokratie," in *Indeologiekritik und Demokratietheorie bei Hans Kelsen*, 216–217.

35. Stephen Holmes, "Kelsen, Hans," in *The Encyclopedia of Democracy*, ed. Seymour M. Lipset (London: Routledge, 1995), 689.

36. For the anti-positivist resurgence after World War II see the comments in: Jestaedt-Lepsius, "Der Rechts- und Demokratietheoretiker Hans Kelsen. Eine Einführung," in Hans Kelsen, *Verteidigung der Demokratie*, hrsg. Matthias Jestaedt und Oliver Lepsius (Tübingen: Mohr Siebeck, 2006), IX.

37. For a recent study on the Habsburg Monarchy: Peter Judson, *The Hapsburg: A New History* (Cambridge: Belknap of Harvard University Press, 2016).

38. Robert A. Kann, *A History of the Hapsburg Empire 1526–1918* (California: California University Press, 1974), 367 ff.

39. Stewart, "The Critical Science of Hans Kelsen," 276–277; Clemens Jabloner, "Kelsen and His Circle: The Viennese Years," *European Journal of International Law* 9, no. 2 (1998): 372–373.

40. Hans Kelsen, *Reine Rechtslehre: Einleitung in die rechtswissenschaftliche Problematik. Studienausg. Der 1. Er. Auflag. 1934*, hrsg. Matthias Jestaedt (Tübingen: Mohr Siebeck, 2008), 50 ff; 76 ff; 116–126. For an overview of the connections between Kelsen's legal positivism and his theory of democracy: Matthias Jestaedt, "La science come vision du monde: science du droit et conception de la démocratie en Hans Kelsen," in *Hans Kelsen. Forme du droit et politique de l'autonomie*, sous la direction de Olivier Jouanjan (Paris: Presses Universitaire de France, 2010), 171–220.

41. On this point see: Georg Jellinek, *Gesetz und Verordnung* (Tübingen: Mohr Siebeck, 1887).

42. See: Bruce Haddock, *History of Political Thought. 1789 to the Present* (Cambridge: Cambridge Polity Press, 2008), 9–41; Maurizio Fioravanti, *La costituzione democratica. Modelli e itinerari del diritto pubblico nel ventesimo secolo* (Milano: Giuffré, 2018), 53 ff.

43. Kelsen, *Die Hauptprobleme der Staatsrechtslehre entiwickelt aus der Lehre vom Rechtssatze* (1st ed.), 57–72; 162–188.

44. Ibid., 469–477.

45. Ibid., 468 ff; 473–474.

46. Hans Kelsen, "Wählerlisten und Reklamationsrecht," in Hans Kelsen, *Veröffentliche Schriften 1905–1910 und Selbstzeugnisse*, hrsg. Matthias Jestaedt (Tübingen: Mohr Siebeck, 2007), 317–330.

47. William Jenks, *The Austrian Electoral Reform of 1907* (New York: Columbia University Press, 1950), 27–40.

48. Kelsen, *Die Hauptprobleme der Staatsrechtslehre entiwickelt aus der Lehre vom Rechtssatze* (1st ed.), 472.

49. Ibid., 479.

50. For Rousseau see: Margaret Canovan, "Arendt, Rousseau and Human Plurality in Politics," *Journal of Politics* 45, no. 2 (May 1983): 286–302.

51. Dreier, *Rechtslehre, Staatssoziologie und Demokratielehre bei Hans Kelsen*, 41–42.

52. Kelsen, *Die Hauptprobleme der Staatsrechtslehre entiwickelt aus der Lehre vom Rechtssatze* (1st ed.), 472.

53. This aspect emerges clearly from the *Stenographische Protokolle der Österreichichen konstituirenden und provisorischen Nationalversammlung*.

54. See: Kelsen, "Vom Wesen und Wert der Demokratie" (1st ed.), in *Verteidigung der Demokratie*, 1–33; Kelsen, "Vom Wesen und Wert der Demokratie" (2nd ed.), in *Verteidigung der Demokratie*, 149–228; Kelsen, "Foundations of Democracy," in *Verteidigung der Demokratie*, 248–386.

55. Hans Kelsen, "Der Proporz im Wahlordnungsentwurf," *Neue Freie Presse* (December 1, 1918): 54.

56. Ibid., 55–57; Hans Kelsen, "Ein Einfaches Proportionalwahlsystem," *Arbeiter Zeitung* (November 24, 1918): 2–6.

57. Kelsen, "Der Proporz im Wahlordnungsentwurf," 56–57.

58. Ibid., 55 and also Hans Kelsen, "Das Proportionalwahlsystem," *Der österreichische Volkswirt* (December 7, 1918): 116–117. The term "Personalitätsprinzip" evokes a relevant part of Habsburg history and the history of the Austrian nationality question. Since the late nineteenth century, there had been thinkers—such as, for example, the social democratic leader and Kelsen's friend Karl Renner—who advocated the necessity to reform the Empire according to the *Personalitätsprinzip*: every nationality had to be legally and politically considered as an individual equipped with full rights and freedom, regardless of the territory where they actually lived. On this basis, the contrasts among the Habsburg nationalities could be neutralized. In my opinion Kelsen's idea of the "Personalitätsprinzip" replacing the *Territorialprinzip* recalled such tradition of thought. See: Karl Renner, *Staat und Parlament. Kritische Studie über die österreichische Frage und das System der Interessenvertretung* (Wien: Genossenshaftsbuchdruckerei, 1901).

59. Kelsen, "Das Proportionalwahlsystem," 117. I think that his extraordinary sensitivity toward the issue of minorities and the necessity to provide them with an appropriate political representation somehow depended on the fact that he was born

and grew up within a State—the Habsburg Empire—which was actually made up of (national) minorities.

60. Kelsen, "Das Proportionalwahlsystem," 116.

61. Ibid., 118.

62. Ibid., 115–118.

63. Brian Peterson, "Workers' Councils in Germany, 1918–1919: Recent Literature on the Rätebewegung," *New German Critique* 4 (Winter 1975): 113–124; In general see: Francis Carsten, *The First Austrian Republic 1918–1939* (Aldershot: Gower Publishing Company, 1986).

64. Kelsen, "Vom Wesen und Wert der Demokratie" (1st ed.), 1–2. Kelsen was referring in particular to Lenin's *State and Revolution* (1917).

65. In the very first version of *Vom Wesen und Wert der Demokratie*, that is, Kelsen's *Vortrag* of 1919, we can observe that Kelsen's anti-bolshevik position was even much more emphasized. Kelsen, "Vom Wesen und Wert der Demokratie," 378–380.

66. Kelsen, "Vom Wesen und Wert der Demokratie," (1st ed.), 3–6.

67. Gabriele De Angelis, "Ideals and Institutions: Hans Kelsen's Political Theory," *History of Political Thought* 30, no. 3 (Autumn 2009): 530.

68. Kelsen, "Vom Wesen und Wert der Demokratie" (1st ed.), 1–2.

69. See: William Galston, "Realism in Political Theory," *European Journal of Political Theory* 9, no. 4 (October 2010): 385–411.

70. Gaetano Mosca (1858–1946) was a jurist, a public servant, and the founder of political science in Italy; Vilfredo Pareto (1843–1923) was a prominent economist and sociologist; Robert Michels (1876–1936) was a sociologist, particularly interested in political parties behavior. Mosca formulated the theory of "political class," Pareto that of the "circulation of the élites," whereas Michels investigated in depth the behavior of mass parties, in particular the German Sociali Democratic Party, while developing the "Iron Law of Oligarchy." They argued that any kind of association and notably democracy were inevitably and necessarily ruled by a structured minority of individuals (the élite). See: Claudio Martinelli, "Gaetano Mosca's Political Theories: A Key to Interpret the Dynamics of Power," *Italian Journal of Public Law* 1 (2009): 1–21; Giovanni Busino, "The Signification of Vilfredo Pareto's Sociology," *Revue européènne de sciences sociales* XXXVIII, 117 (2000): 217–228; David Beetham, "Michels and his Critics," *European Journal of Sociology* 22, no. 1 (1981): 81–99.

71. Michels was a militant of the German Social Democratic Party. He joined the Italian Fascist Party in the 1920s. Pareto's attitude toward Mussolini and fascism was complex and controversial. It is maybe exaggerated to define him a pro-fascist, but he was undoubtedly a conservative thinker. See also: Tim Gennet, *Der Fremde im Krieg. Zur politischen Biographie von Robert Michels 1876–1936* (Berlin: Akademie Verlag, 2008).

72. In both editions of *Vom Wesen und Wert der Demokratie* as well as in his last work on democratic theory: *Foundations of Democracy*, Kelsen identified the existence of "Führer" ("Leaders," "Chiefs") as an integrative characteristic of real democracy. In the last chapter of this book, "Democracy and Proceduralism," I will focus on this particular aspect of Kelsen's democratic theory. Also, I will argue how

his particular view of such relationship is an essential component of his procedural conception of democracy. See: Kelsen, "Vom Wesen und Wert der Demokratie" (1st ed.), 24–27; Kelsen, "Vom Wesen und Wert der Demokratie" (2nd ed.), 210–220; Kelsen, "Foundations of Democracy," 290–294.

73. Kelsen, "Vom Wesen und Wert der Demokratie" (1st ed.), 3.

74. On this point see: Lino Rizzi, "Il problema della legittimità democratica in Kelsen e Rousseau," *Il Politico* 57, no. 2 (aprile-giugno 1992): 228.

75. Antonio Martins, "Sobre o Pensamiento politico de Hans Kelsen. Notas Marginais a Da Essencia e valor da democracia (1920)." Paper for *Poética da Razão. Homenagem a Leonel Ribeiro dos Santos*, orgnized by Adriana V. Serrão et al. (Lisboa: Centro de Filosofia de Universidade de Lisboa, 2013), 596–597.

76. In his *Contract social* Rousseau stated that Englishmen were free only when they elected the Parliament. Jean Jacques Rousseau, *Du Contract social. Ou Principer du Droit Politique* (Paris: Flammarion, 2012), 88; Kelsen, "Vom Wesen und Wert der Demokratie" (1st ed.), 2–5. On Kelsen and Rousseau, Vinx, *Hans Kelsen's Pure Theory of Law. Legality and Legitimacy*, 114–116.

77. On Kelsen's "obsession" for the issue of "heteronomy" see: Vinx, *Hans Kelsen's Pure Theory of Law. Legality and Legitimacy*, 104–112.

78. On the difference between the English and German meaning of *Finktion* (fiction) see: De Angelis, "Ideals and Institutions," 530–531.

79. Kelsen, "Vom Wesen und Wert der Demokratie" (1st ed.), 6–9.

80. Ibid., 11–12.

81. Ibid., 12; see also: Kelsen, *Allgemeine Staatslehre*, 40–46.

82. On Pareto and Michels see: Kelsen, "Vom Wesen und Wert der Demokratie" (2nd ed.), 183–184.

83. Bernard Manin, *The Principles of Representative Government*, Eng. Trans (Cambridge: Cambridge University Press, 2010), 26–28; 197–199.

84. On Kelsen and Weber see: Bobbio, *Diritto e potere. Saggi su Kelsen*, 159–177.

85. See: Hans Vaihinger, "Mitteilungen über das dem Kongress überreichte Werk '*Die Philosophie des Als ob*'," in *Atti del IV Congresso internazionale di Filosofia* (Modena: Formiggini, 1911), 297–309.

86. See: Hans Kelsen, "Zur theorie der juristischen Finktionen. Mit besonderer Berücksichtigung von Vaihnigers Philosophie des Als Ob," *Annalen der Philosophie* 1 Bd. (1919): 630–658; 200–234.

87. Kelsen, "Vom Wesen und Wert der Demokratie" (1st ed.), 12–13.

88. Hans Kelsen, *Sozialismus und Staat: eine Untersuchung der politischen Theorie des Marxismus*, 2. Erw. Aufl (Leipzig: C. L. Hirschfeld, 1923), 57. *Sozialismus und Staat* was not the only Kelsen's work devoted to the critique of marxism and bolshevism. After his moving to the United States in 1940, he published—for example—two long essays on this issue: *The Political Theory of Bolscevism. A Critical Analysis* (1948) and *The Communist Theory of Law* (1955). I will refer to both works in the last chapter on "Democracy and Proceduralism" when analyzing his writing on the *Foundations of Democracy* (1955). On Kelsen and his relation to marxism and Bolscevism: Norbert Leser, "Kelsens Verhältnis

zum Sozialismus und Marx," in *Ideologiekritik und Demokratietheorie bei Hans Kelsen*, 423–437. Mozetič gives an account of the controversy between Kelsen and two prominent Austro-Marxists (Max Adler and Otto Bauer). The dispute between Kelsen and Adler—who were in fact friends—essentially concerned the meaning of the "proletarian dictatorship," which Adler as a Marxist considered in positive terms, whereas with regard to Bauer, Kelsen criticized his concept of "Gleichgewicht der Klassen" (equilibrium of classes), that is, his conviction that at a certain level of social and political development there could be a sort of temporary alliance between the bourgoise and the Social Democratic Party. In this Kelsen saw the proof that the gradual political integration of socialist forces into democratic institutions tended to weaken the anti-system and fundamentally anarchist tendency that he attributed to marxism. Gerald Mozetič, "Hans Kelsen als Kritiker des Austromarxismus," in *Ideologiekritik und Demokratietheorie bei Hans Kelsen*, 446–456.

89. Kelsen, "Vom Wesen und Wert der Demokratie" (1st ed.), 12–15.

90. Ibid., 14.

91. Ibid., 13–14; 20–21.

92. Ibid., 14–15.

93. A further proof of this might be the very first version of *Vom Wesen und Wert der Demokratie* (the *Vortrag* of 1919). Here the references to Lenin and to the Bolsheviks were numerous and extremely critical: Kelsen stated that Lenin had justified the transformation of the soviet regime in a dictatorship, by using "the fiction of representation." See the whole Hans Kelsen, "Vom Wesen und Wert der Demokratie. Vortrag vor der Wiener juristischen Gesellschaft," *Juristische Blätter* 48 (1919): 376–389. A similar critique in Kelsen, *Sozialismus und Staat*, 92 ff and 123. On Marx's and Lenin's political thought: Haddock, *History of Political Thought. 1789 to the Present*, 210–229.

94. Rousseau, *Du Contract social*, 250. On the issue of majority and minority in Rousseau see: Robin Douglass, "Rousseau's Critique of Representative Democracy: Principled or Pragmatic?," *American Journal of Political Science* 57, 3 (July 2013): 740–745. Also, David M. Estlund, Jeremy Waldron, Bernard Grofman, and Scott L. Feld, "Democratic Theory and Public Interest: Condorcet and Rousseau Revisited," *The American Political Science Review* 83, no. 4 (December 1989): 1317–1340. There is an extensive literature on the authoritarian implications of Rousseau's political thought and idea of "general will": some of the leading representatives of such an interpretative line were Karl Popper, *Open Society and its Enemies*, vol. 1 and 2 (London: Routledge 1952); Jacob Talmon, *The Origins of Totalitarian Democracy* (London: Secker & Walburg, 1952); Isaiah Berlin, "Two Concepts of Liberty," in Isaiah Berlin, *Four Essays on Liberty* (Oxford: Oxford University Press, 1969), 118–172.

95. As I am going to discuss in the third chapter of this book, "Democracy and Relativism," Kelsen could not follow Rousseau's reasoning because he rejected the existence of a universally valid and universally comprehensible "common good." In any theory advocating an objectively valid and true principle, Kelsen saw the expression of "absolutism" as opposed to "relativism." On this point see: Eerik

Lagerspetz, "Kelsen on Democracy and Majority Decision," *Archiv für Rechts und Sozialphilosophie* 103, no. 2 (March 2017): 155 ff.

96. Kelsen, "Vom Wesen und Wert der Demokratie" (1st ed.), 9–10. On the connection between proportional voting system and the respect/protection of the minority see: Urbinati, "Editor's Preface," 16–19.

97. Kelsen, "Vom Wesen und Wert der Demokratie" (1st ed.), 9–10; 27–31.

98. See: Michael Gallagher and Paul Mitchell eds., *The Politics of Electoral Systems* (Oxford: Oxford University Press, 2005). An interesting Kelsen's predecessor for the defense of the proportional was John Stuart Mill with his *Considerations on Representative Government* (1861), in which the British thinker identified—although on theoretical basis which were different from Kelsen's ones—a deep connection between parliamentary democracy and the proportional voting system. See: John S. Mill, *Considerations on Representative Government* (Oxford: Oxford University Press, 1975).

99. I am specifically referring to Luigi Ferrajoli's and Pasquale Pasquino's interesting and keen objections to Kelsen's way of theorizing the democratic process. See: Ferrajoli, *La logica del diritto. Dieci aporie nell'opera di Hans Kelsen*, 211–225; Pasquino, "Penser la démocratie: Kelsen en Weimar," 119–131. More recently, Pasquale Pasquino, "Condorcet, Kelsen et la règle de majorité," *Journal of Interdisciplinary History of Ideas* 7, no. 14 (2018): 3–18. In general, for an overview of the concept of "ideal and real democracy" within Kelsen's reflection see: Thomas Olechowski, "Von der Ideologie zur Realität der Demokratie," in *Hans Kelsen. Eine politikwissenschaftliche Einführung* (Wien: Manz, 2009), 113–123.

100. David J. Manning, *Liberalism* (Worthing: Littlehampton Bookservices Ltd., 1976), 15.

101. Tocqueville, *Democracy in America*, 2004.

102. Kelsen, "Vom Wesen und Wert der Demokratie" (1st ed.), 15.

103. See: Edmund Fawcett, *Liberalism. The Life of an Idea* (Princeton, New Jersey: Princeton University Press, 2015). On Kelsen as a liberal thinker see: Van Ooyen, *Der Staat der Moderne. Hans Kelsens Pluralismustheorie*, 71.

104. Kelsen, "Vom Wesen und Wert der Demokratie" (1st ed.), 10.

105. See in general: George Sabine, *A History of Political Thought* (New York: Henry Holt Company, 1951); Bruce Haddock, *History of Political Thought. From Antiquity to Present* (Cambridge: Cambridge University Polity Press, 2005), 168–186.

106. For a critical reflection on the complexity of Kelsen's relation to liberalism see: Carlos G. Herrera, "Kelsen et le libéralisme," in *Le droit, le politique. Autour de Max Weber, Hans Kelsen, Carl Schmitt* (Paris: L'Harmattan, 1995), 60 ff. The debate on the relationship between pluralism and liberalism is complex and long-term. If we look at the history of European political thought, we can observe that such a relationship seems particularly relevant within the English tradition of thought (Mill is an excellent example). Conversely, continental thinkers, who are classically associated to liberalism such as the German Immanuel Kant in the eighteenth century or the Italian Benedetto Croce in the twentieth century, did not put the issue of pluralism at the center of their philosophical reflection. For a critical understanding of liberalism

in relation to pluralism see: George Crowder, *Liberalism and Value Pluralism* (London New York: Continuum, 2002).

107. It is interesting to observe that only the second edition of *Vom Wesen und Wert der Demokratie* was translated in English. Kelsen, *Essence and Value of Democracy*, 2013.

108. The status of parliamentary democracy was at the center of a widespread intellectual debate at that time in Europe. See: Boris Barth, *Europa nach dem grossen Krieg: die Krise der Demokratie in der Zwischenkriegszeit 1918–1938* (Frankfurt-New York: Campus Verlag, 2006).

109. For an informative picture of such as complex historical situation see: Jan Werner Müller, *Contesting Democracy: Political Ideas in the Twentieth Century* (New Haven: Yale University Press, 2011), 9–16; Detlev J. K. Peuckert, *The Weimar Republic. The Crisis of Classical Modernity* (New York: Farrar, Starus, Giroux, 1993) and generally Hans Mommsen, *The Rise and Fall of Weimar Democracy* (Frankfurt am Main-Berlin: The University of North Carolina Press, 1996). Also: Hans Joachim W. Koch, *A Constitutional History of Germany in the 19th and 20th century* (London: Longman, 1984), 278 ff.

110. Carsten, *The First Austrian Republic 1918–1939*, 121–148. See also, for a general view of the first postwar political, social, and cultural Austrian context: Günther Bishof, Fritz Plasser and Peter Berger, ed. *From Empire to Republic: Post World War I Austria* (Innsbruck: Inssbruck Universität, 2010).

111. Hans Kelsen, "Selbstzeuginisse," in *Veröffentlichen Schriften 1905–1910 und Selbstzeugnisse*, hrsg. von Matthias Jestaedt (Tübingen: Mohr Siebeck, 2007), 29–91; 30–91. See: Chapter 2.

112. Both concepts were clearly developed by Marx in his *Manifesto of the Communist Party* (1848). See. Kelsen, "Zur Soziologie der Demokratie," *Der Österreichische Volkswirt* 19 (1926): 209.

113. Ibid.

114. Ibid., 210.

115. Hans Kelsen, "Allgemeine Staatslehre," in *Verteidigung der Demokratie*, 75–78. The issue of compromise is also present in his *General Theory of Law and State* (London and New York: Routledge, 2006), 288 ff. On the *General Theory of Law and State* within the corpus of Kelsen's works see: Treves, "Intorno alla concezione del diritto di Hans Kelsen," 190–197.

116. Nicoletta Bersier Ladavac, "Biographical Note and Bibliography," *European Journal of International Law* 9, no. 2 (1998): 391–392; Carsten, *The First Austrian Republic 1918–1939*, 121–148; Ernst Topitsch, "Kelsen, Demokrat und Philosoph," in *Ideologiekritik und Demokratietheorie bei Hans Kelsen*, 12.

117. Kelsen, "Vom Wesen und Wert der Demokratie" (2nd ed.), 153–154.

118. Ignaz Seipel (1876–1932) was a Catholic priest, a politician, one of the most prominent representatives of the Christian Social Party, whose conservative soul he effectively embodied. Heinrich Triepel (1868–1946) was a legal theorist and scholar of public and international law who played a relevant role in the Weimar intellectual life. He participated in the *Methodenstreit* (debate on method) on the status of public law, which took physically place in the German Association of scholars of public

law, within which Treipel was involved in 1928 in a frontal debate with Kelsen on the "constitutional jurisdiction." The latter—unlike the first—was supportive of it. Carl Schmitt (1888–1980) was one of the leading jurists and philosophers of the twentieth century. He developed a philosophical and legal reflection on the concept of sovereignty as the "decision on the exception" and on the concept of the political as based upon the distinction between "friend and enemy." His political thought was characterized by a frontal attack against liberalism and the traditional principle of the *Rechtsstaat.* See: Caldwell, *Popular Sovereignty and the Crisis of German Constitutional Law*, 125 ff. See also in general: David Dyzenhaus, *Law and Politics. Carl Schmitt's Critique of Liberalism* (Durham, North Carolina: Duke University Press, 1998) and Friedrich Rennhofer, *Ignaz Seipel, Mensch und Staatsmann. Eine biographische Dokumentation* (Wien: Hermann Böhlaus, 1978).

119. Kelsen, "Vom Wesen und Wert der Demokratie" (2nd ed.), 155–158.

120. Ibid., 162–170.

121. Ibid., 164. On the difference between the legal and sociological meaning of "people" within Kelsen's work, see: Oliver Lepsius, "Kelsens Demokratielehre," in *Hans Kelsen. Eine politikwissenschaftliche Einführung* (Wien: Manz, 2009), 73 ff.

122. Pasquino, "Penser la démocratie: Kelsen en Weimar," 119–131.

123. Kelsen, "Vom Wesen und Wert der Demokratie" (2nd ed.), 165–166.

124. Ibid., 166.

125. This effectively stressed by Baume, "Rehabilitating Political Parties: An Examination of Hans Kelsen's Writings," *Intellectual History Review* 28 (January 24, 2018): 427–430.

126. Ibid., 430.

127. See: Heinrich Triepel, *Die Staatsverfassung und die politische Parteien* (Berlin: Druck der Preussischen Druckerei und Verlags-Aktiengesellschaft, 1927).

128. Koch, *A Constitutional History of Germany in the 19th and 20th century*, 251–272; Manin, *The Principles of Representative Government*, 212–214.

129. Kelsen, "Vom Wesen und Wert der Demokratie" (2nd ed.), 167–170.

130. Ibid., 166–173.

131. Ibid., 172.

132. On the foundation of political parties within the constitution according to Kelsen's perspective see: Filippo Scuto, *La democrazia interna dei partiti: profile costituzionali di una transizione* (Torino: Giappichelli editore, 2017), 11 ff.

133. See: Robert Michels, *Soziologie des Parteiwesen* (Stuttgart: Alfred Kröner Verlag, 1989); In his *Sozialismus und Staat*, Kelsen denounced the "aristo-autocratic" of the soviet system. Kelsen, *Sozialismus und Staat*, 188–191.

134. Kelsen, "Vom Wesen und Wert der Demokratie" (2nd ed.), 153–154.

135. Ibid., 175.

136. Ibid., 174–177.

137. Ibid., 176.

138. Ibid., 184–189.

139. It is important to notice that Kelsen used "professional representation" as synonymous with corporatist representation.

140. Kelsen, *Vom Wesen und Wert der Demokratie*, 1929. For a general overview of corporatism and the debate about corporatist representation in the early twentieth century in Europe see: Peter Williamson, *Varieties of Corporativism: A Conceptual Discussion* (Cambridge: Cambridge University Press, 1985), chiefly: 64–74.

141. Kelsen, "Vom Wesen und Wert der Demokratie" (2nd ed.), 190–191.

142. Ibid., 190–192.

143. On the relevance of compromise in Kelsen's thought see: Baume, "Rehabilitating Political Parties: An Examination of Hans Kelsen's Writings," 427–430 and more recently Ragazzoni, "An Overlooked Puzzle in Kelsen's Democratic Theory," 96–118.

144. Hans Kelsen, "Der Drang zur Verfassungsreform," *Neue Freie Presse* (October 6, 1929): 29–30.

145. Kelsen, "Vom Wesen und Wert der Demokratie" (2nd ed.), 193–204.

146. Ibid.

147. Ibid., 174–182; 193–204.

148. See: Chapter 2.

149. See on this point: Heller, "Politische Demokratie und soziale Homogenität," in *Gesammelte Schriften*, Bd. 3, 426–432.

150. Ibid. and also: Heller, "Rechtsstaat oder Diktatur?," in *Gesammelte Schriften*, Bd. 3, 426–432.

Chapter 2

Democracy and Constitution

THE AUSTRIAN CONSTITUTIONAL JURISDICTION: THE PROBLEM OF FEDERALISM

The first edition of *Vom Wesen und Wert der Demokratie* was published in the year the promulgation of the first democratic and republican constitution of Austria was announced. Kelsen participated in the constitutional process as a legal adviser for the Subcommittee for Constitutional Affairs, and he formulated a system of constitutional control, called *Verfassungsgerichtsbarkeit* (constitutional jurisdiction), which would have a considerable impact on European post–World War II democratic states, such as Italy. In general terms, we can say that "modern European constitutional court is the invention of [. . .] Hans Kelsen."[1] Kelsen's contribution to the creation of a constitutional jurisdiction mechanism had—as we are going to see—an important and interesting predecessor in the Habsburg Reichsgerichtshof (Imperial Court),[2] and it was fundamental not only from the concrete and operational point of view but also from a theoretical one. During the entire 1920s Kelsen elaborated on the meaning (legal and political) of constitutional jurisdiction, on its relevance and in the early 1930s he was also involved in a famous dispute with Carl Schmitt on the *Guardian of the Constitution.*[3]

It was in fact in the 1920s that Kelsen published some essays on the significance and characteristics of modern and representative democracy. Yet, we would be disappointed if we searched for references to the problem of constitutional protection in Kelsen's writings on democracy. Simply, none of his popular essays on democracy openly refers to his system of constitutional control enforced in Austria in 1920. Do we thus have to assume that there is no connection between them, as if they represented two clear-cut separate dimensions within his intellectual production? Do we thus have to think that such a "separation" corresponds to that developed between "Sollen" and "Sein," between the realm of Law and that of politics? Therefore that his whole work on constitutional jurisdiction and even his personal contribution to the creation of the Austrian Constitutional Court is essentially an appendix of his legal philosophy?

I argue, rather, that in some crucial respects Kelsen's model of constitutional jurisdiction is profoundly intertwined in the concrete historical and political context characterizing post–World War I Austria and that after 1920 his major essays on constitutional jurisdiction can be seen as his personal effort to keep reflecting on the meaning of parliamentary democracy. I will seek to show how in this effort Kelsen outlined a political justification for constitutional jurisdiction, implying a particular view of democracy and more precisely a series of concepts discussed in the previous chapter.

It would be impossible to fully understand the final aim and meaning of Kelsen's constitutional jurisdiction system unless we seriously take into account the historical background and the major political dynamics characterizing his country, Austria, between 1918 and 1920. The collapse of the Habsburg Monarchy meant a transition toward a democratic Republic, and more precisely the establishing of a National Provisional Assembly, which hosted three major political forces, the Christian Socials, the Nationalists, and the SocialDemocrats.[4] The first two had a conservative orientation and were both anti-socialist, whereas the Christian Socials were fundamentally pro-monarchy and pro-Habsburg, the Nationalist group had always promoted republican ideals like the Social Democrats.[5] The latter, and precisely their leader Karl Renner, who was also the chief of the National Assembly,[6] played a crucial role in the very first sessions of the National Assembly. On October 30, 1918—a few days before Emperor Charles I's abdication (November 11, 1918)—Renner discussed his constitutional law draft on "Staatsgewalt" ("sovereignty") in front of the Assembly, while advocating (in the name of his party) the establishment of a democratic and republican State, based on the principle of people's sovereignty. More precisely—as Renner argued— the National Assembly held and exercised the legislative power, whereas the State Council was provided with the executive power. The latter was basically conceived as subordinated to the first: the primacy of the legislative power was considered by Renner as one of the most remarkable differences with the monarchic past. In ideological terms, Renner looked at the birth of an Austrian democracy as a unique opportunity to create and guarantee a future of peace and prosperity for all. On that same day (October 30) the law was officially enforced.[7] On the basis of such premises, it was inevitable for Renner to opt for a Republic and formalize the end of the Monarchy as, in his opinion, the Emperor Charles I had already done with his "Manifesto" of October 16, 1918.[8]

It was thanks to the Nationalists' support that the SocialDemocrats (SPÖ) could prevail over the Christian Socials (CSÖ) and could pass a law (November 12, 1918) transforming Austria into a republican State.[9] The republican and democratic choice did not put an end to the institutional issues. A complex political debate took shape about whether or not the new Austrian Republic had to be a unitary-centralized State or a federal State and whether or not the new democratic institutions had to be "protected" by means of a special jurisdiction.[10] Within the National Provisional Assembly (and further within the National Constituent Assembly elected on February 16, 1919)[11] a clear opposition emerged between Social Democrats and Christian Socials precisely on the institutional future of the country. Such a division reflected a complex and long-term network of political elements, which involved the relationship between Vienna—the political heart of the country before and after the end of the Monarchy—and the so-called Länder (Regions),[12] that is, the relationship between the Center and the Periphery of the nation. While the SPÖ, which was traditionally embedded in Vienna, was in favor of a unitary and centralized institutional design, the conservative forces, likewise strong in the peripheral areas, pushed for a federal solution granting extensive freedom to the Länder.[13]

The political relevance of the clash between those supportive of federalism versus those supportive of centralism emerged clearly from Renner's words.[14] Faced with the end of the Empire, it was necessary for him (and his party) to prevent the Länder from taking advantage from this situation of political and institutional transition to act as independent entities in contrast with the decisions taken from the Center (the National Provisional Assembly).[15]

Renner was, in fact, concerned about the capabilities of self-government, which the Regions were showing in administrative and organizational terms and which, in his opinion, might push the country toward federalism.[16] There was thus an evident tension between the November 12 law, which imagined a centralized kind of State, and the Länder which instead claimed a federalist system.[17] It is interesting to observe that Renner himself had contributed to the shaping of such tension by proposing the so-called "Beitrittserklärungen" (declarations of accession), which had been enforced on October 29, 1918. Concretely, the Regions were asked to formalize their membership of the new Austria. That implied to conceive the Länder as subjects equipped with a certain amount of autonomy. Yet, once they declared their membership, they were automatically defined as mere "provinces." By this way, the "Beitrittserklärungen" implied a substantially centralized vision of Austria.[18] Immediately after the election of the Constitutional Assembly on February 16, 1919,[19] the social democratic position in favor of a unitary and centralized solution for the new Austrian State seemed to prevail.[20]

As a proof of their dominance within the Constitutional Assembly, I would mention the constitutional law of March 14, 1919, which established a parliamentary government and enforced the principle of "Bundesrecht bricht Landesrecht" (federal Law prevails over the regional one), according to which laws issued by the regional assemblies were enforced only after being ratified by the State Council. The content of such constitutional law corresponded to socialists' *desiderata*.[21] It is not just a coincidence that the March 14 law was also known as that on "the assumption of State authority in the Länder." In other words, such a law granted administrative autonomy to the Regions, while affirming the predominance of central government toward them. This revealed a counter-strategy against the Regions' and Christian Socials' claims for full federalism. It is within the context of head-on antagonism between the supporters of the unitary-centralized solution and those of the federal one that some of the political and historically conditioned implications of Kelsen's contribution to the making of *Verfassungsgerichtsbarkeit* become clearer. Already in 1918 Social Democrats and chiefly their leader Karl Renner took a stand not only in favor of a unitary institutional design but also in favor of a Constitutional Court. As Renner himself clearly stated—during a speech delivered at the National Provisional Assembly on October 30, 1918—the Constitutional Court would "occupy itself not only with the protection of the citizens, but also with State provisions, the freedom to vote, and our public law."[22] In Renner's view, the new Constitutional Court had to be the "democratic" version of the past monarchic "Reichsgerichtshof," that is, the past Imperial Court.[23]

From an historical perspective, Renner and Kelsen did not speak and act within a vacuum. Both were well aware of the tradition of the Austrian Imperial Court, which had been established after the constitutional and political reform of 1867, when the Empire became the Dual Austrian-Hungarian Monarchy.[24] The Imperial Court had played a key role in defending and preserving constitutional liberties and therefore the Austrian "liberal constitutional order": it had to, in fact, protect the constitutional rights of the Austrian citizens.[25] It also had to supervise the boundaries between administrative and judicial authorities, as well as the ones between the regional (Länder) and State administration. More precisely, it had to fix conflicts between the central government and the Länder.[26]

As I have tried to show, the latter aspect was perceived by the Austrian post–World War I political forces as a major political and legal issue to address. They knew that the particular solution to that specific problem—that is, the relationship between Center and Regions—would condition the institutional design of the whole nation. Kelsen was perfectly aware of this too. Like Renner, Kelsen began to discuss publicly about the making of the Constitution and the opportunity of establishing a Constitutional Court already in late 1918, when he published a "memorandum," entitled *Entwurf eines Gesetzes über die Einrichtung eines Verfassungsgerichtshofes* (*A Draft for the Establishment of a Constitutional Court*). Here he stated that following the end of the Monarchy, full sovereignty had been taken by the National Provisional Assembly, which exercised it in the name of the people. From such a premise, Kelsen argued that the Austrian State was not to be intended as the result of a contract between the Länder, and also that—on a legal level—it was impossible to reestablish the old "Reichsgerichtshof." It was the time to transform it into a "Verfassungsgerichtshof," that is, a Constitutional Court of a democratic and republican State.[27] Kelsen was in fact embracing the SPÖ position and notably Renner's one. This shows us how Kelsen himself was connecting the issue of creating such a Court for the concrete historical and political development of his country and more precisely how sensitive and receptive he was to the inputs coming from the leading political force of that time. The weight of political and historical context concerning Kelsen's contribution to the making of the Austrian constitutional jurisdiction emerges both from Kelsen's role as a legal adviser of the Subcommittee of the Constitutional Assembly and from at least two of his writings, which he published during the constituent process.

First, between May and September 1919 Kelsen—as legal adviser and also personally close to Renner—produced six constitutional drafts on the request of Karl Renner, which had to include the "input" of the latter who thought that it was necessary to figure out how the Constitutional Court would work if Austria were to become a federal Republic. The social democratic leader was realistic enough to realize that within a game of reciprocal concessions and compromises between his party and the conservatives, it was likely that the federalist option would prevail. Kelsen was thus asked to develop a constitutional jurisdiction mechanism both in the case Austria would be a centralized State and in the case it would be a federal one. As regards the latter possibility, Kelsen had to reflect on the role of the Constitutional Court in relation to federal government and the Regions. Ideally, if we follow the content of Kelsen's drafts we will see that the first of them was the most "länderfreundlich" (Länder friendly), whereas the following ones designed a federal system where—similar to the Weimar constitution whose Article 13 established the principle of "Bundesrecht bricht Landesrecht"—the Länder Chamber would be subordinated to the federal Chamber, which would likewise imply a subordination of the regional legislation to the federal one.[28]

The varying content of Kelsen's drafts reflected not only Renner's influence but also how the *ratio* behind them and Kelsen's activity itself was to find a political compromise between federalists and anti-federalists. In the light of the necessary (although difficult) negotiations between such different views, Kelsen sought to identify legal mechanisms within a federal framework to avoid and neutralize the potentially centrifugal tendencies coming from the Länder. In this respect, constitutional jurisdiction would have a sort of anti-Länder implication, as wanted by the SPÖ. The issue of creating a Constitutional Court for Austria was evidently everything but one of the many aspects of a struggle for political power.

Kelsen thus initially imagined a "Bundesverfassungsgerichtshof" (federal Constitutional Court) whose task would be to be appealed to by the Bund (the federal Government) against unconstitutional laws of the Länder.[29] This is exactly what he suggested in his *Stellung der Länder in der künftigen Deutschösterreich* (*The Position of the Länder in the Contemporary German-Austria*), which was initially written following the constitutional law of March 14, 1919, and published later. Here he imagined three probable scenarios for Austria: as a fully centralized State; as a unitary State with a decentralized administrative system based on regional autonomy; and as a federal State. The fact that—Kelsen observed—the Regions were pushing so hard in favor of federalism made the latter possible, but this did not necessarily imply that the new Austria had to be considered as a Confederation. For him, any claim of that type was contradicted by the law of October 30, 1918, on "sovereignty."[30] Like in his previous *Entwurf eines Gesetzes über die Einrichtung eines Verfassungsgerichtshofes*, Kelsen replied against those political forces (mainly the conservative ones) and the Regions claiming the contractual origin of power in the post-monarchic Austria that the Austrian Republic was established following the assumption of sovereignty by the National Assembly.[31] That was a good reason—that is, the no-contractual origin of the Austrian Republic—why, for Kelsen, if there were a federal solution, the Austrian State would need a Constitutional Court in order to nullify unconstitutional laws issued by the Regions.[32]

By focusing only on Kelsen's brief but dense comments, we risk however losing the bigger picture, which began to change during the fall of 1919, precisely in relation to the issue of constitutional jurisdiction. Between January and October 1919, Renner regularly met the Länder's governors to discuss with them about the future and the definitive institutional form of the Austrian Republic. During the official meetings of September and October, the governors who most firmly and strongly promoted the federal solution were those of the Tirol (deep southeast Austria), of Voralberg (bordering Switzerland) and of Salzburg.[33] It was in fact Salzburg's governor, Gustav Rehrl, who compared the "Beitrittserklärungen" to "contracts," which—in his opinion—the Regions had subscribed as "sovereign subjects." On this basis, he argued that there had to be a perfect equality between Center and Regions. The idea of a Regions' Chamber subordinated to the federal government was unconceivable for him. Such positions were shared by the Tirol's vice-governor Schlegel, who advocated a direct participation of the Austrian Länder in the writing of the constitution. In front of such request, Renner was unwavering: he stated that only the Constituent Assembly, since democratically elected, had the exclusive right to write and approve the final constitution.[34]

The Regions—or at least some of their representatives—were pushing for a strong idea of federalism and Renner tried to oppose it. This complex and delicate phase of the Austrian constituent process did not only involve Renner (as the Chief of the Constituent Assembly) and the Regions' governors; Christian Socials and Social Democrats as parties played a crucial role too. In the spring of 1920 the Christian Social Michael Mayr, responsible for constitutional affairs of the Constituent Assembly, promoted the first Länder Conference in Salzburg, during which just Mayr proposed a constitutional draft[35] which tried to mediate between extreme federalism (that, for example, supported by Tirol's governor) and the clear inclination for centralism expressed by most of Social Democrats.[36]

Kelsen stressed Mayr's attempt of mediation in a brief article, published anonymously on the eve of the Salzburg Conference for the "Neue Freie Presse" and entitled *Der Vorentwurf der österreichischen Verfassung* (*The Draft of the Austrian Constitution*), in which Kelsen, however, restated his position—in line with the social democratic one—against a contractual origin for the new Austrian Republic.[37]

Fundamentally, behind the clashing vision between socialists and conservatives there was a different concept of sovereignty. If for the Christian Socials the new State was based on a contract with originally sovereign entities, that is, the Regions, for the Social Democrats sovereignty belonged to the Austrian people who exercised it indirectly through the assembly. Mayr's draft was unsuccessful because it essentially disappointed both the members of his same party for being too moderate and Social Democrats who still seemed unwilling to accept a co-equal Chamber of Länder.[38] It was however Mayr who sought to overcome the *impasse* by calling another Länder Conference in Linz some weeks after that in Salzburg. His intention was still to propose a constitutional draft as a form of compromise between socialists and conservatives as well as between the Center and the Regions. He referred to two of Kelsen's constitutional drafts, which—although they included the federal option—were basically pro-Bund rather that pro-Länder. Mayr's draft in fact included the principle according to which the Regions' Chamber had the right only to oppose draft-laws coming from the federal Parliament (Bundestag). Yet, as a concession to Regions, the draft outlined a full reciprocity between the federal government and the Regions in appealing to the Constitutional Court in case of anti-constitutional laws. The federal government could appeal to the Court in case of an anti-constitutional law issued by a regional assembly (Landtag) and a regional government could appeal to the Court in case of an anti-constitutional law issued by the federal Parliament.[39]

It is noticeable that such a principle of full reciprocity was included in none of Kelsen's constitutional drafts and therefore that such a principle should primarily be read as a (political) means to find a compromise between federalists and anti-federalists.

The Linz Conference was a turning point: during the summer, the writing of the Constitution passed to the political forces gathered in the Assembly. The process leading to the promulgation of the constitution can be divided into three major phases, whose main figures were SPÖ, CSÖ, the Nationalists, and Kelsen as a legal adviser.[40] During the first phase the three major political parties presented their own constitutional drafts. All the three projects accepted the federal solution, which would imply a federal Parliament, a Chamber representing the Regions and a Constitutional Court. Full reciprocity in appealing to the Court was recognized, although the Social Democratic projects promoted by the deputy Joseph Dannenberg restated the primacy of the Federation over the Länder. The second phase began when Renner and Mayr published another constitutional project, with the purpose to find a balance between Mayr's project discussed in Linz and Dannenberg's one.[41]

Afterward, the Constitutional Subcommittee was given the task of referring to the Renner-Mayr project, that of Linz, and Danneberg's one to draw up the constitution. Within the Subcommittee the confrontation between Social Democrats and Christian Socials was, however, again harsh. The main issues discussed were (again) federalism and the relationship between legislative and executive power. Some socialists expressed their doubts and critiques about the federal solution, whereas—in clear opposition to Christian Socials—they supported the primacy of the legislative power over the executive one, in the form of a parliamentary government.[42]

On that occasion, Kelsen endorsed social democratic positions. He thought that Austria had to adopt a coherent system of parliamentary government, which represented, for him, one of the major elements of rupture with the monarchic past. Yet, he argued that it would be indispensable—as he had already clearly stated in his articles on the *Proportionalwahlsystem*[43]—to grant the protection of minorities. Among effective mechanisms useful to enhance such protection, Kelsen proposed to provide parliamentary minorities with the right to require committees of inquiry.[44] Evidently, his stance in favor of parliamentary democracy was not born with the first edition of *Vom Wesen und Wert der Demokratie*. It began to take shape during the Austrian constituent process. The final phase coincided with the introduction of constitutional jurisdiction into the constitutional text. The Federal Constitutional Court would become a mechanism by means of which the Center and Periphery would reciprocally control the constitutionality of their laws. In other terms, the Federation was granted the initiative for control over the Länder while the latter was recognized the initiative for control over the Federation.[45]

We have seen how Kelsen was fundamentally more inclined toward the SPÖ anti-federalist view, although, as legal adviser, he could do nothing but accept the choices of the Constitutional Assembly. Yet, Kelsen's work within the Subcommittee Commission for Constitutional Affairs was not confined to legally formalizing and accepting political inputs and guidelines. In fact, he played a more proactive role by introducing the "ex officio procedure," according to which the Constitutional Court became the "objective defender of the constitution."[46]

The major legal and political implications of such a concept was that the constitution of 1920 introduced the primacy of constitutional law over the law of the Federation and the law of the Regions. Three years later, in a long essay on *Verfassungs und Verwaltungsgerichtsbarkeit im Dienste der Bundesverfassung* (*Constitutional and Administrative Jurisdiction in the Service of Federal State*), Kelsen would explain the reciprocity between Bund and Länder in the light of the "ex officio procedure" principle with the following words:

> In calling for the examination and nullification for the unconstitutionality of a law, the federal government and the governments of the Länder are not required to demonstrate that the contested law had transgressed against a particular interest of theirs. That which the Federation and the Länder—by means of a reciprocal control—assert is the interest of the constitutionality of the law.[47]

The right to appeal to the Court, recognized both to the Federation and to the Regions, found its ultimate legal motive in the primacy of the constitution, which had to be considered as "total."[48] Such a way of conceiving and justifying the Austrian constitution of 1920 somehow implied Kelsen's legal monism: to him the federal constitution was in fact the law of a "unitary State federally organized."[49] In this specific case, I would rather recall attention on how he connected the principle of "total constitution" to the issue of federalism, which was everything but an abstract or merely academic problem, between 1918 and 1920. In fact we read in his work on constitutional and administrative jurisdiction:

> The solution that the Austrian Constitution offered to the conflict between federal and Länder Law appears [. . .] to also be in accordance with the principles of the federal State. Not Federation Law such that prevails over the Law of the Land but constitutional Law prevails over that which is unconstitutional, that it would consist of the Law of the Federation and of the Land.[50]

Undoubtedly, as we have seen, Kelsen was more inclined—like Social Democrats—toward a centralized solution for Austria rather than a federalist one, but, once the latter prevailed, he seemed to pose himself, as legal theorist and adviser, the question of how to make the Federation work properly and strengthen the balance between Bund and Länder. The primacy of the constitutional law through the "ex officio procedure" can be interpreted as his response. In other words, the creation of the Constitutional Court, the recognition of the full reciprocity between Bund and Länder for appealing to the Court, and the "ex officio procedure" itself cannot be fully understood regardless with the particular Austrian historical-political context of that time and with the problem of federalism. Yet, during the 1920s, Kelsen continued to elaborate on the legal and political significance of the constitutional jurisdiction and on the principle of the "total constitution," mainly not in relation to federalism but rather to the protection of parliamentary democracy and minorities. In the next paragraphs, I will argue that his idea of constitutional jurisdiction is related to his democratic theory, which he was developing just at the same time.

KELSEN'S CONSTITUTIONAL JURISDICTION: RETHINKING IT ON THE FOOTSTEPS OF HIS DEMOCRATIC THEORY

In 1929 Kelsen, who was a member of the Austrian Constitutional Court, tried to reflect on constitutional jurisdiction from the perspective of "constitutional politics."[51] This specific aspect emerges from one of Kelsen's major works on constitutional theory, *La garantie jurisdictionelle de la constitution* (*The Jurisdictional Guarantee of the Constitution*) (1929), which can be considered as an attempt at conceptualizing the concrete experience of the Austrian constitutional process while going beyond it.[52] Looking back at the founding experience of the first democratic Austrian constitution, Kelsen defined the legal and political meaning of the constitution with the following words:

> The notion of constitution has retained a permanent core: the idea of a supreme principle that determines the whole State order. [. . .] The constitution is ever the foundation of the State, [. . .] the essence of the established community by this order [. . .] What is intended in the first place and in each case by constitution [. . .] is a principle in which the balance of political forces is legally exerted in a given moment.[53]

Such a passage is, in my opinion, rich in implications: Kelsen described the constitution, in the first instance as a result of a "balance of political forces."

With such an expression, he did not only refer to the force and relevance of political dynamics in the making of the constitution itself—a remark made by a thinker who advocated the separation between politics and Law—but wanted also to stress that the constitution was not the product of one, specific subject.

It was rather the result of a complex "process," the outcome of a "balance" involving a plurality of interests, views, and plans. Maybe, his personal and direct experience of the Austrian constituent process influenced and strengthened his particular view of constitution as an outcome of a complex and articulated game of compromises. As previously seen, the Austrian federal configuration of the country itself was, for example, mostly the result of long confrontations and negotiations involving the major political forces of that time. As sovereignty had no subject, the constitution had no subject either. With the *Hauptprobleme der Staatsrechtslehre* (1911) and with *Das Problem der Souveränität* (1920) he had de-personalized the concept of sovereignty (as well as that of the State); eight years later he de-personalized the concept of constitution. With that, Kelsen clearly broke with the idea that there was one single subject behind the constitution, that is, the people equipped with a well-defined and unitary will because, in his opinion, the people as a homogeneous unit simply did not exist. In "La garantie jurisdictionelle de la constitution" Kelsen's reflection on the concept of constitution implied a definition of the people, which he had already adamantly expressed in the first edition of *Vom Wesen und Wert der Demokratie*.[54]

Moreover, he outlined a concept of constitution that was extremely distant from that classically expressed in the tradition of democratic European political thought at least since the French Revolution, when the people was recognized as the subject of constituent power and as such it used that power to establish new institutions.[55] From then onward, the constitution was seen as the product of the sovereign people, assumed as a single entity. Historically speaking, such a view was deeply influenced by Rousseau's political theory and particularly by his idea of the "general will."[56] During the nineteenth century, European legal and political thought was instead characterized by a deliberate attempt at conceptually neutralizing the principle of people's sovereignty (since evoking the image of the French Revolution) and of the constitution as created by the people. Yet, the latter concept had already powerfully reemerged from post–World War I democratic constitutions and from those promulgated after 1945.[57]

With his writing of 1929, Kelsen proposed an explanation of how democratic constitutions took shape, which implied rather the existence of a pluralism of "political forces" capable of reaching a final compromise upon which institutions were concretely established. That final, big compromise was the constitution itself.[58] In other words, the plural connotation of the constitution coexisted—as we read in the aforementioned passage—with its being "the foundation of the State, [. . .] the essence of the established community by this order." Following Kelsen's reasoning, the constitution appeared as that supreme rule which could not be violated: "the legislator's freedom was subordinated to the Constitution" and the constitutional text itself contained both specific "rules" concerning the proper functioning of the State, the legislative process, and also a "series of fundamental rights": "when the constitution," Kelsen wrote, "establishes the equality in front of the Law, fundamental liberties etc., it is stating that laws are not allowed to violate any of such rights."[59] In this sense, according to Kelsen, "the constitution was a procedural rule and a substantial rule."[60] Constitutional jurisdiction thus had to defend and preserve the constitution as the supreme foundation of the State. The way in which Kelsen argued the constitutional jurisdiction mechanism had both a legal and political aspect.

Against those stating that the Constitutional Court was incompatible with Parliament because it would undermine the power of the latter, Kelsen replied that this was not the case because both the Parliament and the Constitutional Court were subject to the constitution. The primacy of the constitution—which Kelsen had already theorized as a guarantee of balance between the Austrian Bund and the Länder[61]—was also the guarantee of the balance of powers between the legislative body and the jurisdictional one.[62]

At the same time, against those who saw a threat to the Montesquiean principle of the "separation of powers"[63] in the constitutional jurisdiction functions, Kelsen replied by following two lines of reasoning. On the one hand, he stressed that the ultimate role of the Constitutional Court had to be situated within the context of "control" rather than of "separation." On the other, he argued that the Court's primary and main task was to nullify an unconstitutional law rather than "creating it." The latter function belonged exclusively to the legislative body.[64]

In this sense, Kelsen posed a fundamental distinction between the Constitutional Court as "negative legislator" and the Parliament as "positive legislator." Just because the Court had a "negative" rather than a "positive" function, the laws (unconstitutional) could be nullified only *after* they were enforced.[65] Also, the function of nullification and the powers of the Constitutional Court were strictly regulated, like for all tribunals, according to constitutional principles.[66] Kelsen's final position left no doubt: "a constitution which did not contain the guarantee of the nullification of unconstitutional laws and acts was not fully compulsory." For him, if it was not compulsory, there was no true chance to preserve democratic institutions and citizens' fundamental rights.[67] The ultimate objective of the Constitutional Court was, for Kelsen, to defend a specific form of government, that is, parliamentary democracy, and a likewise specific form of State, democratic

Republic. In other terms, he was posing a direct link between the latter and "institutions of control."[68]

The connection between Kelsen's constitutional theory and political theory emerges in all its clarity, when focusing just on the major political implications of the concept and function of "nullification." For him, nullifying unconstitutional laws provided the minorities (inside and outside the Parliament) with a concrete protection against the majority: "the Constitutional Court," Kelsen argued, "can represent a suitable instrument into the hands of the minority to prevent the majority from violating its legally granted rights. In this way the minority can oppose to the dictatorship of the majority, which is no less dangerous than that of the minority for social peace."[69]

The Constitutional Court had to nullify unconstitutional laws and in doing so it worked as a "bulwark" against liberticidal tendencies of the majority.[70] Once the law was nullified, the majority was in fact obliged to review the content of the law taking into account the minority's interests.[71] He justified his aversion to the tyranny of the majority with the following argumentation: "if the essence of democracy does not so much consist in the omnipotence of the majority as in the steady compromise between groups, which the majority and the minority represent within the Parliament and thus in social peace, constitutional jurisdiction seems to be a suitable instrument."[72] The closeness of such reasoning to the first and second edition of *Vom Wesen und Wert der Demokratie* is evident. More precisely, in both editions of his writing Kelsen described the relationship between majority and minority within the legislative body as a distinct component of modern, representative democracy and chiefly as a result of that process of "integration" by means of which the plurality of interests, ideas, and aspirations characterizing society could be "rationalized."[73]

The existence of such a duality (majority and minority) in the Parliament posed—according to Kelsen—the issue of how effectively to protect the latter: a parliamentary democracy where the majority oppressed the minority was its exact opposite, that is, a dictatorship. As a political thinker Kelsen emphasized this crucial issue using two relevant argumentations. As seen in the previous chapter, the first one was purely—so to say—theoretical; that is, he stated that a majority was simply unconceivable without a minority in terms of democratic theory. The second one was, in my opinion, more persuasive and consistent: within the Parliament, laws had to be considered—Kelsen argued—as the result of a "compromise between majority and minority." This was, for him, one of the crucial and distinctive elements regarding modern and representative democracy: here, the content of the "State will" (laws) was not the "diktat" of the majority to the detriment of the minority. For Kelsen, this process of compromise and balance could be even more effective if the electoral system was proportional, simply because the latter—differently from the pure majority electoral system—would grant a wide and articulate representation of minority interests and views within the Parliament. He thought that the stronger the representation was, thanks to the proportional mechanism, the easier a compromise between majority and minority would prove to be.[74]

In both argumentations, the legislative assembly turned into a "space" within which the dialectic between the majority and the minority, which was for him a key feature of a well-functioning democratic system, took shape. In his essays on *Vom Wesen und Wert der Demokratie* Kelsen argued that the particular interplay between the majority and the minority could work so well—chiefly if supported and integrated by a proportional representative system—that the minority would be provided with a tangible protection per se, that is, thanks to the intrinsic logic of the parliamentary activity. Yet, if we turn our attention to, for example, *La garantie jurisdictionelle de la constitution*, we can observe that—as a constitutional theorist—Kelsen identified constitutional control as that special, legal mechanism that might offer an extra and more concrete guarantee to protect the minority against the majority. As a constitutionalist and a legal theorist—despite his claims of scientific neutrality and objectiveness—he was justifying constitutional jurisdiction with a liberal argumentation: the protection of the minority. In other words, in this writing of 1929, his legal and his political reflection seemed to be intertwined. Kelsen emphasized the key role played by the Constitutional Court in the active protection of the minority, and more precisely, he related this special and relevant function to the protection of the Constitution itself, because significant changes to the constitutional text could not be allowed without the support and "agreement" of the minority:

> The revision of the constitution requires a reinforced majority. [It] signifies that some fundamental issues can be resolved only by the agreement of the minority; the simple majority, at least on some matters, does not have the right to impose its will on the minority, in the sphere of guaranteed constitutional rights. Any minority—of class, religion or nation—whose interests are in any way protected by the constitution has an eminent interest in the constitutionality of the law.[75]

In this passage, Kelsen connected constitutional control, protection of minorities, and protection of rights. In doing so, we can see the relevant *political implication of his constitutional control mechanism* one more time. Moreover, I argue that the two editions of *Vom Wesen und Wert der Demokratie*, along with *La garantie jurisdictionelle de la constitution*, represent—as a whole—an important contribution to the twentieth-century liberal-democratic theory combining the liberal principle of the protection of the minority and fundamental rights with the guarantee of the primacy of a democratic constitution. This within a conceptual and theoretical framework recognizing a central role to the idea of social and political pluralism as a presupposition to the actual writing of the constitution itself. The interesting point is that Kelsen was formulating such a theory as a response to the period of democratic crisis involving—in the late 1920s—the major European countries, including his. Do we have to assume at this point of reasoning that Kelsen was proposing and outlining a coherent and convincing constitutional theory of democracy?[76] It depends on the way we conceive the significance of constitutional democracy itself.[77]

If we start from the assumption that the validity and legitimacy of democratic decisions should be bound to "fulfill" human rights or particular principles established by a rigid constitution regulating the "content" of laws, then Kelsen's view of democracy seems not to match such a definition.[78]

If we look at *La garantie jurisdictionelle de la constitution* we can identify several aspects testifying to the lack of a constitutional theory of democracy according to the aforementioned sense of the term. First, when arguing that the constitution was also a "substantial rule" Kelsen was referring rather to the fact that civil and political rights included in the constitution itself had to be granted and protected.[79] Second, Kelsen stressed that "constitutional norms which have to be applied by the court should not include vague words such as liberty, justice, equality" because in this case, according to him, a shift of power from the Parliament to the Court might occur.[80] Among examples of such "vague" principles Kelsen identified human rights, which were for him nothing but forms of "natural law": he rejected the idea of inserting "enforceable human rights" into the constitutional text because this would inevitably, radically change the role and functions of constitutional judges—the latter would change into more or less concealed lawmakers.[81]

In this sense, that is, if we focus on the internal logic of *La garantie jurisdictionelle de la constitution*, we can identify a direct connection between his concept of constitutional jurisdiction and legal positivism.[82] For Kelsen, the constitution did not have to contain an excess of general principles and values because the latter were concretely created by the political subjects acting within the Parliament and legitimized through a democratic vote. In Kelsen's perspective, the constitution first of all had to include those "procedures" underpinning the correct functioning of democratic institutions and legally "stipulated."[83]

Also, and in logical relation to both points just mentioned, the Constitutional Court did not possess any right to reformulate the content of unconstitutional laws, because—according to Kelsen—"the organization of the courts is determined by very different considerations from those that determine the legislative body." He was arguing again that the Court had to be seen and considered as nothing but a "negative legislator."[84] He objectively ascribed relevant tasks to the Court regarding the protection of the constitution and democratic institutions, while reaffirming the non-political identity of the Court itself: it had to limit itself to offering "one among the guarantee of legality."[85] Such a guarantee was functional to the protection of the minority, but this did not imply that the constitutional text would include specific and particular well-defined values or principles to carry out and in whose realization the constitutional judges had to play a key role.[86]

Focusing on this specific aspect of his reasoning, there is no doubt—as correctly stressed—that Kelsen's concern was to preserve the Parliament's political primacy. His democratic theory as well as his constitutional theory were related to the "traditional theory of parliamentarism."[87] After all, already with his *Hauptprobleme der Staatsrechtslehre*,[88] Kelsen had re-evaluated the legislative body in open controversy with the traditional public law theory of the German language,[89] and during the Austrian constituent process he had openly supported the creation of a parliamentary government, in line with social democratic positions. Do we thus have to argue that Kelsen did not elaborate any form of constitutional theory of democracy? I aim to look at his theory of constitutional jurisdiction from two perspectives. His idea of constitutional jurisdiction could be seen as (1) the expression of a particular way of conceiving the relation between the constitution and the legislative body and (2) an integrative part of his personal defense of pluralism. Within the political debates on the future of Austria between those supporting the contractualistic foundation of the Austrian Republic and those instead defending the full assumption of sovereignty by the central institutions in the name of the people, Kelsen took a stance in favor of the latter.[90]

In particular, as previously seen, he was supportive of a parliamentary government which implied two aspects: the political responsibility of the government toward the Parliament and more generally the centrality of the legislative body (democratically elected) in the new Austria. Kelsen shared with the SPÖ a sort of legislative-centric vision of politics and more precisely of democratic life. He always remained loyal to this concept both as a legal thinker and as a political thinker. As a proof of that, in 1929, Kelsen published a legal comment on the constitutional reform—which was enforced on that year—in his *Die Grundzüge der Verfassungsreform* (*The Lines of Constitutional Reform*), in which he expressed in fact a strongly critical opinion on those aspects of the reform aimed at weakening precisely the Parliament. Among them, he mentioned the "Notverordungsrecht" (right to issue emergency decrees), which had to be attributed to the president of the State (elected by the people) and which, in his opinion, would allow the president himself to share legislative power with the Parliament.[91] Also, moving from a legal standpoint to a political one, the fact that Kelsen's view was centered on legislative aspects is also widely testified by his democratic theory: to him, the core of political life, the place where values and principles continuously took shape through a peaceful, rational dialogue and compromise was essentially the Parliament.[92]

Yet—as observed so far—along with this optimistic attitude toward the parliamentary debate, Kelsen, as a constitutional thinker, seemed to offer a more stringent vision, when highlighting the relevance of the Constitutional Court as a mechanism to protect the minority.

By that, in my opinion, he was proposing the idea of constitution as a limit to the power of the legislative body and particularly to the potential "tyranny of majority" rather than as the source (in terms of absolute values) of the content of the legislation itself. His legislative centricism and even his trust in the peaceful and rational dialogue between the majority and the minority within the Parliament coexisted with the consciousness that it was likewise useful to establish some form of limit. It is not by chance that in *La garantie jurisdictionelle de la constitution* Kelsen reminded how it was neither realistic nor possible to count on the Parliament for its willing and spontaneous subordination to the constitution.[93]

The legislative organ was not allowed to violate the constitution: the problem itself of protecting the minority against the majority through the Constitutional Court can been interpreted as a problem of posing a limit to legislative activity and more particularly to its dangerous implications for the existence of democracy itself, that is, the tyranny of the majority. In his writing of 1929, Kelsen did look at the constitution in terms of the supreme foundation of the State and also as a supreme limit, which had to be granted through a special jurisdictional system.[94]

The first concept of constitution had a democratic connotation, within a legal and political theory which—as we have seen—rejected (since the *Hauptprobleme der Staatsrechtslehre*) the principle of the people as a unitary political subject. The second concept of constitution had a more liberal significance. If we approach *La garantie jurisdictionelle de la constitution* from the latter perspective, and if we assume that constitutionalism refers to a set of mechanisms to "constrain democracy," that is, in this specific case the tyranny of the majority, then Kelsen's theory of democracy can also be considered as constitutional.[95] In posing himself the problem of how to prevent the minority from being oppressed, Kelsen embraced one of the fundamental issues characterizing the history of European liberalism and, more generally, liberal constitutionalism, referring to those constitutional tools and principles protecting citizens from political oppression. Among these tools, Kelsen identified constitutional jurisdiction.[96] Yet, the closeness between Kelsen's vision of constitutional jurisdiction and that of democracy is not confined to the issue of minorities. There is a second, crucial aspect to take into account, which emerges from the definition of constitution provided by Kelsen at the beginning of his *garantie jurisdictionelle de la constitution.*

For Kelsen, the constitution was essentially "a principle in which the balance of political forces is legally exerted in a given moment."[97] In other words, the concepts of compromise and balance, which are eminently political, underpinned both his democratic theory and his constitutional theory. Behind Kelsen's frequent recalling of compromise and balance there is, however, an even more substantial kind of problem, assumed by his idea of constitution and democracy itself: pluralism (social, political ideal). The recognition of the dialectical relationship between the majority and the minority as a distinctive component of parliamentary democracy as well as the recognition of the constitution as the result of a complex compromise and balance involving a variety of political forces implied—I believe—the admission of a plurality of interests, ideas, and projects within society and politics. Precisely in his essays on *Vom Wesen und Wert der Demokratie*, when addressing the concrete process and mechanism of parliamentary life, he indeed stressed the issue of party pluralism as one of the main components of modern democracies.[98] In my opinion, his refusal to include determined and once for all defined principles to be carried out within social and political life into the constitutional text might be considered—from his viewpoint—as a condition to grant and preserve pluralism inside and outside the Parliament. In the next chapter we will see how this view of pluralism was interrelated with his defense of relativism as the proper "Weltanschauung" of democracy, but for now I would recall attention not only to the relevance of pluralism for Kelsen but chiefly on how it represents one of the key connections between his democratic and constitutional theories. This aspect emerged again from another major contribution of Kelsen to constitutional theory, *Wer soll der Hüter der Verfassung sein?* (*Who Should Be the Guardian of the Constitution?*), which was his personal reply to Carl Schmitt's *Der Hüter der Verfassung* (*The Guardian of the Constitution*).[99] Both were published in 1931, when Kelsen—after being fired from the Constitutional Court and leaving his country for Germany—began to teach international law at the University of Cologne where Schmitt would work.[100] It is hard to imagine two such different intellectuals and personalities sharing the same space.

CONSTITUTIONAL JURISDICTION AS AN ANTI-AUTHORITARIAN CHOICE

The dispute between Kelsen and his rival Schmitt on the "guardian of the constitution" has been at the center of a wide range of literature.[101] My intention is not to demonize Schmitt or to sanctify Kelsen: the first was undoubtedly one of the major German legal theorists of the 1920s and 1930s.

Rather more simply, I aim to outline the analysis of Kelsen's democratic theory precisely by identifying some of the crucial concepts making his constitutional and political view profoundly different from that of Schmitt.[102] It was in 1929 that Schmitt published an article, *Der Hüter der Verfassung*, which would then be re-edited two years later as an essay with the same title, as a response to Kelsen's defense of *Verfassungsgerichtsbarkeit* during the Annual Meeting of German Public Law Teachers in 1928.[103] It was precisely between 1929 and 1931 that Schmitt and Kelsen were involved in a controversy on who had to be the guardian of the constitution—Schmitt, who looked at the Weimar Republic and advocated such a function for the president of the Republic, or Kelsen, who essentially referred to the Austrian experience and kept defending his idea of constitutional jurisdiction. Behind each vision, as we are going to see, there was a diametrically different way of conceiving parliamentarism and democracy.

Schmitt's writing on the *Hüter der Verfassung* was published when the Weimar Republic was already in the grips of social and political turmoil, which was nurtured and radicalized by the 1929 world financial collapse. The constitutional crisis officially began in 1932, although, in some respects, post–World War I Germany had always lived in a condition of crisis: just think that since its foundation there had been twenty-one cabinets.[104] Between the late 1920s and the early 1930s the Weimar political system showed all its fragilities and weakness. A part of that instability depended on the fact that the Weimar democracy was created within a context characterized by a general mistrust if not hostility toward "parties and parliamentary politics."[105]

We should, however, make a distinction between concrete politics and political-legal theory. With regard to the first aspect, parliamentarism and parliamentary democracy were seen with suspicion by three major subjects: traditionalists, who were nostalgic for the Monarchy and the Hohenzollern; the radical right, who at a certain point began to rally to the Nazis; and the radical left, who aspired for a revolution and "proletarian dictatorship" based on the soviet model. With regard to the second aspect, there were prominent Weimar intellectuals, such as the Social Democrat jurists Gustav Radbruch and the already mentioned Hermann Heller, who were critical toward the way in which German parliamentarism had developed but not toward parliamentarism and parliamentary democracy per se. Radbruch criticized, for example, the pressures of extra-parliamentary groups on parties and the progressive mistrust of the citizens toward their representatives, whereas Heller denounced the missed integration of the working class into the new Weimar democracy, while investigating how to carry out a true people's sovereignty within a democratic and parliamentary system. Yet, they were both in favor of a parliamentary democracy and clearly committed against authoritarianism.[106] Even Erich Kaufmann, another prominent jurist of that time who had initially embraced the democratic turn of Germany only as a way to avoid the "proletarian dictatorship," became supportive of parliamentarism.[107] One thing was clear in 1920s Weimar: the Parliament and parliamentarism were at the center of an articulated intellectual debate. On the opposite side of the barricade, Carl Schmitt contributed to such a debate with his *Die geistgeschichtliche Lage des heutigen Parlamentarismus (The Crisis of Parliamentarism)*—dating back to 1923—in which he attacked parliamentarism and liberalism, establishing a series of concepts useful to better comprehend the clash between him and Kelsen. Parliamentarism was ideologically based, according to Schmitt, on principles such as the faith in rationality, politics as dialogue, and tolerant, open discussion, the ability to find truth by means of rational discussion as well as the belief in the separation of powers and the provision of fundamental liberties.[108]

Liberalism was itself nothing but the ideology of parliamentarism, which—as he stressed—contained two main meanings: on the one hand, it signified a particular form of government, in which the latter was controlled by the parliamentary majority. On the other, it referred more generally to the absolute centrality, which the legislative body had acquired in politics, chiefly since it began to be conceived as functional to democracy.[109]

Yet, looking in particular at the history and politics of his time, Schmitt argued that the discrepancy between ideological construction and reality was huge. As a result of the mass-democracy development, the Parliament had progressively lost "its foundation and its meaning": parliamentarism as a virtuous political practice based on a rational and fruitful open discussion did not exist anymore. It had been replaced by the power of "party coalitions which make their decisions behind closed doors" and the influence of "capitalist groups" which "are more important for the fate of millions of people than perhaps of any political decisions."[110]

The fast degeneration of the Weimar situation in the late 1920s seemed to confirm Schmitt's merciless diagnosis and above all posed the capital issue of how (and whether) to fix it. That solution, for Schmitt, hinged on the identification of the true guardian of the constitution.

With a critical reference to Kelsen's theory of constitutional jurisdiction, Schmitt commenced his essay on *Der Hüter der Verfassung* by legally explaining, in a controversy with Kelsen, why judges could not be the guardians of the constitution. Each time a Constitutional Court was called to express its own judgment on the content of a law, more exactly on its constitutionality, the judges operating within this Court became sort of legislators: "a strange connection," Schmitt wrote, "between legislation and legal advice."[111] This risk had to be firmly prevented because, for Schmitt, it was a violation of the principle of the distinction between constitution and constitutional laws. The first was the expression of the political unity of a people and was immutable, at least until it was radically changed through, for example, a revolution, whereas constitutional laws could be numerous and could be changed by means of a special procedure. Above all, since such laws disciplined and regulated jurisdiction, a court could not be provided with the task of guarding the constitution.[112]

Who could play such a relevant and delicate role for the faith of a democracy? Schmitt's answer assumed a radically critical view of liberal parliamentarism. For Schmitt, since its foundation in the Modern Age, the State stayed in front of society as a neutral subject: State and society constituted a "duality" exactly like "government and people" had done for a long time.[113] In particular, since the nineteenth century—Schmitt argued—a profound transformation concerning just the State-society duality had taken place that assumed growing power to the Parliament. As the latter became the center of gravity of political life, as the principle of popular representation by means of the legislative body strengthened, as individual liberties were granted, as political parties and public opinion developed, and as economic forces advocated the self-regulation of the market, the State drew back whereas society began to push forward.[114]

As a result of this, according to Schmitt, the ancient and traditional duality between State and society vanished: society became the State and the State changed into "the self-organization of society." Also, since society continued to structure and organize its interests through political parties, there was no more difference or separation, for Schmitt, between State-society and parties.[115] Schmitt could thus argue that over centuries we had passed from the "absolutistic State of seventeenth and eighteenth century to a nineteenth century liberal State" which, in some respects, still assumed a duality between State and society until the "perfect identity between State and society."[116]

More precisely, liberalism, liberal parliamentarism, and the predominance of political parties generated its exact opposite in the early twentieth century. The Parliament had no more rivals, it controlled the government but de facto—Schmitt stressed—it was in the grips of a plurality of political parties, which had no more limits, which did not have to confront the State because the latter was nothing but a "pluralistic State of political parties" itself. For him, the Weimar Republic was an excellent example of such new typology of State and above all of its "perverse" outcomes: instability and political weakness. Such outcomes depended, according to his interpretation, on two main factors, both related to liberal parliamentarism "losing its foundations." The first factor was the progressive impairment of the relationship between representatives and represented. In the twentieth century citizens were in fact called to vote for "lists" previously designated by the party and more precisely by the élite of the party itself, which often pushed for the interests of single "social groups of power."[117] Already in *Die geistgeschichtliche Lage des heutigen Parlamentarismus*, Schmitt identified this particular role of political parties as an integrative and distinctive component of mass democracy, which challenged, in his opinion, the primacy of individual liberties and the concept of "argumentative public discussion," considered as core presuppositions (philosophical and political) to liberalism and liberal parliamentarism.[118] The second factor directly concerned the problem of creating the "unitary will of the State." It was a (liberal) illusion for Schmitt to think that it was sufficient to have a plurality of democratically elected parties within the Parliament to reach that will. It was another illusion for him to think that the mere existence of such plurality within the context of rights and freedoms could facilitate discussion and compromises and that laws would be the result of a successful game of compromises.[119]

The impact of powerful lobbies and organizations of interests on them, the excess of political parties, and their continuous splitting, for Schmitt, made the creation of a true "State will" capable of acting for the good of the people and thus of overcoming "egoistic interests" impossible.[120] In other words, the new form of State was the victim of its own "pluralism." Against the "pluralistic State of parties" he opposed the only figure who, in his opinion, truly embodied political unity in Weimar Germany: the president of the Republic. Schmitt justified this specific role of the president following two lines of reasoning: firstly, he drew inspiration from Benjamin Constant's theory of the "pouvoir neutre" (neutral power), according to which the King, just because he was above the other powers, could preserve and restore the balance between them in case of necessity. In this sense, the King's power had a "restorative" connotation.[121] Schmitt recognized the same kind of power just to the president of the Republic who thus became a major bulwark against the "dissolution of a pluralistic system."[122]

Yet, the true reason for the president being the guardian of the constitution was intrinsically related to the particular nature of his designation. The fact to be democratically elected made the president the only guarantee of political unity, which was concretely embodied, for Schmitt, by the German people itself. The latter was a unitary entity, equipped with a "substantive equality" and the supreme subject of "constituent power," which could act—beyond the pluralism of social and political organizations—as a unity through the president. Hence, for Schmitt the "fact that the president of the Republic is the guardian of the constitution corresponds to the democratic principle upon which the Weimar is based."[123]

The president's right to appeal to Article 48 in the case of emergency decrees had to be considered, according to Schmitt, within this framework. The issue of who had to protect the constitution assumed to identify the real source of democratic legitimacy. Schmitt's concept of the guardian of the constitution was based on the connection between the president and the people. Protecting the constitution through the president for him was coherently functional and logically subsequent to the principle of people's sovereignty and unity, which he opposed to pluralism (political and party).[124] On such premises, Schmitt argued against constitutional jurisdiction (and notably against its main supporter, Kelsen) that a group of "professional and immovable judges" like those of a Constitutional Court, designated to examine constitutional issues, would inevitably change into a "second Chamber." Although without a democratic legitimacy, they would become a special organ with a "highly political" connotation, because they would have "functions of constitutional legislation," inevitably allowing them to impose their own values.[125]

They would end up representing a sort of "aristocracy" inside the body of the democratic Republic. In other words, Schmitt blamed constitutional jurisdiction not only for being a serious threat to the classical separation of powers but chiefly for being a danger for the preservation of the democratic principle of people's sovereignty.[126]

With his *Die geistgeschichtliche Lage des heutigen Parlamentarismus* and *Der Hüter der Verfassung* Schmitt was tracing a line of division between parliamentarism and democracy, between pluralism and the sovereign people as a unity, between constitutional jurisdiction and the president of the Republic as the guardian of the constitution.[127] In this way, he was proposing his personal solution to the Weimar crisis. In the late 1920s, the Austrian political situation was no less problematic than the German one: the Constitutional Court, in which Kelsen himself was a judge, was at the center of attacks from conservative forces. Already since 1927 the latter had been seeking to widen the powers of the federal President and strengthen executive power to the detriment of the Parliament, where the Socialists were still numerous.[128]

According to Kelsen himself, one of the major obstacles on the road toward the constitutional reform was the Constitutional Court itself, which the Christian Socials wanted to "reorganize" on the basis of their interests.[129] The conflict between the two powerfully erupted at the end of the 1920s about the "so-called Sever-Marriage," that is, about permitting divorced Catholics to re-marry: the judges "appointed by the Christian Social Party" voted against such granting, whereas the other judges voted in favor of it. Among the latter, there was Kelsen: his vote reflected in part his personal commitment in support of the reform of the marriage law.[130]

He paid for his position: he was insulted and blamed for being everything but *super partes*. He was seen as in the service of the SocialDemocrats who were pro-divorce and with whom he had always had good personal relations, chiefly with Karl Renner.[131]

The clash about the "Sever-Marriages" and the attacks against the person
of Kelsen were the background of the constitutional reform of 1929. By
some measure, Kelsen's vote, which was considered "politically motivated,"
contributed to "providing the political backdrop to the re-organization of
1929."[132] Such interpretation stresses the more political connotation of the
Constitutional Courts' judges (including Kelsen) and seems to give some support to Schmitt, according to whom the Constitutional Court was everything
but neutral. The point is not, however, so much that there might be a gap
between what Kelsen wrote on *Verfassungsgerichtsbarkeit* and the reality of
the Austrian Constitutional Court, as the fact that in his reply to Schmitt's
Hüter der Verfassung Kelsen again defended constitutional jurisdiction as
part of a particular concept of democracy. Their controversy was essentially
on the meaning of democracy in a time of crisis.

In his *Wer soll der Hüter der Verfassung sein?* Kelsen realized that at the
core of Schmitt's anti-constitutional jurisdiction theory was the role of the
president of the Republic as the true and sole guardian of the constitution.
If Schmitt considered the Constitutional Court and its judges as a concealed
form of political power, infringing the separation between political and jurisdictional functions, Kelsen looked at Schmitt's theory as a refined way of
legitimizing a soft dictatorship, led by the president of the Republic. The idea
itself of "neutral power" invoked by Schmitt was, for Kelsen, nothing but a
shield to hide one specific political purpose, that of justifying the figure of the
president as the most powerful subject of the State.[133]

It is not a matter of establishing who was right or who was wrong (at
least, this is not the objective of my analysis) as to show that Kelsen's
reply to his rival contained some core conceptual aspects of his democratic
vision as it was developing at that time. Against Schmitt's critique of constitutional jurisdiction, Kelsen followed two directions: on the one hand, he
restated the principle of the Constitutional Court as a "negative legislator."
Like in *La garantie jurisdictionelle de la constitution*, he argued that one
of the main conditions to preserve the role of the Constitutional Court as a
"negative legislator" was to avoid constitutional norms, including "vague"
concepts and words like "justice," "social equality," and so on.[134] On the
other, he identified Schmitt's theory as a drastic refusal of any form of
pluralism, which, for Kelsen, took two main shapes. First, the attack on
liberal parliamentarism and party pluralism. Second, the idea of the intrinsic unity and homogeneity of the people—developed in contrast to that of
pluralism—which needed to be embodied by a likewise unitary entity: the
president of the Republic.[135]

We have previously seen that the latter—since democratically elected—
was, for Schmitt, the only legitimized to represent "the unitary, collective
interest" of the sovereign people.

The particular link between the people and the president was—as Kelsen stressed—precisely the principle upon which Schmitt justified the role of the president as the supreme guardian of the constitution.[136] According to Kelsen, Schmitt did nothing but formulate a political theory centered on a clear-cut dichotomy, that between the Parliament and the president of the Republic: the former was intended as an "enemy of the State," the source of steady conflicts because of party pluralism, whereas the latter was a "friend of the State," which protected the constitution.[137]

In the late 1920s, Kelsen argued, Schmitt's critique of constitutional jurisdiction had to be seen as an attempt to justify a plebiscitary democracy—based essentially on the direct election of the president of the Republic along with the idea that the latter was the sole guardian of the constitution—and therefore to promote the interests and views of reactionary forces. For Kelsen, Schmitt was in fact one of the most iconic representatives of an authoritarian political thought just because of his refusal of pluralism and his attack on parliamentarism. At that time, another prominent Weimar intellectual, the jurist and legal-positivist Richard Thoma, was criticizing Schmitt with an argumentation very similar and close to that of Kelsen. After all, Thoma, like Kelsen, supported a liberal, parliamentary democracy, based on a political representation.[138]

In ideological terms, Kelsen and Schmitt blamed each other for not being: for Schmitt Kelsen's constitutional jurisdiction was nothing but a threat to the principle of people's sovereignty and thus to democratic legitimacy, whereas for Kelsen Schmitt's theory was nothing but the expression of an authoritarian mentality in contrast with what he thought was the *essence* of parliamentary democracy. Regardless of the reciprocal blaming for being "ideological," we can see how—historically speaking—Schmitt' pro-plebiscitarian democracy and Kelsen's pro-parliamentary democracy embodied the two distinctive souls of the Weimar Constitution itself: the powers recognized to the president of the Republic (chiefly in the form of the Article 48) and his democratic designation can be traced back to the plebiscitarian aspect of the constitution, whereas parliamentarism can be traced back to the representative and liberal aspect.[139]

Indeed in 1932 Kelsen and Schmitt again confronted each other about the guardian of the constitution in relation to the German constitutional crisis. Everything began in the spring of 1932 when frictions emerged in Prussia between the local Landtag (legislative assembly),[140] whose majority was formed by Communists and Nazis, and the local government, which was made up of Socialists and Catholics. The head-on contrast between the two powerfully emerged when Prussian ministers issued a decree banning the Nazi storm troopers and the Blackshirts from the streets. As a reaction, the new chancellor Franz Von Papen, who belonged to the right wing of

the Catholics, promised the Nazis new political elections for the federal
Parliament (Reichstag), which was actually dissolved in June 1932. In the
same month, the ban on the nazi storm troopers was lifted. The consequences
of such decision were devastating for Prussia: Nazis were responsible for
violent street fightings and physical assaults, which lasted two months and
radicalized the political atmosphere even more.[141] This situation offered Von
Papen a unique opportunity to try to get rid of the Prussian ministers, particularly the Socialist ones, who were blamed also for being maneuvered by
the Communists. In July the federal government issued an emergency decree,
subscribed by the president of the Republic, Von Hindenburg, and based
on Article 48, in order to restore order in Berlin and Brandenburg. Legally
speaking, Article 48 (notably points 1 and 2), in fact, gave the president the
right to act in the case of a Land failing its duties and it also gave him the
power to adopt emergency measures if the situation required, in the name of
public order and safety.[142]

The next step was the Prussian government's decision to contest the
decree, which was evidently aimed at submitting Prussia to the central government, while overthrowing the Socialist opponents. Prussia appealed to the
Staatsgerichtshof (Court of the State),[143] which recognized that Prussia was
fulfilling its duties, although order was not restored yet. Hence, the decree,
which was however considered as wrongly enforced, was not unjustified.[144]
The ambiguity of the State Court judgment revealed two things: first, the
institutional paralysis characterizing the Weimar Republic and chiefly how
the Court was unwilling to "review discretionary actions by the executive."[145]
Schmitt and Kelsen were involved in such an event: Schmitt was a member
of the Reich's legal team, while Kelsen belonged to the opposite legal team.
Once again, whereas Schmitt argued legitimate use of Article 48, stating his
idea that the restoration of order was not a matter for judiciary bodies, Kelsen
suggested to establish a serious Constitutional Court in Germany, blaming the
Staatsgerichtshof for its controversial and ambiguous decision.[146] Their interpretation of the Staatsgerichtshof decision again reflected their distance in
considering the problem of protecting the constitution. The dispute between
Kelsen and Schmitt is an excellent example of the head-on contraposition
between two radically different ways of conceiving democracy: parliamentary and pluralistic democracy, including a constitutional jurisdiction mechanism for Kelsen, and a plebiscitary and monist democracy characterized by
the president of the Republic as the supreme incarnation of the people's unity
and defender of the constitution for Schmitt. As I have sought to show, each
of the two assumed two likewise radically different ways of conceiving the
people and the constitution: the pluralist definition of the people (which was
unitary only in legal terms) and of the constitution, which was seen as the
result of compromises and debates, allowed Kelsen to re-valuate and affirm

party and political pluralism. For him, political unity was something continuously created within the Parliament. Instead, for Schmitt the unity of the people was something real and preexisting, even compared to the constitution itself.[147] As a unitary and uniform entity the people exercised the power of giving themselves a constitution. From this perspective pluralism was considered a dangerous threat to the "unitary will" of the people and thus to the unity of the State.[148]

Kelsen considered pluralism a positive force, although he thought that a mechanism of jurisdictional control was needed chiefly to avoid that within a context of pluralism and freedom the tyranny of the majority emerged. Schmitt looked at pluralism as a negative force, while posing the problem of granting the political unity of the State, which implied no concern—differently from Kelsen—for the dialectic relationship between the majority and the minority. The fact that Kelsen was interested in the problem of the tyranny of the majority whereas Schmitt was not reflects how the first developed a theory of democracy from the perspective of freedom—more precisely of how to avoid the majority oppressing the minority—whereas the latter viewed the same issue from the perspective of political unity.[149] For Kelsen it was thus necessary to understand which tools were most useful and adapt to grant freedom and therefore the dialectic between the majority and the minority, this for him being the core of legislative process itself. Among these tools, there was constitutional jurisdiction. For Schmitt it was instead essential to understand how to preserve the unity of the State—which presupposed the already existing unity of the people as sovereign subject—from conflicts and political instability generated, in his opinion, within a parliamentary and pluralist kind of democracy.

To sum up, Schmitt believed in a monist, anti-liberal theory of democracy, while Kelsen believed in a pluralist, parliamentary, and liberal one. Kelsen's theory of constitutional jurisdiction—which was initially strongly related to the Austrian constituent process and the issue of federalism—his dispute with Schmitt, and his particular way of replying to *Der Hüter der Verfassung* enlighten us further on Kelsen's democratic view and his personal political choice in favor of parliamentary democracy. So far, we have analyzed specific aspects of his democratic theory, such as the concept of political representation, the voting system, the dialectic between the majority and the minority, the issue of protecting the minority against the tyranny of the majority, parliamentarism, and constitutional jurisdiction, all presupposing—as I have tried to demonstrate—the principle of pluralism. The point is that, for Kelsen, real democracy was not only a problem of which (good) institutions to choose and make it work properly but also one of which vision of the world ("Weltanschauung") to have. As we are going to see in the next chapter, for Kelsen, democracy could not be effective without a relativist

"Weltanschauung". I will thus discuss how and to what extent Kelsen's concept of relativism is connected with the core elements of his democratic theory discussed so far.

NOTES

1. See on this point: Alec Stone Sweet, "Constitutional Courts and Parliamentary Democracy," *West European Politics* 25, no. 1 (January 2007): 78–80; Costanza Margiotta-Broglio, "La Corte costituzionale italiana e il modello kelseniano," *Quaderni costituzionali* 2 (Agosto 2000): 333–370. Sweet stresses that the basic difference between the American judicial review mechanism and the European constitutional review consist of a different way of conceiving the role of the legislative power. In the United States the judicial review was introduced as an effect of the refusal of "legislative sovereignty," whereas Europe—more precisely after the end of World War II—constitutional review was based on a sort of "suspicion" toward judicial power. That was the reason why constitutional review was recognized to a special Constitutional Court. According to Sweet such difference between the American and the European systems also derives from a likewise diverse interpretation of the "separation of powers" principle. In the United States that principle has been basically seen in terms of "checks and balance" among the "co-equal branches of the government," whereas in Europe that same principle has been often applied in terms of rigorous separation among the main powers. To European eyes, the American judicial review has appeared as a dangerous source of "confusion of powers" for a long time. Alec Stone Sweet, *Governing with Judges: Constitutional Politics in Europe* (Oxford: Oxford University Press, 2000), 2; Sweet, "Constitutional Courts and Parliamentary Democracy," 79. I would add that the European way of interpreting Montesquieu's principle is not an invention of the post–World War II period. Already during the French Revolution it was clear that—differently from the American ones—French political leaders were fundamentally inclined to enforce a clear-cut separation of powers which, over a long period, nurtured the instability of the French revolutionary governments, which were never be able to find a true and effective balance between legislative power and executive power. On this specific issue see in general: Maurice Duverger, *Les constitutions de la France* (Paris: Presses Universitairs de France, 2004).

2. See: Wilhelm Brauneder, *Österreichische Verfassungsgeschichte. Einführung in Entwicklung und Strukturei* (Wien: Manzsche Verlag, 1992), 738–739.

3. For a critical approach to Kelsen's concept of constitutional jurisdiction see: Michel Troper, "Kelsen et le controle de constitutionalité," in La controverse *sur "le gardien de la constitution" et la justice constitutionelle. Kelsen contre Schmitt,* 157–182.

4. See: chapter 1.

5. On the republican orientation of the Austrian nationalist force of that time see: Anton Wandruska, *Österreichspolitische Struktur. Die Entwicklung der Parteien und politischen Bewegungen* (Wien: Verlag für Gesellaschaft und Politik), 370–371.

6. See: chapter 1.

7. *Stenographische Protokolle der Österreichischen Provisorischen Nationalversammlung (1918–1919)*, 31–38. With his draft, Renner restated the commitment of his political party in favor of democratic institutions. His party had contributed to the introduction of male universal suffrage in 1907 and that event had been considered by most Austrian Social Democrats as their own political victory over conservative and reactionary forces. During the Annual Conference of 1917, the party's support of the democratic system was declared again, although with a difference to notice between the moderate and the revolutionary wing of the party. The first—led by Renner—believed in the quality of democratic institutions per se, whereas the latter—led by Otto Bauer—tended to see full democracy essentially as a necessary step toward the creation of a true socialist society. If we look at the rich history of Continental European social democratic parties since the mid-nineteenth century, we can see that they were always marked by this kind of internal split, which derived both from a different way of interpreting Marx's theory of revolution and also from the necessity to apply that particular theory to the reality of their nations. See: Norbert Leser, "Austro-Marxism. A Reappraisal," *Journal of Contemporary History* 11, no. 2/3 (July 1976): 117–133; Melanie Sully, *Continuity and Change in Austrian Socialism. The Eternal Quest for the Third Way* (New York: Columbia University Press, 1982), 14–17 and the recent Mark E. Blum and William T. Smaldone eds., *Austro-Marxism: The Ideology of Unity* (Leiden: Brill, 2015), in particular: 39–56.

8. *Stenographische Protokolle der Österreichischen Provisorischen Nationalversammlung (1918–1919)*, 38.

9. Charles A. Gulick, *Austria from Habsburg to Hitler* (New York: New York University Press, 1984), 50; *Stenographische Protokolle der Österreichischen Provisorischen Nationalversammlung (1918–1919)*, 65.

10. Felix Ermacora, *Österreichischer Föderalismus vom patrimonialen zum kooperativen Bundesstaat* (Wien: Braumüller, 1984), 41.

11. See: Eric Roman, *Austria-Hungary and the Successor States: A Reference Guide from the Renaissance to the Present* (New York: Fact on File Inc., 2003), in particular: 93–141.

12. In 1918 by Länder one meant the territory up and below the river Enns. Since 1867 the Habsburg Empire, which was transformed into the Austro-Hungarian Monarchy, was "divided" between the Crown Länder, which corresponded to the Western half of the Empire (Cisleithania or Austria), and the Lands of the Hungarian Crown (Transleithania). Both parts were unified under the Crown of the Habsburgs. Ariel Roshwald, *Ethnic Nationalism and the Fall of the Empires* (London and New York: Routledge, 2000), 8–11. See in general: Kann, *A History of the Habsburg Empire 1526–1918*, 1977.

13. Ernst Hanisch, *Österreichiche Geschichte 1890–1990. Der lange Schatte des Staates. Österreichiche Gesellschaftsgeschichte im 20. Jahrhundert* (Wien: Carl Überreuter, 1994), 74–75.

14. For an introduction to federalism through an historical perspective: John Boogman and Gees N. Van der Plaat eds., *Federalism: History and Current Significance of a Form of Government* (Netherlands: Springer, 1980). For a general

overview of federalism in terms of political science: George Anderson, *Federalism: An Introduction* (Oxford: Oxford University Press, 2008).

15. *Stenographische protokolle der Österreichischen provisorischen nationalen Versammlung (1918–1919)*, 76.

16. Ibid., 77–78. The point is however that the Regions subscribing those "declarations" saw themselves as full "sovereign subjects." Ferdinand Karlhofer and Günther Bischof, eds. *Austrian Federalism: History-Properties-Change* (Innsbruck: Innsbruck University Press, 2015), XXI–XXII.

17. Another example of the complex relationship between the Center and the Regions were the vehement protests made by a delegation of representatives of Austrian Regions against the National Provisional Assembly on October 22, 1918. They strongly criticized the Assembly for advocating the monopoly of the whole administrative re-organization and for wanting to cut the Regions out of the subsequent writing of the constitution. Alfred Ableitinger, "Die Grundlegung der Verfassung," in *Österreich 1918–1938. Geschichte der ersten Republik*, Zwei Bände, hrsg. Erika Weinzierl and Kurt Skalnik (Graz, Wien: Styria Verlag, 1983), 151.

18. Brauneder, *Österreichische Verfassungsgeschichte*, 192–193; Gerald Schmitz hrsg., *Die Vorentwürfe Hans Kelsens für die Österreischiche Verfassung* (Wien: Manz Verlag, 1981), 22 ff.

19. The Social Democrats gained the relative majority of votes within a proportional type of electoral system. The political success of Renner's party induced the Christian Socials to abandon the tones of "religious crusade," which they used against their rivals during the electoral campaign, in order to re-open a dialogue with them. The CSÖ was realistic enough to comprehend that head-on opposition to the Socialists would affect its ability to influence the writing of the constitution. Norbert Leser, *Genius Austriacus. Beiträge zur Geschichte und Geistesgeschichte Österreichs* (Wien, Köln, Graz: Hermann Böhlhaus Nachf., 1986), 180–181.

20. In this sense, the best source to effectively realize the predominance of the Social Democrats within the National Provisional Assembly are the *Stenograhische Protokolle* of the Assembly itself.

21. *Stenographische protokolle der Österreischichen konstituirenden Nationalversammlung*, 65–66.

22. Ibid., 33.

23. It was not the first time that Renner took a stance on the introduction of a constitutional jurisdiction mechanism. In his *Das Selbst-bestimmungsrecht der Nationen* (*Right of Self Determination of Nations*) (1917), he outlined the transformation of the Austro-Hungarian Empire into a big democratic Federation of the Habsburg nationalities and suggested to establish a federal Constitutional Court, whose task would be to protect citizens' constitutional rights, verify the constitutionality of member states laws, and safeguard the correct division of competences between the federal government and the single member states. It is to be notice that, once the Empire collapsed and even the most remote chance to change the Empire into a sort of super-Danubian Federation vanished, the Social Democrats and Renner himself embraced the unitary-centralized option against their conservative opponents. See: Karl Renner, *Das Selbstbestimmungsrecht der Nationen* (Leipzig, Wien: J. Deuticke, 1917), 75ff.

Ermacora, *Österreischicher Föderalismus vom patrimonialen zum kooperativen Bundesstaat*, 48 ff.

24. The Imperial Court was valid only within the western part of the Empire (Cisleithania), that is, the territories called Austria.

25. Andrzey Dziadzio, "The Role played by the Constitutional Tribunal in Preserving the Liberal Nature of the Habsburg Monarchy in the Turn of the 19th Century," in *Constitutional Developments of the Habsburg Empire in the Last Decades Before its Fall*, ed. Kazimierz Baran (Krakow: Jagiellonian University Press, 2010), 25–28.

26. Brauneder, *Österreichische Verfassungsgeschichte*, 738–739. The powers and the tasks of the Imperial Court were accurately analyzed by Georg Jellinek in his *Ein verfassungsgerichtshof für Österreich* (1885).

27. This was the position of those supporting the federal option.

28. Schmitz, *Die Vorentwürfe Hans Kelsens für die Österreischichen Bundesverfassung*, 114 and Gerald Schmitz, *Karl Renners Briefe aus St. Germain und ihre rechtspolitischen Folgen* (Wien: Manzsche Verlag und Universitätsbuchhandlung, 1991), 49–59.

29. Theo Öhlinger, "Verfassungsgerichtsbarkeit und parlamentarische Demokratie," in *Im Dienste an Staat und Recht. Festschrift für Erwin Melichar*, hrsg. Hans Schäffer (Wien: Manz Verlag, 1983), 125 ff.

30. Hans Kelsen, "Die Stellung der Länder in der künftingen Deutschösterreich," *Zeitschrift für Öffentliches Recht* (1919–1920), 98–122.

31. Ibid. He would repeat the same concept one year later in *Der Vorentwurf der österreichischen Verfassung* (*The Draft of the Austrian Constitution*) (1920), in which Kelsen argued in fact that the Austrian State was a unitary entity, established solely to fight against the centrifugal thrust coming from the Regions. Hans Kelsen, "Der Vorentwurf der österreichischen Verfassung," in *Die Vorentwürfe Hans Kelsens für die Österreischiche Verfassung*, hrsg. von Gerald Schmitz (Wien: Manz Verlag, 1981), 1–33.

32. Kelsen, "Die Stellung der Länder in der künftingen Verfassung Deutschösterreichs," 125 ff.

33. Felix Ermacora, *Die Entstehung der Bundesverfassung 1920. Die Sammlungen der Entwürfe zur Staats- bzw. Bundesverfassung* (Wien: Braumüller, 1989), 6. Peter Bussjäger, Christoph. Schrameck, and Mirella M. Johler, "Federalism and Recent Dynamics in Austria," *Revista d'estudis autonòmics i Federals* 28 (2018): 74–75.

34. Felix Ermacora, *Die Bundesverfassung und Hans Kelsen. Analyse und Materiale* (Wien: Universitätsbuchhandlung, 1981), 19, in particular: 15–19. On the meetings with the Regions' governors, see also: Clemens Jabloner, "Die Gerichtshöfe des öffentlichen Rechts im Zuge des Staatsumbaues 1918 bis 1920," in *Beiträge zur Rechtsgeschichte Österreichs*, Bd. 2, hrsg. Thomas Olechowski (Wien: Verlag der Österreichischen Akademie der Wissenschaft, 2011), 213–222.

35. Mayr's draft was based on one of Kelsen's constitutional drafts. Hans Kelsen, *Österreichisches Staatsrecht. Ein Grundriss entwicklungsgeschichtlich dargestellt* (Tübingen: J. B. C. Mohr, 1923), 161.

36. Ermacora, *Die Entstehung der Bundesvrfassung 1920. Die Sammlungen der Entwürfe zur Staats- bzw. Bundesverfassung*, 6.

37. Kelsen, "Der Vorentwurf der österreichischen Verfassung," 314–317.

38. Karin M. Schmidleichner, "Die steirische Presse und die Bundesverfassung," in *Studien zur Zeitgeschichte der österreichischen Länder. Demokratisierung und Verfassung in den Ländern 1918–1920* (Wien: St. Polen, 1983), 148–160.

39. Ermacora, *Quellen zum österreichischen Verfassungsrecht (1920). Die Protokolle des Unterausschusses des Verfassungsausschusses* (Wien: Österreichisches Staatsarchiv, 1967), 139 and Schmitz, *Karl Renners Briefe aus St. Germain und ihre rechtspolitischen Folgen*, 73–74.

40. Stanley L. Paulson, "Hans Kelsen and Carl Schmitt. Growing Discord Culminating in the Guardian Controversy of 1931," in *The Oxford Handbook of Carl Schmitt*, ed. Oliver Simons and Jens Meierheinrich (Oxford: Oxford University Press, 2016), 522.

41. "Gross-deutscher Entwurf," 97; "Zweiter Christsozialischer Entwurf," 142–143; "Sozialdemokratischer Entwurf," 151. They are all included in Ermacora, *Quellen zum österreichischen Verfassungsrecht (1920). Die Protokolle des Unterausschusses des Verfassungsausschusses*, 1967.

42. Ibid., 298–311.

43. See: chapter 1.

44. Ermacora, *Quellen zum österreichischen Verfassungsrecht (1920). Die Protokolle des Unterausschusses des*, 354–356. The principle of establishing committees of inquiry was accepted but not in the form imagined by Kelsen, because of the Christian Social opposition. Ibid., 352.

45. Ibid., 354.

46. Thanks to such a "procedure," the Constitutional Court self-activated on laws, which constituted the premises of its rulings. See: Giorgio Bongiovanni, *Reine Rechtslehre e dottrina giuridica dello Stato. Hans Kelsen e la Costituzione austriaca del 1920* (Milano: Giuffré, 1998), 190–192. See also Schmitz, "The Constitutional Court of the Republic of Austria," 240–265.

47. Hans Kelsen, "Verfassungs und Verwaltungsgerichtsbarkeit im Dienste des Bundesstaates, nach der neuen österreichischen Bundesverfassung vom 1. Oktober 1920," *Zeitschrift für Schweiz. Recht* 52 (1923): 185–186.

48. Ibid., 192.

49. Kelsen, "Der Vorentwurf der österreichischen Verfassung," 318; Kelsen, "Verfassungs und Verwaltungsgerichtsbarkeit im Dienste des Bundesstaates, nach der neuen österreichischen Bundesverfassung vom 1. Oktober 1920," 175–177.

50. Ibid., 192.

51. This is the core principle underpinning Kelsen's work on "La garantie jurisdictionelle de la Constitution," 1929.

52. Kelsen defended the principle of constitutional jurisdiction during the 1928 meeting of the Association of German Public Law.

53. Hans Kelsen, "La garantie jurisdictionelle de la constitution," in *Annuaire de l'Institut Internationelle de droit publique* (Paris: Les Presses Universitaires de France, 1929), 63–64.

54. He would re-state the same concept in the second edition of the essay as well. See: chapter 1.

55. In this sense, just think about the figure of Emmanuel Joseph Sieyés with his pamphlet *Qu'est-ce que le Tiers-État?* (1789).

56. Petra Gümplova, *Sovereignty and Constitutional Democracy* (Baden-Baden: Nomos Verlag, 2011), 10 ff; See also: Lucien Jaume, "Constituent Power in France: The Revolution and its Consequences," in *The Paradox of Constitutionalism: Constituent Power and Constitutional Form*, ed. Martin Loughlin and Neil Walker (Oxford: Oxford University Press, 2008), 67–85.

57. Maurizio Fioravanti, *Costituzione* (Bologna: Il Mulino, 1998), 99 ff.

58. Kelsen, "La garantie jurisdictionelle de la constitution," 63–64. Against, for example, the Rousseauian concept of the people considered as unitary entity, Kelsen stated that the people was sociologically a plurality and a multiplicity of individuals, interests, and visions, and that it became a unity only from a legal point of view, that is,—as we can read in *Vom Wesen und Wert der Demokratie*—only when its members "were subjected to the same legal-normative order."

59. Kelsen, "La garantie jurisdictionelle de la constitution," 65.

60. Ibid.

61. With regard to the relationships between the federal government and the Regions, Kelsen emphasized—in line with what he stated during the constituent process—that constitutional jurisdiction was essential to preserve and respect the separation of responsibilities between the Bund and the Länder: "every violation—Kelsen argued—of the federal responsibilities from the Länder and vice versa represents an attack on the constitution." The protection of the constitution allowed—according to him—the preservation of the intrinsic unity of the State. The latter presupposed thus a perfect equality between Federation and Regions in terms of appealing to the Constitutional Court. Kelsen, "La garantie jurisdictionelle de la constitution," 95.

62. Ibid., 95 ff.

63. See: Charles L. Montesquieu (Baron de Secondat), *L'Esprit des lois* (Paris: Classique Garnier, 2011).

64. Kelsen, "La garantie jurisdictionelle de la constitution," 92–95. The relevance of political compromise clearly emerged also from the fact that the members of the Constitutional Court, who were appointed by the Parliament, belonged (in part) to the two major political parties of Austria: from 1921 onward, four members of the Court came from the Christian Social Party, three came from the Social Democratic Party, and four were "neutral." Among the latter there was Kelsen himself. Tamara Ehs, "Felix Frankfurter, Hans Kelsen and the Practice of Judicial Review," *Zeitschrift für Öffentliches ausländisches Recht und Völkerrecht* 73 (2013): 461; Stephan G. Hinghofer-Szalkay, "The Austrian Constitutional Court: Kelsen's Creation and Federalism's Contribution?," *Féderalism Régionalism* 17 (2017), https://popups.ulieg e.be:443/1374-3864/index.php?id=1671.

65. Kelsen insisted a lot on the difference between "positive and negative legislator." Kelsen, "La garantie jurisdictionelle de la constitution," 77 ff; 89; 92–97 and also 133.

66. Ibid., 110.

67. Ibid., 99.
68. Ibid., 136.
69. Ibid., 136–138.
70. Ibid.
71. On this aspect: Renaud Baumert, "Audiatur at altera pars: justice constitutio-nelle et decision démocratique dans le pensée de Hans Kelsen," in *La controverse sur "le gardien de la constitution" et la justice constitutionelle. Kelsen contre Schmitt*, 143–152.
72. Kelsen, "La garantie jurisdictionelle de la constitution," 137–138.
73. See: chapter 1.
74. Ibid.
75. Kelsen, "La garantie jurisdictionelle de la constitution," 137.
76. See for this aspect the recent: Ferrajoli, *La logica del diritto. Dieci aporie nell'opera di Hans Kelsen*, 227 ff. Also: Ferrajoli, *La democrazia costituzionale* (Bologna: Il Mulino, 2016), 9–65.
77. I refer to Richard Bellamy's essay *Constitutional Democracy*, in which he identifies four major meanings of constitutional democracy according to the particu-lar way of interpreting the relation between constitution and democracy: that is, if in terms of "constraint" (of constitutionalism on democracy) or if in terms of "con-stitutionalism enabling democracy." Richard Bellamy, "Constitutional Democracy," in *The Encyclopedia of Political Thought*, ed. Michael Gibbons (New Jersey: John Wiley & Sons, 2015), 2–13. On the same issue see also: Richard Bellamy, *Political Constitutionalism. A Republican Defence of the Constitutionality of Democracy* (Oxford: Oxford University Press, 2007), 90 ff.
78. This is for example Luigi Ferrajoli's opinion. He argues that after the end of World War II Europe (and other parts of the world) have been marked by the promulgation of democratic constitutions including what he defines as "substantial principles." According to these new democratic constitutions (among which he men-tions the Italian one of 1948), laws are valid because they are coherent with those principles and implement them. For him this is the true significance of constitutional democracy. On the other hand, we have Richard Bellamy's position, identifying four major meanings of constitutional democracy, in terms of political theory. Ferrajoli, *La democrazia costituzionale*, 2016; Bellamy, "Constitutional Democracy," 1–15. For an effective analysis of contemporary debate on constitutionalism: Luigi Lacché, "Rethinking Constitutionalism between History and Global World: Realities and Challenges," *Giornale di Storia costituzionale/Journal of Constitutional History* 32, no. 2 (2016): 5–31.
79. Kelsen, "La garantie jurisdictionelle de la constitution," 71.
80. Ibid., 118.
81. Ibid., 118–120; on this point see: Stone Sweet, "Constitutional Courts and Parliamentary Democracy," 81–82. For a different interpretation of this specific aspect see: Invernizzi-Accetti, "Reconciling Legal Positivism and Human Rights: Hans Kelsen's Argument from Relativism," 220–228. Applying a perspective of political philosophy, the author argues instead that in Kelsen's work we can find credible theoretical foundations for a defense of human rights on the basis of his legal

positivism and relativist attitude. It is however interesting to observe that the article's author does not take into account Kelsen's writing on "La garantie jurisdictionelle de la constitution" and more generally those on constitutional jurisdiction.

82. Kelsen, "La garantie jurisdictionelle de la constitution," 63 ff.

83. Ibid., 91–92. On this point see: Dyzenhaus, *Legality and Legitimacy. Carl Schmitt, Hans Kelsen and Hermann Heller in Weimar*, 151.

84. Kelsen, "La garantie jurisdictionelle de la constitution," 92 ff.

85. Ibid., 53–58; 66–67.

86. Kelsen, "La garantie jurisdictionelle de la constitution," 118–119. On this point see also: Ferrajoli, *La democrazia costituzionale*, 29–31.

87. Pasquale Pasquino, "Verfassungsgerichtsbarkeit und Demokratietheorie," in *La controverse sur "le gardien de la constitution" et la justice constitutionelle. Kelsen contre Schmitt*, 28.

88. See: chapter 1.

89. Ibid.

90. See the previous paragraph of this chapter.

91. The president's new power according to the constitutional reform implied—Kelsen stressed—that he could issue emergency decrees when there was no time to wait for the Parliament's decisions. Kelsen, "Die Grundzüge der Verfassungsreform," *Neue Freie Presse* (October 20, 1929), 6–7.

92. See: chapter 1. In the next chapter on "Democracy and Relativism" I will argue how profoundly such particular concept—that is, the legislative body as a space for the creation of values and principles—was intertwined with Kelsen's defense of relativism. I will also seek to show the controversial implication of such a view in relation to the concrete historical-political context of the late 1920s and the early 1930s, in which Kelsen published his last writings on the essence and meaning of democracy before leaving Europe for the United States in 1940.

93. Kelsen, "La garantie jurisdictionelle de la constitution," 92.

94. Ibid., 53 ff.

95. Bellamy, "Constitutional Democracy," 2 ff.

96. See the fundamental: Guido De Ruggiero, *History of European Liberalism*, Engl. trans (London: Peter Smith Publ., 1977); David Harris, "European Liberalism in the 19th Century Europe," *The American Historical Review* 60, no. 3 (1955): 501–526. It is true that De Ruggiero's interpretation of liberalism was conditioned by his closeness to Italian idealism but his book remains one of the best sources for an understanding of European liberalism in a historical perspective. For a more recent work see: Richard Bellamy, *Liberalism and Modern Society. An Historical Argument* (London: Blackwell, 1992), which offers an analysis of some great "liberal" thinkers of the following countries: Italy, England, France, and Germany, from a perspective between history of ideas and political theory.

97. Kelsen, "La garantie jurisdictionelle de la constitution," 65.

98. See: chapter 1.

99. Carl Schmitt, *Der Hüter der Verfassung* (Tübingen: Verlag von J.C.B Mohr (Paul Siebeck, 1931); Hans Kelsen, *Wer soll der Hüter der Verfassung sein?*(Tübingen: J. C. B. Mohor, 1931).

100. Métall, *Hans Kelsen. Leben und Werk*, 55–57.

101. See: Michael Haybäck, *Carl Schmitt und Hans Kelsen in der Krise der Demokratie in der Zwischenkriegszeit: eine rechtsphilosophische und historische Analyse*, Dissertation (Salzburg, 1999); Carlos G. Herrera, "La polemica Schmitt-Kelsen sobre el guardian de la constitucion," *Revista de Estudios Politicos* 86 (October, December 1994): 195–277. Herrera, *Le droit, le politique. Autor de Max Weber, Hans Kelsen, Carl Schmitt*; Dyzenhaus, *Legality and Legitimacy: Carl Schmitt, Hans Kelsen and Hermann Heller in Weimar*; Vinx, *Hans Kelsen's Pure Theory of Law: Legality and Legitimacy*; Beaud-Pasquino, *Le controverse sur "le gardien de la Constitution" et la justice constitutionelle: Kelsen contre Schmitt*; Lars Vinx, "Introduction," in Lars Vinx, *The Guardian of the Constitution: Hans Kelsen and Carl Schmitt on the Limits of Constitutional Law* (Cambridge: Cambridge University Press, 2015), 1–21; Oliver Simons and Jens Meierhenrich, eds., *The Oxford Handbook of Carl Schmitt*; Giovanni Bisogni, *La politicità del giudizio sulle leggi. Tra le origini costituenti e il dibattito giusteorico contemporaneo* (Torino: Giappichelli, 2017); Josu De Miguel Bárcena, *Kelsen versus Schmitt: política y derecho en la crisis del constitucionalismo* (Madrid: Guillermo Escolar Editor, 2018).

102. For a comparison between Kelsen and Schmitt on the issue of constitutional jurisdiction from a perspective of legal philosophy see. Stanley L. Paulson, "Arguments conceptuelles de Schmitt à l'encontre du controlle de constitutionalité et response de Kelsen. Un aspect de l''affrontement entre Schmitt et Kelsen sur le gardien de la constitution," in *Le controverse sur "le gardien de la Constitution" et la justice constitutionelle. Kelsen contre Schmitt*, 244–262.

103. During the annual meeting of the association in 1928, there was a discussion between Kelsen and Triepel on constitutional jurisdiction: the first reasoned on its meaning and implications in purely abstract terms, the second in historical terms. Caldwell, *Popular Sovereignty and the Crisis of German Constitutionalism*, 80 and Stolleis, *Geschichte des öffentlichen Rechts in Deutschland. Staatsrechhtslehre und Verwltungswissenschaft 1914–1945*, Bd. 3, 193–195.

104. See on the Weimar collapse since the late 20s the fundamental: Mommsen, *The Rise and Fall of Weimar Democracy*, 1996.

105. Ellen Kennedy, "Introduction: Carl Schmitt's *Parlamentarismus* in Historical Context," in Carl Schmitt, *The Crisis of Parliamentary Democracy* (Eng. trans. 1st and 2nd ed.), ed. and trans. Ellen Kennedy (Cambridge Massachusetts and London England: MIT Press, 1998), XXV.

106. See: Gustav Radbruch, "Goldbilanz der Reichsverfassung," *Die Gesellschaft* 1 (1924): 57–69; Heller, "Politische Demokratie und soziale Homogeneität," 421–434.

107. Kaufmann opposed tenaciously to Kelsen's legal positivism, as the Annual Meetings of the Association of German Public Law Teachers between 1926 and 1929 testify. Yet, he shared with him a political view in favor of democracy. See: Stanley L. Paulson, "Some Issues in the Exchange between Kelsen and Kaufmann," *Scandinavian Studies in Law* 48 (2005): 274–276 and Baume, *Hans Kelsen and the Case for Democracy*, 28–29.

108. Schmitt, *The Crisis of Parliamentarism*, 35–42.

109. Ibid., 34–35.

110. Ibid.

111. Schmitt, *Der Hüter der Verfassung*, 37.

112. Ibid., 37 ff.

113. Ibid., 73–78.

114. Ibid.

115. Ibid., 77–82.

116. Ibid., 82–84.

117. Ibid., 84–91.

118. Particularly see: Carl Schmitt, "Preface to the Second Edition," in *The Crisis of Parliamentary Democracy*, 2–17.

119. Schmitt, *Der Hüter der Verfassung*, 86 ff. On Schmitt and his attack on pluralism see: Van Ooyen, *Der Staat der Moderne. Hans Kelsens Pluralismustheorie*, 163–177.

120. Schmitt, *Der Hüter der Verfassung*, 86 ff.

121. See: Benjamin Constant, *Principles of Politics Applied to all Governments*, Eng. trans. (Indianapolis: Liberty Fund Inc., 2003). On this aspect: Valentino Lumowa, "Benjamin Constant on Modern Freedom: Political Liberty and the Representative System," *Ethical Perspectives* 17, no. 3 (2010): 391–405.

122. Schmitt, *Der Hüter der Verfassung*, 132–141. Schmitt argued that one of the "fathers" of the Weimar constitution, Hugo Preuss, had always seen the president of the Republic as a counter-weight against the Parliament. For Schmitt, Preuss was conscious that in the new Germany, the president of the Republic could be a strong point of reference and an element of unity against political fragmentation. Ibid.

123. Ibid., 157–158. Article 48 allowed the president, in case of emergency, to take measures without the prior consent of the Parliament. Among such measures there were the "emergency decrees."

124. Schmitt, *Der Hüter der Verfassung*, 158.

125. For a reflection on the role of constitutional judges as subjects "imposing values" see David Robertson, *The Judge as Political Theorist: Contemporary Constitutional Review* (Princeton, New Jersey: Princeton University, 2010), 19.

126. Schmitt, *Der Hüter der Verfassung*, 155–156.

127. Ibid. This concept was already present in his essay on *Parlamentarismus*. Kennedy, "Introduction: Carl Schmitt's *Parlamentarismus* in Historical Context," XXXII–XXXIII.

128. Kelsen paid a special attention to such dynamics and particularly to the Christian Socials' proposal to modify the constitutional text of 1920. In his *Die Grundzüge der Verfassungsreform* (*The Lines of the Constitutional Reform*) (1929) he identified all the major legal and political aspects of such proposal: the Conservatives asked to strengthen the powers of the majority, those of the federal president, while changing the structure of the legislative assembly by creating a professional Chamber. If it is true that Kelsen positively accepted the proposal of limiting the parliamentary immunity and reinforcing the popular initiative, he criticized the idea of passing constitutional reforms through a popular referendum at the condition that the latter was requested by the majority of the National Counsel. The latter formed along with the

Länder Counsel, the federal Assembly. This kind of procedure would be to the detriment of the minority. Yet, the proposal scaring Kelsen the most were that concerning the establishment of a professional (that is, not political Chamber) for the reasons already clarified in the previous chapter and that concerning the role of the president of the Republic. The latter would be elected directly by the people (like in Weimar Germany) and would be attributed the power of enforcing "Notverordungsrecht" (emergency decrees) which could even modify the content of laws when it was not possible (because of a declared state of emergency) to wait for the Parliament's resolution. The point was that it was the president's right to determine when it was the case to enforce an emergency decree or not. This gave the president significant discretionary power. Kelsen, "Die Grundzüge der Verfassungsreform," 6–7.

129. Métall, *Hans Kelsen. Leben und Werk*, 47–50.

130. Kelsen supported for many years the activity of the Society for the Reform of the marriage. He was sensitive to the problem of marriage legislation. Ehs, "Felix Frankfurter, Hans Kelsen and the Practice of Judicial Review," 464.

131. Ibid.

132. Ibid. To reconstruct Kelsen's work in the Court, see in general: Walter, *Hans Kelsen als Verfassungsrichter.*

133. Kelsen, *Wer soll der Hüter der Verfassung sein?*, 8 ff.

134. Ibid., 14–28.

135. Ibid., 36 ff.

136. Ibid., 36–52.

137. Ibid., 47–56.

138. See: Richard Thoma, "Sinn und Gestaltung des deutschen Parlamentarismus," in *Recht und Staat*, hrsg. Bernard Harms, Bd. 1 (Berlin: Reimar Hobbing, 1929), 98–126.

139. Christoph Möllers, "We are (Afraid of) the People": Constituent Power in German Constitutionalism," in *The Paradox of Constitutionalism: Constituent Power and Constitutional Form*, ed. Martin Loughlin and Neil Walker (Oxford: Oxford University Press, 2008), 87–92.

140. Weimar Germany was a federal State, made up of Länder.

141. Caldwell, *Popular Sovereignty and the Crisis of German Constitutionalism*, 164–165.

142. Vinx, "Introduction," 2015, 1–4.

143. The Staatsgerichtshof was designated to decide special cases, including those with a constitutional connotation. Yet, it was not a true constitutional court and in fact "it never exercised significant control over government" and "rarely challenging state action, particularly that under article 48." Carl Schmitt, *Legality and Legitimacy*, Eng. trans. Jeffery Seitzer (Durham and London: Duke University Press, 2004), 139.

144. Vinx, *Introduction*, 2015, 4–5.

145. Caldwell, *Popular Sovereignty and the Crisis of German Constitutionalism*, 168.

146. Schmitt, "Prussia contra Reich: Schmitt's Closing Statement in Leipzig," 222–227 and Kelsen, "Kelsen on the Judgment of Staatsgerichtshof 25 October 1932," 228–253. Both in Vinx ed., *The Guardian of the Constitution*, 2015.

147. The concept of "political unity" was likewise crucial in his 1928 essay "Der Begriff des Politischen" ("The Concept of the Political").

148. On this point: Caldwell, *Popular Sovereignty and the Crisis of German Constitutionalism*, 86–87.

149. On the centrality of freedom in Kelsen's concept of constitutional jurisdiction see Lepsius, "Der Hüter der Verfassung demokratisch betrachtet," in *La controverse sur "le gardien de la constitution" et la justice constitutionelle. Kelsen contre Schmitt*, 118–120.

Chapter 3

Democracy and Relativism

ANTI-JUSNATURALISM AND RELATIVISM: A GENERAL OVERVIEW

In 1930 Kelsen lived in Germany and—as previously seen—he was involved in the controversy with Schmitt, a colleague at the University of Cologne.[1] A few years later, Kelsen witnessed the fall of the Weimar Republic and Hitler's political victory in 1933, which made his professional and personal life in Germany more and more difficult.[2]

On April 7, 1933, the nazi regime passed a law expelling from German universities all those professors who were politically undesirable. Kelsen's expulsion was motivated by his alleged proximity to marxist groups, which sounds sadly paradoxical and ironic, if one thinks that for all his life Kelsen was admittedly anti-marxist.[3] He then decided to move to Switzerland where he taught at the Institute of International Studies (Geneva).[4] Here he remained until 1940 when he left Europe with his family for the United States.[5] In scientific terms, the early 1930s were however undoubtedly a fruitful and intense period for Kelsen. His interests and publications ranged from the theory of legal and formalist positivism—which was officially systemized in his *Reine Rechtslehre* (*Pure Doctrine of Law and State*)—to the theory of international law with works such as *Fragen des Völkerrechts* (*Questions on International Law*) (both published in 1934) and *Das Primat des Völkerrechts* (*The Primacy of International Law*) in 1936.[6]

After his second exile to Switzerland (the first one had been from Austria to Germany) Kelsen again faced the issue of democracy in a very brief essay entitled *Wissenschaft und Demokratie* (*Science and Democracy*), published in 1937. After that, he would elaborate on democratic theory in 1955 when— already in the United States—he published *Foundations of Democracy*.[7] His last contribution to democratic theory, while still living in Germany, was not the second edition of *Vom Wesen und Wert der Demokratie*, but rather two writings—respectively published in 1932 and 1933—that is, *Verteidigung der Demokratie* (*Defence of Democracy*) and *Staatsform und Weltanaschauung* (*Forms of State and World Outlook*). Both were brief, concise, and—maybe because of the particular political situation in Germany moving to the nazi dictatorship—also characterized by an atypical (at least for Kelsen) "emotional" attitude.[8] If we ideally match the latter essays with Kelsen's second edition of *Vom Wesen und Wert der Demokratie* we can see how for him real democracy was also a matter of world vision.

I have already shown how, for Kelsen, the essence of democracy was its being a form of political organization based on representative and parliamentary institutions, the provision of fundamental liberties, the dialectical relationship between the majority and the minority, which could be facilitated by a particular voting system—the proportional one—and which needed a constitutional jurisdiction mechanism. I have also argued that all these components—constituting the essence of democracy for Kelsen—assumed the concept of pluralism. Real democracy was, for Kelsen, liberal and pluralist. Yet, real democracy was not only a problem of granting (positive) rights or recognizing party pluralism as *conditio sine qua non* to make bills the result of compromises rather than *diktats*.[9] It was also a matter of the way one looked at life and considered oneself in relation to the others. For Kelsen, any political system presupposed a precise way of seeing and understanding life and human relations. His theory of democracy had thus a cognitive dimension, which was perfectly coherent with his legal theory philosophically based on the neo-Kantian assumption, according to which the way we know determines the object we know.[10]

To Kelsen, democracy dealt with a particular "Weltanschauung": the relativist one. In all of his works on political theory Kelsen identified the connection between relativism and democracy, both when living in Europe and when—after 1940—living in the United States.[11] By relativism Kelsen mainly intended that epistemological and philosophical view refusing "absolute truth" and "absolute values," meant as universally valid, just, and therefore immutable.[12] In the next pages, I will argue that Kelsen's stance in favor of relativism did not imply moral indifference or indifference toward which form of government might be the best to preserve individuals' freedom and dignity. For now, I am interested in stressing how the ultimate roots of Kelsen's conception of relativism are, in part, embedded in his legal theory.[13]

I have previously argued that his (ultra) positivist view of Law, State, and sovereignty worked as a relevant condition to a broader reformulation of the meaning of the legislative body, to a likewise important reformulation of the meanings of people and constitution, which were both crucial for his democratic and constitutional theory.[14] In the same way, behind his definition of relativism and his refusal of "absolute" values and truth, there was a likewise drastic critique of natural law and natural law doctrine.[15] In other words, Kelsen's legal theory, or at least some of its core assumptions, actually represents an important theoretical pre-condition to his idea of relativism in relation to his democratic theory. Kelsen's particular definition of relativism itself can in fact be better comprehended by taking into account his attack on natural law. All his work was characterized by a strong critique of the latter[16]: from the *Hauptprobleme der Staatsrechtslehre* (1911) to his essays *Der soziologische und juristische Staasbegriff* (*The Sociological and Legal Conception of the State*) (1922) and *Die philosophische Grundlagen des Naturrechtslehre und des Rechtspositivismus* (*The Philosophical Foundations of Natural Law Doctrine and Legal Positivism*) (1928) passing through the *Allgemeine Staatslehre* (1925); from the first edition of the *Reine Rechtslehre* (1934), to works of the American period such as *Society and Nature* (1943), the *General Theory of Law and State* (1945), *Law, State and Justice in the Pure Theory of Law* (1948), *The Natural Law Doctrine before the Tribunal of Science* (1949), and *What Is Justice?* (1957).[17] Just to mention some of his most relevant writings in order to reconstruct his anti-jusnaturalist position.[18]

In the 1920s as well as almost thirty years later when already moved to the United States, Kelsen took his distance from natural law and natural law doctrine coherently with his legal positivism. Taking the abovementioned works into consideration we would immediately realize that his anti-jusnaturalist argumentation developed in the European period remained fundamentally unchanged in the American one. That is the reason why I will outline such argumentation by primarily referring to one of his European major writings on this issue, that is, *Die philosophische Grundlagen des Naturrechtslehre und des Rechtspositivismus*, and—where possible—to some equally relevant works from his American phase. Kelsen admitted as law only a positive one, considered as creation of human will and as a "coercive order," which "brought about a certain behavior of men" and sanctioned "in case of opposite behavior."[19] The legal validity of such process of creation and therefore the legal validity of any legal norm depended, in his opinion, on its correspondence to particular procedures, relying on the constitution.[20] Instead, for Kelsen, natural law implied the idea that legal norms were such because their validity derived from their perfect correspondence to "nature" ("nature of men," as living beings equipped with "human reason," or from "nature in general"), which contained objectively "just norms" prescribing how people had to behave, live etc.[21] in his *Die philosophische Grundlagen des Naturrechtslehre und des Rechtspositivismus* of 1928 the laws were thus "just" because their content reflected the norms/principles inscribed in the "nature" in one of the aforementioned meanings.[22] Many years later in *The Natural Law Doctrine before the Tribunal of Science* would stress that the "nature" became the "legislator."[23]

As we can read in his work of 1928 and in many other published later on this issue, both those tracing the validity of positive norms to "nature" and those tracing it to the "nature of men," that is, to "human reason," were making a mistake for Kelsen: the first because "nature" was rather per se a dimension based on mere "causal" relations, that is, it "has no will" and therefore no "prescriptions" and "orders" for humans can be deduced from nature; the latter because "the norms prescribing human behavior" derived from "human will" rather than from "human reason," which was also a very complex concept to define.[24] If reason "described" human behavior, will "prescribed" them. To Kelsen, the "mistake" of the whole natural law doctrine was thus to overlap two dimensions which his legal theory maintained as rigorously separate: that of "Is" and that of "Ought to." In other words, in his opinion, the natural law doctrine inferred legal (positive) norms, which corresponded to the "Ought" dimension, from the "Is" one.[25] For Kelsen, behind the doctrine of natural law and such an overlapping mechanism there was the necessity to identify a universal, objective, immutable source of validity for positive and human norms. In natural law doctrine such a source of validity was inevitably meta-juridical, just because it was embedded in "nature."[26] According to Kelsen, the need and the aspiration to find an ultimate, definitive, and universally valid explanation or foundation to reality (in this case to law) was the effective expression of a "metaphysical-religious" kind of mentality, which he opposed to a "scientific," "positivist," and "critical" one.[27] His emphasis on the dichotomy "metaphysical-religious mentality" and "scientific mentality" is considered as an important intellectual affinity with the Vienna Circle, which Kelsen knew, and which had a strong anti-metaphysical connotation.[28] If a "metaphysical-religious" kind of mentality was the typical of natural law doctrine, the "scientific" one characterized legal positivism and particularly his *Reine Rechtslehre*, which—as he would affirm later in *Law, State and Justice in the Pure Theory of Law*—"restricts itself to a structural analysis of positive law based on a comparative study of the social orders [. . .] The problem of the origin of the law—the law in general or a particular legal order—meaning the causes of the coming into existence of the law [. . .] are beyond of the scope of this theory."[29]

Instead, as we can continue to read in *Die Philosophischen Grundlagen des Naturrechtslehre und des Rechtspositivismus*, the "metaphysical-religious" vision was embedded in the persisting human mistrust toward one's ability to understand the world. Men needed to believe in some, final foundation, including of the law, in order to overcome this sense of insecurity.[30] Hence, Kelsen seemed to relate the natural law concept and doctrine to a specific psychological and human inclination. As stressed in scholarly literature, the psychological explanation was particularly visible in his 1920s writings, such as *Die Philsophischen Grundlagen des Naturrechts und des Rechtspositivismus*,[31] maybe as a result of Kelsen's interest in psychology and Sigmund Freud's thought.[32] Yet, if it is true that in his later works the psychological explanation was less emphasized, the anti-metaphysical argumentation—as we can see, for example, in *What Is Justice?* belonging to the American period—remained unchanged and strongly present.[33] Kelsen identified also a fundamental, inner contradiction between the "metaphysical" component of the natural law doctrine and the historical dimension within which that doctrine had concretely developed over centuries. In his opinion, the aspiration of such doctrine to universality clashed with the ever-changing human and historical reality.

The problem was—Kelsen argued—that, beyond the ("metaphysical") aspiration to find the ultimate foundation to reality, just the meaning of "nature" and therefore what the latter "prescribed" varied in history. Kelsen reminded how, for example, the right to property was considered a sacred and inviolable "natural right" or the exact opposite, that is, as not a natural right, according to the different way of considering the meaning of "nature." John Locke's concept of "nature" implied the right to property as natural right, whereas those claiming the elimination of private property as the source of all social evil started from an evidently different idea of the meaning of "nature."[34] As clearly emerged from his *Die Philsophischen Grundlagen des Naturrechts und des Rechtspositivismus*, Kelsen was defining natural law doctrine like nothing but an elegant ideological product: in very general and abstract terms the natural law doctrine stated that "nature" was the objectively valid and just source of positive norms. Yet—Kelsen stressed—precisely the way of interpreting the significance of "nature" and the norms it allegedly prescribed changed according to historical, ideal, and political factors.[35]

Kelsen argued that—over centuries—natural law doctrine had thus served as a powerful instrument to sustain and legitimize specific forms of political and social order. In this sense, for Kelsen, natural law was not so much the source of positive law, as a way to historically and ideologically justify it.[36] Hence, Kelsen's critique of natural law was a critique of ideology: as legal theorist he was arguing that only positive law existed and as political thinker his declared objective was to understand the meaning of democracy beyond any ideological construction or interpretation.[37]

What interests me is not so much the correctness of Kelsen's reasoning or lack thereof as to highlight two aspects: first, Kelsen's critique of natural law took shape through a direct contrast between natural and positive law. Second—and most importantly—he vehemently rejected the idea of "nature" becoming the source of legal norms and order because of its alleged being objectively "just." Kelsen's critical view of natural law, whose roots can be situated within his legal theory, underpinned his idea of relativism itself. Natural law doctrine with its efforts to inscribe the prescriptive component of legal norms within "nature"—the latter assumed as an already given, immutable, perfect, true, just dimension—for Kelsen, implied an epistemological, psychological, and philosophical "absolutist" conception of life and world.

It contained the belief that somewhere, in "nature" exactly, the ultimate, definitive, just principle determining the validity of all positive, legal norms and human conduct could be identified.[38] Instead, legal positivism, with its interpretation of law in terms of the validity of legal creation process and therefore indifferent toward a problem of meta-juridical foundation of legal norms, assumed a relativist one.[39] Many years after *Die Philsophischen Grundlagen des Naturrechts und des Rechtspositivismus*, in his *General Theory of Law and State*, we can find an effective overview of the contraposition between natural law and positive law in terms of the contrast between an "absolutist" and a "relativist" conception of law:

> The essential characteristic of positivism, as contrasted with natural law theory, may be found in the renunciation of an "absolute" material justification and therefore in a [. . .] self-imposed restriction to a merely [. . .] formal foundation of legal validity. . . . Any attempt to push beyond such relative-hypothetical foundation, that is to move [. . .] to an absolutely valid fundamental norm justifying the validity of positive law, means the abandonment of the distinction between positive and natural law. Positivism and [. . .] relativism accordingly belong together just as much as do the natural law doctrine and (metaphysical) absolutism.[40]

Recognizing how central such argumentation—that is, the "formal foundation of legal validity"—was for Kelsen's definition of relativism might turn out supportive of that long series of scholars and intellectuals blaming him for elaborating a dangerous legal theory, reducing the complex problem of legitimacy to a problem of legal norms authorization. Kelsen's critics have often stressed how—according to his pure theory of Law—positive norms were legal and legitimate essentially if they were created according to established procedures. Fully adopting exactly this kind of argumentation we could deduce that Kelsen's defense of relativism was coherent with a legal theory, which was evidently indifferent to the issue of values and founding principles. This is one of the reasons why his legal theory, in particular, and legal positivism in general have often been blamed for potentially justifying any kind of political regime, including the dictatorial ones.[41] Historically speaking—as we are going to see in the next chapter—this kind of critique became incredibly popular just after World War II when the counter-positiv-ist reaction led by neo-jusnaturalist thinkers took place.[42]

Once it is established that Kelsen rejected natural law and that he identi-fied a connection between natural law-absolutism, on the one hand, and legal positivism-relativism, on the other, can we argue that his stance in favor of relativism was the (inevitable) result of a theory mainly oriented to identifying "legal" with "legitimate," that is, mainly focused on the "formal foundation" of legal process? Can we argue that Kelsen's relativism was the ultimate expression of a substantial indifference toward values? Regarding such a question, there is, in my opinion, at least one fundamental objection to take into account, chiefly if assuming the perspective of the history of politi-cal thought.

As I observed at the beginning of this chapter, Kelsen defined relativism above all as proper "Weltanschauung" of democracy. This became particu-larly relevant in both editions of *Vom Wesen und Wert der Demokratie*, which were devoted to the analysis of real democracy, while targeting—respec-tively—the Soviet regime and the rise of reactionary forces in Austria.[43]

Regardless of Kelsen's claim to outline a neutral analysis of parliamentary democracy, what he was actually doing—as I have tried to show in chap-ter 1—was rather to justify representative and parliamentary democracy as a much better option in comparison to those ideologies and regimes which were anti-parliamentary and against fundamental liberties. The same kind of consideration might be applied and extended to his 1930s essays, such as the aforementioned *Verteidigung der Demokratie* until his American works, such as *Foundations of Democracy*. As we are going to see, the first was any-thing but a sterile academic exercise: it represented Kelsen's personal word in favor of democracy, freedom, against absolutism and autocracy, before he left Germany. With the second, Kelsen stated again his choice for representa-tive democracy and relativism in the time of the Cold War period.[44]

His conception of relativism actually assumed a radical critique of natural law and natural law doctrine. Also, it assumed a particular positivist and formalist legal theory (which has arouse numerous critiques), but politically speaking such a conception was consciously inserted by Kelsen—as political thinker—within a broader theory aiming to define the meaning of democracy and defend it against its opponents. The fact that Kelsen elaborated on the significance of relativism as vision of democracy, which he openly consid-ered preferable to the major non-democratic systems of his time (both of the extreme left and extreme right), has a relevance, which is worth being discussed. The point for me is to understand how and to what extent Kelsen's view of relativism, assuming a harsh, with unappealing view and critique of natural law doctrine, was functional and coherent to his view and defense of parliamentary, liberal and pluralist democracy.

THE PARABLE OF JESUS AND PILATE

In both editions of *Vom Wesen und Wert der Demokratie* Kelsen devoted one chapter to "democracy and life visions," although it was in the second edition that, in my opinion, we can better grasp the core political implications of his idea of relativism as "Weltanschuung" of democracy. Kelsen developed his reasoning by establishing a clear-cut dichotomy between relativism and absolutism, as the two philosophical and epistemological views characterizing respectively two specific forms of government: democracy and its opposite, that is, autocracy. Such classification was already clearly present in the *Allgemeine Staatslehre* and in his speech on *Demokratie* held in 1926 for the German Sociological Association. It was again discussed in his essay on *Staatsform und Weltanschuung*.[45] The differences between the two forms of government dealt with both institutional mechanisms and philosophical visions: democracy, differently from autocracy, presupposed, for example, parliamentarism, party pluralism, and the guarantee of fundamental rights. The divide between the rulers and the ruled was ineradicable for Kelsen in real democracy although—unlike autocracy—the ruled could choose their rulers through the elections:

> The creation of numerous leaders becomes the central problem of real democracy—which, contrary to its ideology, is not a collective without leaders—which stands out from real autocracy not so much for the absence as, rather, for the great number of heads. And so, a special method of selecting leaders from the governed community appears element of real democracy. This method is election.[46]

The designation of the "leaders" from below implied a double "rationalization" of the leadership itself: on the one hand, the function of the rulers seemed to be "submitted" to "social order," which meant that rulers were politically responsible for their actions and decisions toward the people. On the other, the relationship between the rulers and the ruled—being based on the electoral mechanism, on the provision of civil and political rights, including the right for the citizens criticize the rulers' behavior—was, so to say, dynamic. For Kelsen, such dynamism was also implemented by the fact that in democracy, at least on paper, every person was supposed to participate in political life and compete for elections.[47] On the contrary, within autocracy, such relationship was rigid and fundamentally immutable, because—Kelsen argued—the "autocratic system [. . .] does not know any method to create leaders." In autocracy, for Kelsen, the complex problem of how to select rulers was in fact reduced and transformed into the question of who should rule.[48] According to Kelsen, once it is established that, for example, the ruler/s had to be "the best," any other problem or issue, including that of political responsibility or the guarantee of freedoms and rights, became of secondary or even irrelevant.[49]

The implications of the dichotomy between democracy and autocracy so far outlined are significant: first of all, the dual classification of the forms of government should be correctly situated within Kelsen's attempt to identify the components and mechanisms of real democracy. Second, the provision of fundamental freedoms was an implicit and essential condition for Kelsen to enact and preserve the political process leading to the creation of the ruling class.[50]

For now and in this specific case, I would rather recall the attention on another, crucial element: to Kelsen, the different relationship between rulers and the ruled—characterizing both democracy and autocracy—assumed a likewise diverging view of life, world, and truth, that is, a diverging episte-mological and philosophical vision. The connection, which he established between relativism-democracy and absolutism-autocracy, was based on the idea that the way we know and interpret reality influences our life and specifi-cally the major forms of political and social organizations. The Kantian and more precisely neo-Kantian influence of such reasoning is evident: Kelsen himself admitted it in his *Absolutism and Relativism in Philosophy and Politics* (1948).[51] With that—as properly stressed, for example, in *Staatsform und Weltanschauung*—Kelsen was far from affirming any "absolute" or "necessary" cause-effect relation between one's philosophical vision and politics or political thought. He was rather tracing a "tendency," according to which a certain way of looking at the world and interpersonal relations impacted one's political belief and even—on a larger scale—political sys-tems' organization.[52]

For Kelsen, behind autocracy there was the firm belief in the existence of "absolute truth," an "absolute reality," or "an absolute value" and the possi-bility to access it, whereas democracy was based on a totally different kind of assumption, according to which human beings could only comprehend "rela-tive truths" and "relative values." The latter—since relative—could change, rise, evolve, and decline.[53] Philosophical absolutism admitted the existence of "the thing in itself," an absolute reality truly existing. Knowing meant thus— Kelsen stressed—to know that "thing in itself."[54] To him, if starting from such assumption (which, for him, was for example typical of the natural law doc-trine), the idea and "cause" of democracy itself would be lost, because faced with someone (a person, a Leader, a Party, a Church) possessing the com-prehension of "absolute truth" only "obedience" was admitted. Such "obedi-ence" was de facto the submission to that person or group of persons who, since they knew what was objectively good and true, unilaterally decided and ruled for the whole community. Within an autocracy, ideologically sustained and nurtured by philosophical absolutism, the one or the ones knowing what is objectively right or wrong would impose their will on the people regardless of their consent.[55] Instead, philosophical and epistemic relativism rejected the "thing in itself," while recognizing the existence of a plurality of "knowing subjects," all equal, who knew and interpreted the world by establishing reciprocal contacts and relations. As Kelsen emphasized, this kind of view was particularly suited for democracy, which—differently from autocracy—was in fact based on equal rights and freedoms, on the indirect participation of the people to political decisions, on the dialectic between the majority and the minority, on pluralism of parties and opinions.[56]

In autocracy, there was a supreme Leader who possessed the truth, indicating which values and principles were "objectively" true and valid. The latter were thus "transcendent." It was precisely their being "transcendent" which provided the autocratic chief with an absolute power: he possessed a truth, which could not be reached or comprehended by the rest of the people, because this truth was embedded in a reality or nature, which only the autocrat could access.[57] The allegedly "absolute truth" possessed by the Leader—Kelsen argued—became a powerful "screen" to hide the true origin of his power, with a "mystic-religious veil." This was vital for autocratic systems just because—differently from democracy—they did not include any method to select the Leader.[58] According to Kelsen, philosophical absolutism was thus coherently and perfectly functional to the scopes and projects of an autocratic Leader. It was a powerful ideological tool to strengthen autocratic power itself.[59] In democracy, instead, values and principles emerged from the political game, which fully developed within Parliament through debates between diverse, plural, and competing ideas, by means of political parties and through the dialectic between the majority and the minority.[60] Values as well as truths were thus "immanent" to human and political life: they were a human creation, and because of this, they could change and evolve.[61] In my opinion, it is in the light of such reasoning that Kelsen greatly insisted a lot, for example, on the "negative" function of constitutional judges, whose task was not to apply a set of pre-ordered values inside the constitutional text but rather to nullify unconstitutional laws.[62]

In democracy, the nature of leadership was "immanent" too, because rulers were chosen by the ruled through elections. It was the mechanism of electoral selection to determine and legitimize their political position, instead of some allegedly "absolute truth." The dichotomy between absolutism-autocracy and relativism-democracy implied thus a likewise diverging idea of the origin of political power and chiefly a divergent way of justifying it. In autocracy, the origin of that power remained a sort of inaccessible mystery for the people: as a result of this, only passive obedience to the one who possessed and understood the supreme truth was admitted. In democracy, on the contrary, the origin of that power was public and known: the rulers were such because selected through elections. As a result of this, for Kelsen, consent instead of obedience became crucial to defining the relationship between the rulers and the ruled in democracy. The fact that consent was required, that rulers were responsible toward the ruled, and that the latter had the similarly capital responsibility to select the ruling class made a serious democratic political education extremely relevant for Kelsen.[63]

He had already spoke about this in a concise essay dating back to 1913: *Politische Weltanschauung und Erziehung* (*Political World Outlook and Education*) and he returned on this crucial issue in the late 1920s, with the second edition of *Vom Wesen und Wert der Demokratie*, not so much for some abstract or academic reason but as a way to reflect on his time. He argued in fact that the many problems experienced by the new ruling classes of the post–World War I period partly arose from a poor democratic education and consciousness.[64]

Kelsen's reference to the problem of education shows us, in my opinion, how his relativism was *relative* itself: in democracy all values and truths were relative—because of their immanence—but to make a democratic system work, with its full meaning, the rulers had to be mentally and culturally prepared, educated to democracy.[65] In *Vom Wesen und Wert der Demokratie*, the dichotomy between relativism and absolutism was thus functional to show that the idea of relative truths and values was coherent with a liberal and pluralist conception of democracy, also based on a fluid, dynamic relationship between the rulers and the ruled. Conversely, belief in the existence of an absolute truth or principle determining social and political life was instead a constituent element of autocracy. Such a dichotomy was based in part—as I have tried to show—on the connection (of neo-Kantian influence), between the way of knowing/interpreting process and reality.[66] This kind of connection underpinned both Kelsen's legal and political theory. As previously discussed, Kelsen's critique of natural law implied the rejection of any "metaphysical," "absolute" foundation of law, in favor of a "formal" and "hypothetical one." Legal positivism could accept only the second one, because law (positive) was a human product and because human reason could not access absolute truths.

Moving from legal to political theory, the terminology changed but the sense of Kelsen's reasoning remained, in my opinion, unchanged: by elaborating the contrast between relativism-democracy and absolutism-autocracy, Kelsen wanted to show what kind of dangerous consequences for individuals' freedom the belief in absolute truth or in some universally valid principle/value/truth embedded in reality or "nature" might imply. Against absolutism and autocracy, Kelsen argued that politics (exactly like law) was a human, immanent product of forces, which—in the specific case of democracy—acted within a plural and free space. As legal theorist, he was firmly against any "absolute" (or "metaphysical" to use his words). As a political thinker he refused any absolutist foundation of political power and leadership, arguing that autocratic systems, sustained by an absolutist philosophical vision, changed people into passive "subjects," whose only task was to obey. In the light of such argumentation, Kelsen's stance in favor of legal positivism (*contra* natural law and natural law doctrine) and in favor of relativism does not appear so much as a way to deny the existence of values/truth per se or even worse as a way to elaborate some anti-democratic or worse pro-dictatorial reflection. It appears rather as an integrative component of his conception of real democracy in contrast to autocracy.

It was just at this point in his reasoning that Kelsen introduced the Parable of Jesus and Pilate in the final part of *Vom Wesen und Wert der Demokratie*: he was referring to Chapter 18 of the Gospel, in which Jesus Christ's trial is narrated. Jesus states to be the one who brings the "truth" and all those who listen to his voice will be participating in the truth. Right in front of him, there is Pilate, the Roman governor, who—Kelsen argued rather ironically—does not know what truth is "because he comes from a skeptical civilization." Since being free from any absolute belief or conviction—that is, since he is a "relativist"—Pilate lets the people decide about Jesus's faith and the people decides to sentence Jesus to death, while saving Barabbas, a thief.[67] Kelsen's comment on such passage of the Gospel did not really aim to stress that the people had made a terrible mistake by consenting to crucify Jesus. Kelsen did not consider the Parable of Jesus and Pilate as the proof that in the absence of absolute values or principles wrong decisions could be made, rather that Pilate with his behavior embodied a true relativist and democratic attitude. He did not know what "truth" was; he did not possess or presumed to possess it. Hence—Kelsen argued—he appealed to the people, rather than imposing his own, personal will.[68] Kelsen seemed to have no doubt about this: Pilate behaved democratically because he left the people the last word on Jesus's life.[69] Yet—as correctly argued in scholarly literature—the use of such Parable risks being counter-productive for Kelsen's argumentation in favor of relativism as a vision of democracy. Pilate relying on the people (or should we say crowd?) to decide Jesus's fate (who moreover for Pilate was legally innocent) maybe should not be taken as the example of a political man with a democratic and relativist attitude but rather as the example of a clever governor who was simply trying to strengthen his own political position. For its part, the people gathered in front of Pilate's palace appeared more like a mass led by emotions rather than a democratic people, as Kelsen imagined it.[70]

Such argumentation is certainly useful to highlight the conceptual (and political) limits of the way in which Kelsen used the Parable of Jesus and Pilate. Yet, it is likewise relevant, in my opinion, to identify two more aspects, which might be helpful to reconstruct some probable reasons why Kelsen used just the Gospel episode. First, in my opinion, at the end of *Vom Wesen und Wert der Demokratie*, Kelsen needed to summarize the dichotomy between relativism-democracy and absolutism-autocracy with a powerful and striking image. The popular and iconic Parable of Jesus and Pilate offered him a good opportunity in this sense. Second, as we can see from some of his writings, the use of such Parable was perfectly coherent with his undoubted tendency to select historical characters, thinkers, figures embodying, in his opinion, one of these two visions (relativism or absolutism). He referred, for example, to Plato, Thomas of Aquin, Dante Alighieri, Leibniz, and Hegel as representatives of an "absolutist" philosophical vision.[71] In particular, Jesus and Plato, for him, shared the belief in the existence of an "absolute justice" founded on a likewise absolute conception of "good."[72] Instead, Locke and Hume—as "founders of anti-metaphysical empiricism"—and Kant, with his preference for methodological issues and with his idea of knowledge as a continuous process, were all considered by Kelsen against "political and philosophical absolutism."[73] Yet, if we confined ourselves to focusing on Kelsen's critique of political and philosophical absolutism in contrast with relativism—expressed in his intentions through the (controversial) Gospel Parable—we would have a still partial understanding of his view. In fact, he took a step forward by arguing that the very refusal of absolute truths or absolute values implied a precise moral and political choice in favor of toler-ance, which was another remarkable aspect of real democracy distinguish-ing it from autocracy.[74] Here, Kelsen passed from analyzing the *essence* of democracy to illustrating its *value*.

For Kelsen, real and parliamentary democracy was based on the dialectic between the majority and the minority. Both were legally provided with full rights to promote their program and ideas. The majority was not such because embodying some allegedly true, objective, and universally valid political principle, because in possession of the only and true meaning of "good," or because it received more votes after an electoral competition, based on equal political rights.[75] For its part, the minority, which was not such because it represented a wrong or unjust vision per se, could become the new major-ity if it conquered people's spirits. The provision and recognition of same freedoms and dignity to the majority and the minority implied—as Kelsen argued—that none of the two had either the power or the right to prevaricate on its counterpart. The particular dialectic existing between the majority and the minority—assuming a relativist view because, for Kelsen, only a person convinced of possessing an absolute truth, believing to be "enlightened" by "a divine inspiration" or a "supranatural light" could "remain deaf" to the others' opinions—expressed at best, in his opinion, the spirit of tolerance as distinctive aspect of democracy.[76]

According to the argumentation developed so far, Kelsen related relativism-democracy and tolerance within one single reasoning. He believed that the consciousness of how relative values and truths were nurtured—within a political system providing citizens with the same rights and freedoms—a tolerant mentality and behavior, which was concretely embodied, in his view, by the particular relationship between the majority and the minority.

Two observations are worth making at this point: in my opinion, Kelsen's relativism was anything but the symptom of moral indifference. Within his democratic and political theory, relativism should rather be considered as a presupposition to tolerance. More specifically, from a perspective of the history of political thought, it is equally interesting for me to observe how by linking relativism with tolerance, Kelsen ended up justifying the first with a classical liberal argumentation: the principle of tolerance is in fact crucial to all liberal tradition.[77] With that I am not trying to cast doubt on the consistency of Kelsen' argumentation but to stress how he seemed to internalize a kind of mindset which can be related—from my viewpoint—to the liberal one. With regard to this specific aspect, I maintain that Kelsen's defense of tolerance and his particular way of establishing the connection between philosophical absolutism-autocracy and philosophical relativism-democracy presents interesting connections with the work of some prominent representatives of nineteenth- and twentieth-century European liberalism. Kelsen's praising of tolerance and everyone's right to freely express their opinion within a free and respectful confrontation represents the epitome of classical European liberalism: from John Locke to Karl Popper. Just think about John Stuart Mill: with his works he connected liberalism and democracy by advocating a representative government, tolerance, equal political rights and above all by defending the principle of individual freedom.[78]

In his essay *On Liberty* (1859), he theorized freedom of opinion and of speech, tolerance toward the others' opinions, and the respect of the minority/ies as the blueprint of a truly liberal (and democratic) system. Like another great champion of nineteenth-century European liberalism, Alexis De Tocqueville, he vehemently criticized the tyranny of the majority inside and outside the legislative body.[79] Mill's liberalism assumed, however, a particular way of considering the cognitive process: for him, the "absolute truth" was inaccessible, and he argued that what we call truth or truths commonly resulted in, for example, politics, from open discussions and respectful, rational confrontation among different ideas, even with those which were visibly wrong or false.[80] Mill argued in fact that "though the silenced opinion might be an error, it may [. . .] contain a portion of truth; and since the general or prevailing opinion on any subject is rarely or never the whole truth, it is only by the collision of adverse opinions that the reminder of the truth has any chance to be supplied."[81]

In other words, the nature itself of the cognitive process was one of the reasons why, for Mill, intolerance could have no room within a truly liberal society. No one, not even the most powerful majority, thus had the right to silence the minority or deprive it of its freedoms.[82] If we stopped here, we would already have identified significant similarities between Kelsen's political thought and Mill's one. The following quote from *On Liberty* provides us with a further example of such closeness of viewpoints:

> Truth, in the great practical concerns of life, is so much a question of the reconciling and combining of the opposites, that very few minds sufficiently capacious and impartial to make the adjustment with an approach to correctness, and it has to be made by the rough process of a struggle between combatants fighting under hostile banners. [. . .] Only through diversity of opinion is there, in the existing state of human intellect, a chance of fair play to all sides of the truth.[83]

In Kelsen like in Mill the open, rational dialect among different visions, perspectives, proposals, the respect for diversity of opinion, the respect for the minority, that is, tolerance, were all deeply intertwined. In this sense, both were two genuine liberal thinkers. Kelsen's reflection on the connection between autocracy and absolutism, the way in which he depicted the figure of the autocrat and the path from an absolutist view of the world to an autocratic, repressive, intolerant political system also seemed to be close—not to say precursor of—to Isaiah Berlin's work on the intellectual origins of the twentieth-century dictatorial (or autocratic for Kelsen) regimes.

Between the late 1940s and the early 1950s,[84] the liberal English philosopher, whose work can be situated within the so-called Cold War liberalism,[85] was committed to identifying—through the perspective of the history of ideas—the ideal roots of authoritarian political ideologies nurturing twentieth-century totalitarianism. He outlined a cultural and philosophical process starting with ancient philosophers such as Plato proceeding until Marx with his historical materialism, passing through Enlightenment scientism (embodied by thinkers such as Hélvetius and Condorcet), Hegel's idealism, and Comte's positivism.[86] In his opinion, all these thinkers shared one core element, a substantially identical "Weltanschauung": the belief that the absolutely just way of comprehending life, society, and politics could be obtained, that there was somewhere an "absolute truth" to grasp, and that—once discovered and revealed to the rest of the world—all values could be reconciled. For Berlin, such a granitic vision, which he called "monism," was the basic epistemological and philosophical premise to modern totalitarianism and precisely to soviet communism and nazism.[87] In *Two Concepts of Liberty* (1955), Berlin's definition of monism as the ideological "heart" of anti-liberal and anti-democratic regimes seems to evoke Kelsen's argumentation on philosophical absolutism discussed so far because—like the latter—Berlin believed:

> One belief, more than any other, is responsible for the slaughter of individuals on the altars of the great historical ideals—justice or progress or the happiness of future generations, or the sacred mission or emancipation of a nation or race or class, or even liberty itself, which demands the sacrifice of individuals for the freedom of society. This is the belief that somewhere, in the past or in the future, in the divine revelation or in the mind of an individual thinker [. . .] there is a final solution.[88]

For Kelsen philosophical absolutism was tied to autocracy to the same extent as for Berlin monism was tied to totalitarianism, because for both a political system based on the idea that those ruling possessed the absolute truth, a principle absolutely and universally valid or—in other words—the "final solution" would be inevitably anti-liberal, intolerant, and anti-pluralist. For Berlin like for Kelsen, "absolute truth" politically required nothing but pure, mere, total obedience and submission.[89] Similarly, Berlin—as Kelsen did for absolutism—delineated the exact opposite to monism, that is, pluralism. The latter was the belief that there was not only no ultimate, final solution, no final and absolute truth to reveal and carry out, but also—and as a result of this—a plurality of human ends and values. Berlin could thus argue that.[90]

It is undeniable that Kelsen and Berlin started from different intellectual premises and had different intellectual formations. Kelsen's critique of philosophical absolutism cannot be fully understood without taking into account his critique of natural law doctrine. Instead, Berlin's critique of monism implied first of all a methodological choice in favor of history of ideas.[91]

It is likewise true that in Berlin's case pluralism implied a strong emphasis on individual rights to choose freely among different values and freely determine one's objects, whereas in Kelsen's work the conception of pluralism dealt much more, in my opinion, with party pluralism and pluralism of political opinions as integrative elements of parliamentary democracy. Also, differently from Kelsen, Berlin never took an open stance in favor of relativism, although his conception of pluralism seems to lead in that direction.[92] Yet, for Berlin like for Kelsen the way of interpreting reality and human life influenced the way of interpreting politics and political conduct itself. Starting from such a premise, both demonstrated to be strongly critical toward the concept of "absolute truth," "absolute values," "absolute principles," "final solutions" seen as the ultimate source of despotic, intolerant, and illiberal political systems. Above all, their critique to absolutism (Kelsen) and monism (Berlin) was functional to their declared adherence to liberal democracy.[93]

In my opinion, it was the common liberal spirit which was the ultimate reason for the interesting elements of similarity between Kelsen and Mill and also between Berlin and Kelsen.

So far, I have tried to delineate some significant aspects of Kelsen's dichotomy between democracy-relativism and absolutism-autocracy. Starting from Kelsen's radical critique of natural law doctrine, which is a long-running component of his legal philosophy, I have focused on the main reasons why Kelsen thought that democracy was characterized by a relativist and tolerant vision of the world. There is, however, still one relevant aspect to cover, which is inherent in Kelsen's reasoning. If—as seen so far—relativism implied tolerance and respect toward everyone's opinion, did one have to respect even intolerant (anti-liberal and anti-democratic) ideologies? Did one have to be tolerant toward the intolerant? This question was particularly crucial between the late 1920s and the early 1930s, when in many parts of Europe anti-system movements were taking advantages from liberal and democratic institutions to rise to the power. How did Kelsen (relativist, democratic, and tolerant) respond to such capital question?

THE DEFENSE OF DEMOCRACY IN TIMES OF PERIL

In the early 1930s the German Republic was very distant from the ambitious and progressive goals, which the Weimar constituents had posed themselves and the German people by writing the Constitution of 1919. The Great Depression of 1929 had a destabilizing impact on politics: in 1930, after Brüning's failure to get the Parliament (Reichstag) consent to cut government expenditure and wages as a drastic measure to face the crisis, President Hindenburg used Article 48 of the constitution, allowing him to pass laws by decrees. From then until 1933 "presidential governments" were established, which proved to be a serious blow to the already shaky Weimar parliamentary and democratic institutions.[94] The "authoritarian" turn continued under Chancellor Von Papen (from the constitutional crisis of the "Prussian strike"),[95] who represented the interests of some of the most conservatives social groups—such as, for example, landowners—who had never accepted the democratic principles.[96] Meanwhile—as an effect of the 1929 economic and financial collapse—the radical left, embodied by the Communists, and the radical right with Hitler's Nazis were growing.

The Social Democrats, who might have been a bulwark against the political polarization of the country in defense of that Constitution, seemed paralyzed: they had not been able to increase popular consent, changing gradually into a political force mainly committed in exhausting "parliamentary tactics."[97] Instead, the Nazis had been capable of capitalizing on the state of widespread social and economic instability to such an extent that by July 1932 they had 230 seats in the German Parliament, becoming the major political force. The Nazi victory represented a challenge not only to the leftist parties (from Social Democrats to Communists) but also to the conservatives supporting Von Papen, who like the Nazis wanted to get rid of the Weimar constitution and institutions as soon as possible but unlike the Nazis had no serious popular support. Yet, the "relative loss of votes" from the Nazis during the elections of November 6, 1932, pushed Hitler's party to get closer to the conservative block, which hoped to use the political "deal" with the Nazis to take political advantage of their still substantial mass following. This alliance would turn into one of the main and most disruptive political factors leading to the end of the Weimar Republic and Hitler's rise to power.[98]

It was just in 1932 that Kelsen published *Verteidigung der Demokratie*, which summarized some of the key concepts of his democratic theory, elaborated up to then. More precisely, *Verteidigung der Demokratie* can be read— along with the second edition of *Vom Wesen und Wert der Demokratie*—as a sort of political manifesto against the rising and triumphant anti-democratic regimes inside and outside Europe (in Italy with Mussolini and in Russia with Stalin), although Kelsen's main focus was definitely on Germany on the eve of Hitler's triumph.[99]

If we look at the European political situation of that time from the perspective of political ideas and movements present on the European soil, we will see how Kelsen's position was an exception within a large part of intellectual environment. The political polarization characterized not only Germany but also a large part of the Continent, which had become the stage of a visible contrast between Fascists and anti-Fascists during the early postwar period. Historically speaking, the latter—chiefly when coinciding with the radical left of communist inspiration—were in favor not of parliamentary democracy and fundamental liberties but of the soviet-communist regime which was anything but the aftermath of the "true democracy."[100] Just to mention some relevant figures who perfectly embodied such political and ideological widespread polarization: in France the ultra-nationalist Charles Maurras, who in 1905 had established the monarchic and reactionary movement of the Action Française, was ferociously against parliamentary democracy, so much so that during the 1920s he got closer to Italian fascism. His critique of democracy was characterized also by a clear anti-Jewish content.[101] In Italy, the idealist philosopher Giovanni Gentile theorized the fascist State as an anti-liberal, anti-individualist, anti-socialist, militarist State which had to be "totalitarian."[102] Yet, if looking to the opposite side of the barricade, that is, communist ideology—and just to mention some iconic figures for European history and political thought—the attitude was not substantially different, although obviously inspired by a completely different ideology and scopes.

The Polish communist and militant Rosa Luxemburg founded the Communist Party of Germany, whose objective was to lead a communist revolution which, from her perspective, would be analogous to the Soviet one of 1917. She thought that the chaotic situation of Germany in 1919 would turn into a concrete opportunity to achieve it, but her revolutionary attempt was violently repressed by the extreme right militia of the Freikorps. Her idea was that no sort of compromise could exist between "true freedom"—attainable only within a communist society—and "false freedom," characterizing parliamentary democracies.[103] For his part, the Italian intellectual and communist militant Antonio Gramsci, who was an admirer of Lenin and was, exactly like Luxemburg, against any compromise with the "bourgeois system," was also among the most prominent founders of the Italian Communist Party in 1921. He was imprisoned for his anti-fascism in 1928 and theorized the subversion of the bourgeois democracy (read: parliamentary and liberal democracy) to be replaced with a communist system through a revolution involving workers and peasants.[104]

As previously discussed, within this articulated context typified by attacks on liberal and parliamentary democracy, Carl Schmitt occupied a special place. In his work on *Die Geistesgeschichtliche Grundlage des heutigen Liberalismus* (1923), he argued that traditional liberalism with its rationalist belief in dialogue, compromises, and openness did not exist anymore and that parliamentarism—as specific form of democracy—was an empty formula, while, in his opinion, nurturing a (for him) devastating party pluralism.[105] With his words full of contempt and mistrust toward parliamentarism and liberal democracy, Schmitt effectively expressed a spirit, mentality, and a political and philosophical vision which historically succeeded between the 1920s and the 1930s.[106] In the early 1930s when fascism was already a reality and nazism was about to rise, Kelsen instead took a political stance in support just of parliamentary democracy. If we take into account how strong and widespread the anti-democratic views, inspired both by fascism and communism, were at that time in Europe, he took a largely minority position. One of the very few intellectuals of his generation supportive of parliamentary democracy and chiefly of the connection between relativism and democracy was the legal theorist Gustav Radbruch, although he was distant from Kelsen's ultra-legal positivism.[107]

Considering the historical and political context of that time, *Verteidigung der Demokratie* had a challenging and evocative title: challenging because Kelsen spoke about "defending" democracy in a time of peril and widespread crisis, and evocative because just the term "defense" might induce one to think that Kelsen wanted to advocate some special measure to protect democratic institutions. Kelsen was instead very far from theorizing what is called nowadays a "militant democracy."[108] In the first paragraphs of his essay, Kelsen noted the failure of the Weimar Republic, by stressing the unbridgeable gap between the constitutional text, which for him remained the most progressive and socially advanced ever and the German people. Kelsen argued, in fact, that "Germans no longer seem to want the freedom they had given themselves."[109]

Historically speaking, Kelsen situated the Weimar crisis, which embodied to him the spiritual crisis of a whole people, within a broader historical-political context, characterized by an extreme political polarization between extreme left and extreme right. Kelsen wrote, with a kind of language strangely "emotional" by his standards:

> The ideal of democracy pales and [. . .] on the horizon of our age a new star is born which the more the hope of the masses turn to it, the more it shines: dictatorship. It is its sign that the struggle against democracy is being led on two fronts: from the extreme Left, from the bolshevik movement that is growing ever more and contains ever larger circles of the working class; and from the extreme Right, Fascism [. . .] National Socialism, whose party grew like a storm. [. . .] Today, it unites the great part of the bourgeoisie.[110]

On the one hand was Bolshevism, the "dictatorship of the proletariat," and on the other, fascism and—in Germany—the growing national-socialism, which Kelsen labeled as an unclear and highly dangerous ideological experiment.[111]

Three years after the second edition of *Vom Wesen und Wert der Demokratie* and twelve years after the first edition, Kelsen re-proposed the same schema, which shows again how his interest in democratic theory was concretely related to the major historical events and challenges of his time: he identified those political and ideological forces threatening parliamentary and liberal democracy. In the light of this—that is, in the light of concrete and stringent political problems—Kelsen again elaborated on the meaning of democracy, while defending it against the accusations, coming from "leftist" and "reactionary" camps. In both cases, the problem—for Kelsen—was to defend democracy against the supporters of autocracy and philosophical absolutism.[112] To him, there was no substantial difference between extreme left and extreme right, because both were aiming to create a dictatorship. Yet, Kelsen's reply to the leftist anti-democratic positions was based on a clear and important distinction, between Communists and Social Democrats. It was the former, for Kelsen, and not the latter that invoked and pushed for "dictatorship of the proletariat" and the overthrow of liberal democracy, which was blamed for producing "formal" rather than "substantive" equality. According to the Communists, only by suppressing the capitalist system, and thus private property of production means, would true equality and true democracy would be established.[113] Against this, Kelsen followed three major lines of reasoning: first, he reminded that, historically speaking and despite the communist contempt of democratic institutions, the political and social situation of the German proletariat had improved and evolved within a democratic context and thanks to democratic freedoms. Second, the main and fundamental difference between Communists and SocialDemocrats—that is, between the radical and the moderate left—was the fact that the former categorically rejected parliamentary democracy and fundamental rights (considered as the hatred "bourgeoise democracy"), whereas the latter believed in democracy as that political organization which was fully functional to the implementation of their ideals of social justice.[114] Third, the radicalization of communist intents had to be ascribed, for Kelsen, to the discrepancy between Marx's "prophecy" about the transformation of the proletariat (poorer and poorer) into the absolute majority of the people and sociopolitical reality contradicting just such prophecy.[115] Since there was no chance for the proletariat to become the "absolute majority"—Kelsen argued—Communists pushed for class war aimed at a revolution, that is, opted for political violence against their opponents.[116] On the opposite side of the barricade, the radical right attacked parliamentary and liberal democracy, blaming it for nurturing corruption and arguing that the majority principle along with the classical parliamentary debate was an ineffective way of making political decisions. They asked thus—here, in my opinion, he was mainly thinking on the Austrian case—to replace political representation with a corporative representation, providing "the best" experts with the power to decide on "objective issues."[117]

Regardless of the specific, relevant ideological differences between the Communists and the reactionaries, their anti-democratic programs shared, for Kelsen, some crucial conceptual elements: both refused the parliamentary mechanism with its majority principle and with its debate between the majority and the minority. Above all, both aimed—despite the opposing nature of their ideologies—to become the majority, not respecting of their political competitors, but against them; that is, they wanted to become the majority to suppress the minority.[118] For Kelsen, behind the "class war," invoked by the Communists, as well as behind the rule of "the best" advocated by the reactionaries, there was the same political objective and the same philosophical vision: they both wanted to impose their own political will unilaterally. This firm conviction was based, according to Kelsen, on a common "Weltanschauung", the absolutist one, which was coherent with their dictatorial aims.[119] Parliamentary democracy, with its relativist view, with its political compromises, with its fluid, dynamic relation between the rulers and the ruled, and with its idea of the majority principle relying on a dialectical relationship between the majority and the minority, was the exact opposite of both of extreme right and of extreme left dictatorships. In the latter form—Kelsen argued in *Verteidigung der Demokratie*—freedom was lost, chiefly the freedom to "political self-determination" which could be reached (although not fully) through the provision of fundamental liberties, through the (indirect) participation to the creation of political will. Although the hiatus between the rulers and the ruled persisted, in real democracy— Kelsen stressed like in all of his essays on democratic theory—there was a set of political and institutional mechanisms capable of reducing it. That hiatus would instead inevitably grow and intensify in a dictatorship, of both political colors, not only because people would be deprived of political freedom but also because along with losing the latter, they would lose a series of fundamental rights and above all "intellectual freedom," which meant "freedom of science, freedom of moral, religious, artistic conviction."[120] Kelsen connected thus parliamentary democracy with freedom of thought, that is, with one of the most traditional liberal rights in history. To him, relativism stimulated tolerance and both—not to be empty concepts and words—presupposed fundamental freedoms, in particular "intellectual ones."[121] In the light of this, it is reasonable to argue that Kelsen's conception of relativism was far from affirming moral or value indifference: as correctly stressed, relativism—on the basis of its connection with tolerance, with freedom of thought and expression—was a value per se. It was not only the *forma mentis* of democracy but also its *value*, because it "expressed" and assumed the ultimate principle upon which, for Kelsen, real democracy was founded: freedom and notably freedom of thought and intellectual freedom.[122]

Yet, the fact that democracy was based on and recognized civil and political freedom made it potentially "weak" because anti-democratic movements or ideologies could emerge and even prevail by taking advantage of those same freedoms. "Democracy," Kelsen bitterly argued, "is that form of government which is less capable of defending itself from its enemies."[123] With such words, Kelsen seemed to anticipate, in my opinion, a kind of philosophical and political argumentation—the fragility of democracy as a free and open political system—which would be developed by Karl Popper some years later in his *Open Society and Its Enemies* (1943).[124] More concretely, for Kelsen, in the early 1930s one was witnessing in Germany to the paradox of a democracy, which was destroying itself, whose people had been "convinced" that they could live without those rights, which "they gave themselves."[125] The solution could not, however, be the use of force, the suspension of fundamental liberties, or some sort of soft dictatorship established in the name of democracy itself.[126]

Kelsen's reasoning was rich in its implications: it contains, in my opinion, two levels of interpretation. The first is purely historical-political; the second is related to his way of conceiving real democracy. In the early 1930s, Kelsen and Schmitt were involved in a controversy, which—as we have seen—concerned just the issue of how to protect a democratic system in case of perils inside it. Kelsen's position in favor of the constitutional jurisdiction was not only a matter of coherence with his legal theory or with his past role in the shaping of the Austrian "ex officio procedure"; it was also—politically speaking—a problem of refusing the establishment of an emergency government from the hands of one single person, the President.[127] The final words of his 1932 essay presupposed, in my opinion, a large part of what he theorized against Schmitt on the *Guardian of the Constitution.*

> One wonders even if [. . .] democracy should not be defended even against the people who no longer want it, against a majority, which is unanimous only in its will to destroy democracy. To ask these questions already means to deny them. A democracy that seeks to assert itself by force has ceased to be democracy. [. . .] And it must not even try it: those who are for democracy cannot be caught up in the fatal contradiction of restoring to dictatorship to defend it.[128]

Kelsen's opposition to any emergency measure, to use force in the name of the preservation of democratic institutions, was also intimately coherent with his conception of democracy. Real democracy was pluralist, relativist, and liberal, that is, based on the provision of fundamental rights, on parliamentary debate, and on everyone's right to express their opinion. Starting from such assumptions, there was thus no room, according to Kelsen, for adopting emergency measures, not even in the name of democracy itself. Such a position might be considered very controversial, not to say dangerous and conceptually weak, chiefly if taking the point of view of a "militant democracy," that is, if assuming that democracy can legally adopt undemocratic measures or strategies in order to preserve its existence.[129] The core issue is, however, another one. Faced with the Weimar crisis and the growth of anti-democratic forces, Kelsen chose, politically, to defend with extreme coherence his own view of what the *essence* and *value* of democracy were and therefore of what—as a result of that particular essence and that particular value—it could never be or become. The peril could not justify—Kelsen insisted on this—the elimination or suspension of fundamental rights and freedoms, that is, the elimination of the *liberal* component of democracy. The centrality of the pro-liberal rights argumentation—such as freedom of thought and "intellectual freedom"—in Kelsen's political thought was testified by his essay on *Wissenschaft und Demokratie* of 1937.[130] Even more straightforward than in the previous works on democratic theory, here Kelsen emphasized that for absolutist ideologies the political competitor was perceived as a "Feind" (enemy) and as such he/she deserved to be eliminated. By using the term Feind Kelsen was, in my opinion, referring and not even too implicitly to Carl Schmitt's popular conception of politics as "friend-enemy distinction."[131]

Maybe, just to be in controversy with Schmitt, Kelsen stressed that the "Feind mentality"—typifying absolutist ideologies which, for Kelsen, were both those of extreme left and right—was exactly the opposite to the "Freund (friend) mentality" typical of democracy. Differently from Schmitt, the contraposition between "enemy-friend" for Kelsen was not the essence of politics as a whole but only of autocratic systems. In democracy the opponent was in fact simply a competitor with whom dialogue and compromise—through "argumentations and counter-argumentations"—were possible because he/ she was seen not as someone radically different inferior or wrong but, rather, as a person sharing with other individuals the same rights, among which were those of freely expressing one's opinion, freedom of thought, and also scientific freedom.[132] The latter—that is, scientific research and development—could prosper, for Kelsen, only within a free environment, in which plurality of ideas, open debates, and critical reflections, with all this might imply, existed. The "spiritual energies" leading to progress (social, economic, scientific) could bloom much more and much better within a democratic system rather than in an autocratic one[133]:

> In autocracy, which is not only a form of government but also a form of Church, there can not be any compromise, but only a *Diktat*. Hence, there can not be room for freedom of thought, for spiritual freedom, for freedom of science and tolerance. The Primacy of Will over Knowledge implies that only what is good is true too. Yet, what is good is decided only by the secular or religious authority, to which not only the will but also the belief of its subjects must be submitted. Whoever opposes such authority is not thus only breaking the law but also wrong. So, we can understand that in this political system the freedom of science must be [. . .] eliminated.[134]

Science would inevitably be replaced by religion: the scientific and critical kind of knowledge would be replaced by a mystic-irrational-metaphysical kind of knowledge and mentality, which would serve to strengthen the power of the secular or religious Leader and push the people in a condition of total submission.[135] Instead, the preservation of scientific freedom, as "intellectual freedom," implied the possibility and ability to protect democracy and its relativist outlook against autocracy. In Kelsen's reasoning, liberal rights, democracy, tolerance, and relativism again appeared deeply intertwined.

In his essay of 1937 Kelsen greatly emphasized the issue of freedom of science, to which he referred to delineating a critical outlook on the European condition. He was evidently thinking in particular about two countries: fascist Italy and nazi Germany. In his opinion, "the European crisis of democracy" coincided in fact with the "European crisis of science."[136] Such words had a profound and stringent historical-political connotation, not only in relation to

Kelsen's personal commitment in favor of parliamentary democracy in the time of fascism and nazism on the Continent but also because—as he himself observed—in Europe science and education were granted and provided by the government: they were public. The very particular nature of the European educational system, from the elementary to university, which basically put science under the "care" of the government, posed serious problems precisely for the maintenance of scientific freedom once that the government had turned into something dictatorial. Kelsen was pessimistic: in Europe the rise of anti-democratic and repressive regimes threatened freedom of science more than in other areas of the world just because of the particular government-oriented kind of educational system. To the European situation Kelsen opposed that of the United States—which instead was mostly private—by quoting the speech delivered that same year by the president of Harvard University, Professor James Bryant Conant, who praised intellectual freedom, research freedom, freedom of thought, and tolerance as a necessary condition for a nation to grow spiritually and materially.[137]

To Kelsen, Professor Conant's statements represented a political manifesto in favor of a series of principles, which for him were all typical of a liberal democracy. By referring to such speech Kelsen was, in my opinion, identifying Europe (or at least a part of it) with autocracy (with all this implied for him) and the United States with democracy (with all this implied for him). To Kelsen, the principle of freedom of science, freedom of expression, and freedom of thought was the true dividing line between these two areas of the world, at that time. His essay of 1937, which can be considered as an ideal continuation of his reflection on democracy previously developed, shows us thus the relevance of intellectual freedom for Kelsen as political thinker. Eleven years later, far from Europe and within the new global order of Cold War—distinguished by the opposition between the Western and the Eastern bloc—Kelsen would return to focus on this concept in his *What Is Justice*? Here, Kelsen argued again that democracy was such because it granted freedom of thought, intellectual freedom, and therefore that it had to maintain the principle of tolerance, because "it could not defend itself giving up itself."[138] The historical-political context had changed since the end of World War II, new political challenges had emerged but evidently Kelsen remained loyal to his concept of real democracy. Like in his European essays of the 1920s and 1930s, Kelsen argued that if it was true that democracy—for its very nature—could be potentially threatened from its inside (and the post–World War I European history testified to it), it was equally true that it had to run this risk, because just that risk made liberal democracy as such.[139] The danger for democracy to be subverted by anti-democratic and anti-liberal ideologies or movements had to be accepted, although not passively. That danger was in fact, for Kelsen, the potential consequence of living and acting within a free, pluralist social and political system, based on the idea that—in absence of an allegedly absolute truth, value, or principle and since all individuals were born equal and with the same rights—freedom of thought and expression had to be granted. Unless democracy was not able to accept and run that risk, it would lose its own identity and significance.[140]

NOTES

1. It is interesting to observe, in biographical terms, that Kelsen supported Schmitt's hiring at the University of Cologne, despite their opposite legal and political views. Schmitt was not as fair as Kelsen, since he was among those professors of the University of Cologne who requested to expel Kelsen after the nazi rise to power in 1933. John Mccormick, *Carl Schmitt's Critique of Liberalism. Against Politics as Technology* (Cambridge: Cambridge University Press, 2009), 266.

2. Reut Y. Paz, "Kelsen's Pure Theory of Law as a Hole in Time," *Dans Monde(s)* 1, no. 7 (2015): 80.

3. Métall, *Hans Kelsen. Leben und Werk*, 60–65. For Kelsen's critique of Marx and Lenin see: chapter 1.

4. On the same year—1933—Kelsen was also invited to teach international law at the University of Prague. On Kelsen in Geneva, see: Jürgen Busch and Nicoletta Bersier Ladavac, "Zwischen zwei Welten," in *Hans Kelsen: Leben—Werk—Wirksamkeit*, 167–192.

5. Métall, *Hans Kelsen. Leben und Werk*, 75–76.

6. He would further develop his interest in international law once in the United States. In Geneva, Kelsen followed as a tutor the PhD dissertation of an Italian law student, Umberto Campagnolo (1904–1976), who would become a prominent figure within the post–World War II Italian intellectual environment and one of the first supporters of the European Federalist Movement established by Altiero Spinelli. In Geneva Campagnolo attended Kelsen's lectures. The Austrian jurist examined his dissertation on the meaning and implications of international law. Kelsen and Campagnolo had a completely opposite view of international law: the former was in favor of the absolute primacy of international law over the national one, corresponding to the principles of his legal monism. The latter argued instead that State law had to precede over international law, since only state law actually existed. Despite their opposite visions, Kelsen praised Campagnolo's work. Losano, "La trilogia su Umberto Campagnolo (1904–1976): Kelsen, il federalismo, la Guerra giusta e la guerra europea," 46–47.

7. *Foundations of Democracy* will be at the center of the next Chapter. The *General Theory of Law and State* (1945)—which was however a work of legal theory—could be in some respects considered as another of Kelsen's contributions to political theory since, for example, Kelsen returned to the issue of autocracy. Yet, strictly in terms of democratic theory, *Foundations of Democracy* was, in my opinion, Kelsen's last, systematic work on it.

8. According to Monika Zalewska, "Some Misunderstandings Concerning Hans Kelsen's Concepts of Democracy and the Rule of Law," *Jurysprudencja* 8 (2017):

110, only *Staatsform und Weltanschauung* was characterized by an "emotional" attitude. I would say that this is in part true for *Verteidigung der Demokratie* too.

9. See: chapter 1.

10. See: chapter 1.

11. The relationship between relativism and democracy is already clearly established by Kelsen in the last chapter of his *Allgemeine Staatslehre*, 34–114; in *Demokratie*, 115–148; in both editions of *Vom Wesen und Wert der Demokratie*, 1–33 and 149–228; in *Staatsform und Weltanschauung* 1933; in *Verteidigung der Demokratie*, 229–237; in *Absolutism and Relativism in Philosophy and Politics*, 1–24; in *Foundations of Democracy*, 248–386.

12. Kelsen, "Vom Wesen und Wert der Demokratie" (1st ed.), 31–34; Kelsen, "Vom Wesen und Wert der Demokratie" (2nd ed.), 223–228. For a systematic overview of the conception of relativism in political philosophy see: Graham M. Long, "Relativism in Contemporary Liberal Political Philosophy," in *A Companion to Relativism*, ed. Stefen D. Hales (Blackwell Publishing: New Jersey, 2011), 307–325.

13. For an interesting and pertinent critical analysis of Kelsen's concept of relativism and its theoretical weaknesses see: Anna Maria Pintore, "Democracia sin derechos. En torno al Kelsen democratico," *Doxa* 23 (2000): 119–144.

14. See: chapters 1 and 2.

15. Kelsen's stance in favor of legal positivism characterized all of his work, both in Europe and in the United States. See, for example: Kelsen, *Allgemeine Staatslehre* 1925, Kelsen, *Reine Rechtslehre* 1934, Kelsen, *General Theory of Law and State* 1945, and Kelsen, *What is Justice?*, 1957.

16. Kelsen continued to develop his critique of natural law in a very articulated way just during his American period. Opalek, "Kelsens Kritik der Naturrechtslehre," 74. On Kelsen as critic of natural law see the recent: Langford, Bryan and McGarry eds., *Hans Kelsen and the Natural Law Tradition*, in particular, their "Introduction," 1–55.

17. I think that *The Natural Law Doctrine Before the Tribunal of Science* and *What is Justice?*—the latter was the text of Kelsen's last lecture at the University of Berkeley before taking the leave from teaching—are a concise and clear *summa* of his anti-jusnaturalist reflection as a premise to relativism. That is the reason why I decided to refer to these specific essays to outline some of the key components of Kelsen's concept of natural law and natural law doctrine.

18. *General Theory of Law and State* included some of the pillars of Kelsen's legal positivism as developed in Europe. Yet, it would be constrictive to think that the *General Theory* was a mere restatement of already previously explained concepts. Differently from the European period, now Kelsen admitted the existence of "a plurality of legal sciences," including the sociology of law. This might be ascribed to the fact that he was living in the United States, where the academic audience was generally sensitive to this kind of discipline. Treves, "Intorno alla concezione del diritto in Hans Kelsen," 119.

19. Hans Kelsen, "Law, State and Justice in the Pure Theory of Law," *The Yale Law Journal* 57 (1948): 378. On the same issue see: Hans Kelsen, *Die philosophischen Grundlagen der Naturrechtslehre und Rechtspositivisumus* (Rottenburg: Pan Verlag Rolf Heise, 1928), 8–12.

20. See: Kelsen, "Allgemeine Staatslehre," *Reine Rechtslehre, General Theory of Law and State* and "Law, State and Justice in the Pure Theory of Law."

21. Hans Kelsen, "The Natural Law Doctrine Before the Tribunal of Science," in *What is Justice? Justice, Law, Politics in the Mirror of Science. Collected Essays* (Berkeley and Los Angeles: University of California Press, 1957), 137.

22. Kelsen, *Die philosophischen Grundlagen der Naturrechtslehre und Rechtspositivismus*, 8–12.

23. Ibid.

24. Ibid. and also on this point: Kelsen, "The Natural Law Doctrine Before the Tribunal of Science," 137–140.

25. Kelsen, *Die philosophischen Grundlagen der Naturrechtslehre und Rechtspositivismus*, 8 ff. On this point: Invernizzi-Accetti, "Reconciling Legal Positivism and Human Rights: Hans Kelsen's Argument from Relativism," 218.

26. Kelsen, *Die philosophischen Grundlagen der Naturrechtslehre und Rechtspositivismus*, 41 ff; Kelsen, "The Natural Law Doctrine Before the Tribunal of Science," 137–144.

27. Kelsen, *Die philosophischen Grundlagen der Naturrechtslehre und Rechtspositivisumus*, 41 ff; Kelsen, "The Natural Law Doctrine Before the Tribunal of Science," 137 ff. The critique of the "metaphysical-religious" view, characterizing for Kelsen the natural law doctrine, becomes crucial to understanding his attack on post–World War II neo-jusnaturalism, as we can read in *Foundations of Democracy*. On this aspect see: chapter 4.

28. Kelsen praised the Vienna Circle for its critique of any metaphysics, even though he took clearly distance from its logical empiricism. Jabloner, "Kelsen and His Circle: The Viennese Years," chiefly: 378 ff.

29. Kelsen, "Law, State and Justice in the Pure Theory of Law," 383–390.

30. Kelsen, *Die philosophischen Grundlagen des Naturrechts und des Rechtspositivismus* 40–42.

31. Ravira García-Salmones, "On Kelsen's Sein. An Approach to Sociological Themes," *No Foundations: Journal of Extreme Legal Positivism* 8 (2011): 49–50. According to Garcia-Salmones, since the 1930s "Kelsen transformed the psychological exposition of his antimetaphysical thesis already present in *Grundlagen des Naturrechts* into the evolutionist study of *Society and Nature*." Ibid., 50.

32. In 1921, Kelsen was invited by Sigmund Freud to deliver a speech on the concept of State and mass psychology at the Wiener Psychoanalitische Gesellschaft (Wien Psychoanalytic Society). Some months later, his speech was published as an autonomous essay for the journal *Imago*, entitled "Der Begriff des Staates und die Soziopsychologie mit besonderer Berücksichtigung von Freuds Theorie der Masse" (*The Concept of State and Socialpsychology with Reference to the Freudian Theory of Group Sociology*). Here, Kelsen analyzed the relation between the State and the masses from a psychoanalytic perspective. In 1923, Kelsen published for the journal *Logos* another essay, "Gott und Staat" (*God and the State*), in which—while taking inspiration from Freud' *Totem und Taboo*—Kelsen argued that in democracy the process of submission to the Leader was filtered by the electoral mechanism, through which the ruled could chose the rulers. Kelsen would use a substantially similar kind

of argumentation in the second edition of *Vom Wesen und Wert der Demokratie* and in *Foundations of Democracy*, when discussing the specific democratic method of choosing leaders within democratic systems. Kelsen, "Der Begriff des Staates und die Soziopsychologie mit besonderer Berücksichtigung von Freuds Theorie der Masse," *Imago* VIII (1922): 97–141; Hans Kelsen, "God and the State," in *Essays in Legal and Moral Philosophy*, trans. Peter Heath, selected by Ota Weinberger (Dortrecht: Reidel, 1973), 61–82; Kelsen, "Vom Wesen und Wert der Demokratie" (2nd ed.), 216; Kelsen, "Foundations of Democracy," 292–293. On Kelsen and Freud see: Jabloner, "Kelsen and His Circle: The Viennese Years," 368–385, in particular from page 376 on.

33. García-Salmones, "On Kelsen's Sein. An Approach to Sociological Themes," 2011, 50.

34. Kelsen, *Die philosophischen Grundlagen der Naturrechtslehre und Rechtspositivismus*, 37 ff. The same kind of argumentation in Kelsen, "The Natural Law Doctrine Before the Tribunal of Science," 151–154; Hans Kelsen, "What is Justice?," in *What is Justice? Justice, Law, Politics in the Mirror of Science. Collected Essays* 20–21.

35. Kelsen, *Die philosophischen Grundlagen der Naturrechtslehre und Rechtspositivismus*, 37 ff. Again, the same argumentation in Kelsen, "The Natural Law Doctrine Before the Tribunal of Science," 151 ff; Kelsen, "What Is Justice?," 20.

36. Kelsen, *Die philosophischen Grundlagen des Naturrechts und des Rechtspositivismus* 40; Kelsen, "The Natural Law Doctrine Before the Tribunal of Science," 151.

37. On this point: the comments of Topitsch, "Hans Kelsen- Demokrat und Philosoph," 11–27. Kelsen as a political thinker insisted greatly and often on his anti-ideological commitment. Not only in the two editions of *Vom Wesen und Wert der Demokratie* are a good example of this, but also his "Demokratie" (1926), in *Verteidigung der Demokratie*, 143–144.

38. Kelsen, *Die philosophischen Grundlagen der Naturrechtslehre und Rechtspositivismus*, 37 ff and also: Kelsen, *General Theory of Law and State*, 435 ff; Kelsen, "The Natural Law Doctrine Before the Tribunal of Science," 144 ff. In "What Is Justice?" he sought to synthetize his anti-jusnaturalist thought: "if the History of human thought proves anything, it is the futility of the attempt to establish, in the way of rational considerations, an absolutely correct standard of behavior as the only just one, excluding the possibility of considering the opposite standard to be just too." Kelsen, "What Is Justice?," 21.

39. Kelsen, *Die philosophischen Grundlagen des Naturrechts und des Rechtspositivismus*, 41–60.

40. Kelsen, *General Theory of Law and State*, 437–438. This concept was already clearly expressed in Kelsen, *Die philosophischen Grundlagen des Naturrechts und des Rechtspositivismus*, 41–60.

41. We have already seen how during the early postwar period Kelsen's legal positivism was targeted by major thinkers of that time such as, for example, the previously mentioned Hermann Heller. Another prominent figure to be reminded of is the legal theorist Gustav Radbruch. Just after the end of World War II, Radbruch

frontally attacked just the formalist and positivist legal theory (notably Kelsen's one) for reducing the issue of legitimacy to that of mere legality and thus for becoming perfectly functional to inhuman nazi laws. In cases of an open violation of moral norms, a law could not be considered as such, that is, as binding. See: Radbruch, "Gesetzliches Unrecht und übergesetzlliches Recht," 105–108. On this aspect see also: Stanley L. Paulson, "Radbruch on Unjust Laws: Competing Earlier and Later Views," *Oxford Journal of Legal Studies* 15, no. 3 (1995): 489–500. Radbruch's critical perspective seems to find an echo in the works of other prominent cotemporary thinkers and scholars who are likewise critical to legal positivism and particularly to Kelsen's: David Dyzenhaus, "Why Positivism Is Authoritarian," *The American Journal of Juriprudence* 1, no. 1 (1992): 83–112 and Robert Alexy, "Law, Morality and the Existence of Human Rights," *Ratio Juris* 25, no. 1 (1995): 2012, 2–14.

42. Michael Stolleis, *Der Methodenstreit der Weimarer Staatsrechtslehre—ein abgeschlossenes Kapitel der Wissenschaftgeschichte?* (Stuttgart: Franz Steiner Verlag, 2011), 19.

43. With regard to this aspect—as mentioned in the first chapter—it was already since the early 1910s that Kelsen argued the political and social importance of a proper education to democracy as a "condition to democratic life." See: Hans Kelsen, "Politische Weltanschauung und Erziehung," in *Die Wiener Rechtstheoretische Schule. Schriften von Hans Kelsen, Alfred Merkl, Alfred Verdross*, hrsg. Hans R. Klecatsky, Renè Marcic and Herbert Schambeck (Wien: Franz Steiner Verlag—Verlag Österreich, 2010), 1227–1246; Tamara Ehs, "Erziehung zur Demokratie. Hans Kelsen als Volksbildner," in *Hans Kelsen—Leben—Werke—Wirksamkeit*, 1–2.

44. See: chapter 4.

45. Kelsen, "Allgemeine Staatslehre," 52–63; Kelsen, "Demokratie," 132–136; Hans Kelsen, *Staatsform und Weltanschauung* (Tübingen: J. B. C. Mohr (Paul Siebeck Verlag, 1933), 18–21.

46. Kelsen, "Vom Wesen und Wert der Demokratie" (2nd ed.), 214.

47. Ibid., 214–215; 218 ff.

48. Ibid., 216.

49. Ibid., 214 ff.

50. Also, as we are going to discuss in the next chapter, precisely Kelsen's emphasis on the problem of how to select rulers within democracy represents one of the key elements to take into account when discussing the procedural connotation of his democratic theory.

51. Hans Kelsen, "Absolutism and Relativism in Philosophy and Politics," in *What is Justice? Justice, Law, Politics in the Mirror of Science. Collected Essays*, 198–208.

52. Kelsen, *Staatsform und Weltanschauung*, 7–9; 24–29.

53. Kelsen, "Vom Wesen und Wert der Demokratie" (2nd ed.), 223–228.

54. Ibid. See also: Kelsen, "Absolutism and Relativism in Philosophy and Politics," 198–199.

55. Kelsen, "Vom Wesen und Wert der Demokratie" (2nd ed.), 223–228.

56. Ibid., 225–226.

57. Ibid., 215–228.

58. Ibid., 223–228. With the term "mystic-religious veil" Kelsen was emphasizing what he considered as the "irrational" aspect of autocratic leadership. It was in his 1933 essay on *Staatsform und Weltanschauung* that Kelsen stressed the contrast between "rational" and "irrational" in a more, in my opinion, systematic way. Unlike absolutism, the philosophical vision characterizing democracy was not only relativist but also rational: rationality made respectful and tolerant debate among diverse opinions possible, whereas "irrationality" was typical of autocracy and more precisely of the strategies which, according to Kelsen, the autocratic Leader adopted to justify his power. Kelsen, *Staatsform und Weltanschauung*, 15–18.

59. Kelsen, "Vom Wesen und Wert der Demokratie" (2nd ed.), 223–228. See also: Kelsen, "Absolutism and Relativism in Philosophy and Politics," 198–203.

60. See: chapter 1.

61. Kelsen, "Vom Wesen und Wert der Demokratie" (2nd ed.), 223 ff.

62. See: chapter 2.

63. Kelsen, "Vom Wesen und Wert der Demokratie" (2nd ed.), 210 ff.

64. Ibid., 219.

65. On this aspect see: Tamara Ehs, *Hans Kelsen und die politische Bildung im modernen Staat. Vorträge in der Wiener Volksbildung. Schriften zu Kritikfähigkeit und Rationalismus* (Wien: Manz, 2007).

66. In the shaping of the dichotomy between relativism-democracy and absolutism-autocracy, Kelsen himself admitted to be inspired by the Austrian jurist and historian Adolf Menzel's work on *Demokratie und Weltanschauung* (*Democracy and World Vision*). Kelsen praised Menzel, who had been one of his Professors of Law at the University of Vienna along with Bernatzik, for connecting a metaphysical view of the world and reality to an autocratic power. Kelsen, "Vom Wesen und Wert der Demokratie" (2nd ed.), 225; on this point: Pellegrino Favuzzi, "Hans Kelsen's & Ernst Cassirer's Conception of Natural Law," in *Hans Kelsen and the Natural Law tradition*, 329.

67. Kelsen, "Vom Wesen und Wert der Demokratie" (2nd ed.), 227.

68. Ibid., 227–228.

69. Ibid.

70. I refer to Gustavo Zagrebelsky's work. In his opinion Kelsen's use of the Gospel episode is too superficial and "ideological": to understand the historical context and of Pilate's political role is necessary to realize that the Roman governor's decision to give the people the last word on Jesus was based on very personal and contingent political reasons, rather than with an allegedly relativist and thus democratic view. Pilate wanted to reinforce his political authority, while placating the people. Also, Pilate's decision to rely on the people gathered around his palace is more evocative—according to Zagrebelsky—of a plebiscitary kind of democracy, in which the Leader uses the emotions and hatred of the masses for his own interests. In other words, for Zagrebelsky, the Parable of Jesus and Pilate is more suited for describing a "mass-plebiscitary" democracy, in which the people looks more like a "crowd" than the liberal, relativist, democratic one defended and theorized by Kelsen. Gustavo Zagrebelsky, *Il Crucifice! E la democrazia* (Torino: Einaudi, 1995).

71. See: Kelsen, "Vom Wesen und Wert der Demokratie" (2nd ed.), 225–226; See also: Kelsen, "Absolutism and Relativism in Philosophy and Politics," 204–208; Kelsen, "What is Justice?," 11–24.

72. See: Hans Kelsen, "Platonic Justice," in *What is Justice? Justice, Law, Politics in the Mirror of Science*, 82–109 ; Kelsen, "Absolutism and Relativism in Philosophy and Politics," 204–206.

73. Ibid., 205. It is interesting to notice that Plato and Hegel were considered as two champions of an absolutist, anti-liberal kind of political mentality and government by the Austrian philosopher of science Karl Popper. See: Popper, *The Open Society and its Enemies*. With regard to Dante, Kelsen changed his attitude: in his monographic study on *Die Staatslehre des Dante Alighieri*, he identified the Florentine poet with the medieval supreme theorist of a great Empire, of a "universal monarchy" whose scope was to unify the people. Here, there was no reference to Dante as representative of an absolutist philosophy and politics. See: Hans Kelsen, *Die Staatslehre des Dante Alighieri* (San Bernardino: Ulan P, 2012).

74. Kelsen, "Vom Wesen und Wert der Demokratie" (2nd ed.), 223 ff.

75. Ibid., 193–204; 210–220; 223–228.

76. Ibid.

77. Long, "Relativism in Contemporary Liberal Philosophy," 309–311. Toleration is commonly tied to liberalism and to moral relativism. On this topic see also: Graham Long, *Relativism and the Foundations of Liberalism* (Exeter, UK: Imprint Academic, 2004), 13 ff.

78. Mill, *On Liberty*, 1975; Mill, *Representative Government*, 1975.

79. See in comparison: Tocqueville, *Democracy in America*, vol. I, 2012 and John S. Mill, *On Liberty* (New York: W. W. Norton, 1975). Bellamy, *Liberalism and Modern Society*, 22–35.

80. Alan Ryan, *The Making of Modern Liberalism* (Princeton: Princeton University Press, 2012), 257–278.

81. Mill, *On Liberty*, 65.

82. Gray, *Liberalism: Essays in Political Philosophy*, 23–24.

83. Mill, *On Liberty*, 59–60.

84. See: Isaiah Berlin, "Historical Inevitability," in Isaiah Berlin, *Four Essays on Liberty*, 41–117; Berlin, "Two Concepts of Liberty," 118–172.

85. By Cold War liberalism one means an articulated intellectual movement, which developed during the post-World War II period and whose most significant representatives were Berlin himself, Raymond Aron, Karl Popper, Jacob Talmon, Micheal Oakeshott, and Friederich Von Hayek. They all believed in individual freedom as a value per se to preserve. They were all epistemologically "skeptical," "pluralist," in favor of a liberal-democratic government and admittedly anti-marxist. Their being anti-marxist went beyond the Cold War ideology and political strategy with its bipolar division of the world. What Cold War liberals criticized about marxism was its allegedly claim to find out the true and objective laws of economic and social development. Their declared opposition to marxism was one of the leading components of their likewise strong commitment to understanding the ideal roots of twentieth-century totalitarianism. Jan Werner Müller, "Fear and Freedom: On Cold War Liberalism,"

European Journal of Political Theory 7, no. 1 (2008): 45–64; Terry Nardin ed., *Micheal Oakeshott's Cold War Liberalism* (New York: Palgrave Macmillan, 2015).

86. See: Berlin, "Historical Inevitability," 1969.

87. Hatier, "Berlin and the Totalitarian Mind," 768.

88. Berlin, "Two Concepts of Liberty," 167.

89. Kelsen, "Vom Wesen und Wert der Demokratie" (2nd ed.), 216–217; 223–227; Berlin, "Two Concepts of Liberty," 142–147.

90. Ibid., 168–169.

91. Isaiah Berlin, *Tra Filosofia e storia delle idee. La società pluralista e i suoi nemici. Intervista autobiografica e filosofica*, It. trans., a cura di Steven Lukes (Firenze: Ponte alle Grazie, 1994), 62.

92. On the complex issue of relativism within Berlin's political philosophy see: Jason Ferrell, "The Alleged Relativism of Isaiah Berlin," *Critical Review of International Social and Political Philosophy* 11, no. 1 (2008): 41–54 and Crowder, *Liber*alism *and Value Pluralism*, 2002.

93. *Two Concepts of Liberty*—published in 1958—when the ideological contrast between the liberal-democratic West and the Soviet East was as a matter of fact—could be read as Berlin's personal and political statement in favor of liberal democracy against the Soviet system. See on this point: Berlin, *Tra Filosofia e storia delle idee. La società pluralista e i suoi nemici. Intervista autobiografica e filosofica*, 62.

94. Peukert, *The Weimar Republic: The Crisis of Classical Modernity*, 264.

95. See: chapter 2.

96. Peukert, *The Weimar Republic: The Crisis of Classical Modernity*, 265.

97. Smaldone, *Weimar and the Social-Democratic Challenge*, 12–17.

98. Peukert, *The Weimar Republic: The Crisis of Classical Modernity*, 265–267.

99. The same consideration could be extended to his essay *Staatsform und Weltanschauung*.

100. This, for me, the shareable interpretative perspective emerging from Salvo Mastellone, *Storia della democrazia in Europa. Da Montesquieu a Kelsen (XVIII-XX)* (Torino: UTET, 1999).

101. Olivier Dard, "The Action Française in a Transnational Perspective," in *Reactionary Nationalists, Fascists and Dictatorships in the Twentieth Century Against Democracy*, ed. Ismael Saz, Zira Box, Toni Morant, and Julián Sanz (Berlin: Springer Verlag, 2019), 30 ff.

102. Patrizia Dogliani, "Fascism and Fascists in Italy," in *Reactionary Nationalists, Fascists and Dictatorships in the Twentieth Century Against Democracy*, ed. Ismael Saz, Zira Box, Toni Morant and Julián Sanz (Berlin: Springer Verlag, 2019), 125 ff.

103. See: Jason Schulmann, *Rosa Luxemburg. Her Life and Legacy* (New York: Palgrave and MacMillan, 2013).

104. See: Ernesto Galli Della Loggia, "Le ceneri di Gramsci," *Mondo Operaio* 7 (1977): 69–91.

105. See: chapter 2.

106. On Schmitt's relation to German right and the Nazi Party see for a concise and clear overview: Joseph W. Benderesky, "Carl Schmitt and the Weimar Right,"

in *The German Right in the Weimar Republic. Studies in the History of German Conservatorism, Nationalism and Antisemitism*, ed. Larry Eugene Jones (New York: Oxford Berghahn, 2014), 268–290.

107. During the Weimar Republic—that is, during the first phase of his intellectual production—Radbruch spoke in favor of relativism as a component of democracy and as a condition to tolerance, although he rejected the idea of being tolerant toward intolerant ideologies and political movements. See: Martin D. Klein, *Demokratisches Denken bei Gustav Radbruch* (Berlin: Berliner Wissenschafts-Verlag, 2007), 213 ff. Nathalie Le Boudëc, "Le role de le pensee de Gustav Radbruch dans la refondation de l'État de droit démocratique après 1945," *Revue d'Allemagne* 46, no. 1 (2014): 83–94.

108. By "militant democracy" one means the restriction of democratic freedoms to isolate and neutralize an anti-democratic threat. Jan Werner Müller, "Militant Democracy," in *The Oxford Handbook of Comparative Constitutional Law*, ed. Micheal Rosenthal and András Sajó (Oxford: Oxford University Press, 2012), 1257–1258.

109. Kelsen, "Verteidigung der Demokratie," 229.

110. Ibid., 230.

111. Ibid., 231–232.

112. Ibid., 231.

113. Ibid., 231–232. On this topic see also Kelsen, "Vom Wesen und Wert der Demokratie" (2nd ed.), 220–223. In general, on the same issue see: Kelsen, "Zur Soziologie der Demokratie," 1926.

114. Kelsen, "Verteidigung der Demokratie," 228–231. By identifying such a distinction, which was actually not too far from reality, Kelsen seemed to ignore how complex and multifaceted the German social democratic attitude was toward the issue of revolution and the aftermath of communism. Such complexity emerged from all the main political manifestos of the party: from that of Erfurt in 1891, when the SPD was established, to the last one of Heidelberg in 1932. William Smaldone, *Confronting Hitler. German Social Democrats in Defense of the Weimar Republic, 1929–1933* (Lanham, MD: Lexington Books, 2010), 17.

115. Kelsen, "Verteidigung der Demokratie," 231–232. Here Kelsen's critique of communism seemed to evoke the social democratic Eduard Bernstein's critique of Marx's prophecy about the progressive impoverishment of the working class as part of a growing social polarization between the rich (a few) and the poor, who were the large majority. Bernstein (1850–1832) argued that the improving socioeconomic and political situation of the British working class proved how reforms and not revolutionary overthrown were the key to social democratic political success of the future. The Social Democrats had in fact—in his opinion—to push for a serious reformist project and coherently embrace democratic values, including respect of the minority. See: Robert Mayer, "The Quest for Evolutionary Socialism: Eduard Bernstein and Social Democracy," *History of European Ideas* 23, nos. 2–4 (1997): 137–141.

116. Kelsen, "Verteidigung der Demokratie," 232–233.

117. Ibid., 234 ff.

118. Ibid., 232 ff.

119. Ibid.

120. Ibid., 235–236.

121. Ibid., 236. See also: Kelsen, *Staatsform und Weltanschauung*, 24–30.

122. This aspect is stressed by Ota Weinberger, "Introduction: Hans Kelsen as Philosopher," in *Hans Kelsen: Essays in Legal and Moral Philosophy*, XXV–XXVI; Topitsch, "Kelsen. Demokrat und Philosoph," 12–27.

123. Kelsen, "Verteidigung der Demokratie," 237.

124. It is interesting to observe that both Kelsen and Popper identified in Plato's philosophy the roots of autocratic thought (for Kelsen) and totalitarian (for Popper). For Popper see his *The Open Society and its Enemies*, vol. I, *The Spell of Plato* (London: Routledge, 1952). On Popper's critique of Plato as part of his "commitment to Liberalism" see: Ryan, *The Making of Modern Liberalism*, 413–425.

125. Kelsen, "Verteidigung der Demokratie," 229–230.

126. Ibid., 236–237.

127. See: chapter 2.

128. Kelsen, "Verteidigung der Demokratie," 237.

129. Müller, "Militant Democracy," 1257–1258.

130. The essay of 1937—the last on democratic theory published before moving to the United States—was thus in line with the second edition of *Vom Wesen und Wert der Demokratie* and with *Verteidigung der Demokratie*.

131. See: Carl Schmitt, *Der Begriff des Politischen. Ein kooperativer Kommenta* (Berlin: Walter de Gruyter, 2016); On this topic: Ernst-Wolfgang Böckenförde, "The Concept of the Political: A Key to Understanding Carl Schmitt's Constitutional Theory," *Canadian Journal of Law and Jurisprudence* 10, no. 1 (1997): 5–19.

132. Hans Kelsen, "Wissenschaft und Demokratie," in *Verteidigung der Demokratie*), 239–241. On the contrast between Kelsen's concept of compromise and Schmitt's concept of "enemy-friend" see: Van Ooyen, *Der Staat der Moderne. Hans Kelsens Pluralismustheorie*, 100–104.

133. Kelsen, "Wissenschaft und Demokratie," 242.

134. Ibid.

135. Ibid., 242–243.

136. Ibid., 243.

137. Ibid., 245–246.

138. Kelsen, "What Is Justice?," 23.

139. Ibid., 23–24.

140. Ibid., 22–24.

Chapter 4

Democracy and Proceduralism

KELSEN IN THE UNITED STATES: LAW AND POLITICS DURING THE COLD WAR

In 1940, like many other intellectuals before him, Kelsen left Europe for the United States, where he spent the last part of his professional and private life.[1] Moving to North America meant a radical change for him. Here his legal work was often considered with suspicion, not to say with open hostility. His pure theory of Law was seen as obscure, excessively difficult, and even as a "sterile" scholarly work.[2] As convincingly argued, there are mainly three types of problems to take into account while explaining Kelsen's problematical position in the United States. First, in the early 1940s, legal formalism was totally rejected in American legal departments in favor of "legal realism." On a more political level, Kelsen's political theory did not seem particularly appealing: his relativist vision, related to his legal positivism, was perceived with suspicion too, as was the expression of a potential (and dangerous) indifference toward moral issues. Finally, legal curricula in American universities were much less theoretical and abstract than those in European universities; that is, they were less inclined to give room to excessively abstract and purely theoretical topics.[3] According to this perspective, the fact that in the United States constitutional law was "dominated by a case-based method" might also explain why Kelsen did not continue to elaborate on "constitutional themes."[4]

The problems which Kelsen experienced in the United States and which concerned his status as a scholar and theorist did not however hamper his career, although it is useful for us to remember that he got a position at Berkeley University in 1942 as Professor of Political Science, rather than as Professor of Law.[5] Beyond the not-easy relationships with the American (legal) academic environment, his new life in the United States was rich of

131

events and changes, stimulating his intellectual reflection. He personally witnessed the end of World War II, the Nuremberg Trials for the punishment of
the nazi crimes, the creation of the United Nations, and more generally the
beginning of the Cold War with its ideological contrast between the West
and the East. This historical-political context posed to him relevant issues
about the creation and maintenance of a stable and peaceful international
order, through, for example, international organizations, and about the restoration of a post-totalitarian age democracy. In the post–World War II period,
Kelsen sought, in my opinion, to address all of them. Obviously, his interest
for international law and democracy came from before, from the European
years, but the major international transformations which occurred since the
mid-1940s contributed to revive it. In the United States, Kelsen's scientific
interests ranged from the issue of how to grant peace on an international
level with *Peace through Law* (1944) to sociology with *Society and Nature*
(1945).[6] From the *General Theory of Law and State* (1945),[7] in which, for the
first time, he conceived a plurality of legal sciences (including sociology of
law)—maybe as a way to get closer to U.S. intellectual and academic environment—to works on international law and mainly on the UN law, such as
The Law of the United Nations (1950).[8]

Most interestingly, his American period was marked by the publication of
his last remarkable contribution to democratic theory, that is, *Foundations of
Democracy*.[9] All these scholarly works might be seen as—in part—Kelsen's
personal way of "reinventing" himself as a scholar in the United States, and
his response to concrete stimuli coming from international politics.

Just one year before the end of the war, Kelsen published a long essay
entitled *Peace through Law* which was not only an example of his interest in
international law, characterizing moreover his whole American period, but
also a proposal to reform the "League of the Nations," within a broader plan
for reforming "the international legal community."[10] Already in *Das Problem
der Souveränität* (1920), Kelsen clearly elaborated a monist and formalist
conception of sovereignty, according to which national legal systems (i.e.,
politically speaking, nation-states) were all to be thought of as included
within the "international legal system."[11] In perfect coherence with this,
Kelsen argued in *Peace through Law* that international law had to prevail
over national law. Starting from such monist, legal premises, he argued—on
a more political level—that the ultimate key to international peace was to
replace a system based on nation-states with a global "Federation."[12]

Since he was realistic enough to appreciate the extreme difficulty in
accomplishing such an ambitious goal, he proposed a sort of short-term pro-
gram to the Federation, that is, the creation of a "Permanent League for the
Maintenance of Peace" (which would initially be made up of the countries
winning World War II), equipped with an International Court of Justice and a

police.[13] The task of the Court would be to resolve judicially the contrasts and disputes among the members of the League judicially, and the police would apply the Court's sentences.[14]

The core concept behind such a proposal was that, for Kelsen, any dispute was "justiciable," that is, every dispute could be turned into a "legal" one.[15] In Kelsen's view, the League and the Court would grant peace on the international level. His intellectual and theoretical debt toward Immanuel Kant's *Zur ewigen Friede* (*For the Eternal Peace*, 1795) and the concept of "civitas maxima,"[16] elaborated by the representative of German Enlightenment, Christian Wolff, has rightly been noticed.[17] Yet, Kelsen's pacifism had its own, strong elements of originality. By identifying the Court as an efficacious instrument to neutralize the potential disruptive content of disputes among States, he was in fact delineating a form of "legal or cosmopolitan pacifism," which became also a source of inspiration for prominent European twentieth-century intellectuals such as the Italian Norberto Bobbio or the still-living German Jürgen Habermas.[18] Yet, there are two more aspects worthy of attention: first, similarly to his works on democratic theory, under the guise of a neutral, scientific and *super partes* kind of analysis, Kelsen was in reality defending a specific ideal, that of peace. Also, with his "League," he seemed to foresee the creation of the United Nations and the writing of the U.N. Charter, on both of which in 1950 he published a long and detailed book, *The Law of the United Nations*. Here, Kelsen criticized the U.N. Charter as being vague and "inadequate" in establishing the "legal instruments" to carry out the principles which it expressed and to enforce the rights which it included. In particular, he looked at Article 39 of the U.N. Charter providing the Security Council with the right to "decide measures for restoring peace" as a means to allow a political organ (the Council) to prevail over the legal system. In this way, the assertion of the primacy of international law, which was for Kelsen a condition to grant international peace, was de facto severely hampered.[19]

His detractors considered Kelsen's analysis of the U.N. Charter as nothing but the expression of his pure theory of law, and thus oriented toward a formalist conception of law. In their eyes, the Austrian legal theorist was fundamentally unable to grasp the innovation of that new international organization and of the U.N. Charter.[20] Seemingly more balanced is the opinion of those who recently stressed how Kelsen's work on the UN should be essentially considered as an attempt to elaborate on the elements of "vagueness" of the Charter, on how—in his opinion—it did not clearly establish "legal instruments" to enforce the rights (and the principles) which it contained.[21] Beyond the controversy, Kelsen's book testified—on a theoretical level—to his idea of "legal pacifism" and, on a strictly historical level, to his interest in the developments of the international system. His attention to the creation of the UN was parallel to that of another international major

event, that is, the Nuremberg Trials, on which he published a long and relevant essay, showing again his commitment for international law, *Will the
Judgment of the Nuremberg Trials Constitute a Precedent in International
Law?* (1947). After obtaining American citizenship, Kelsen in 1945 was in
fact appointed as legal adviser for the UN Commission for War Crimes.
His task was to analyze the legal aspects of those trials.[22] His comments on
the Trials were extremely critical, although he agreed "the need to try high-
ranking nazi officials."[23]

He contested the decision to prosecute single individuals for "war crimes"
because—as he argued—that kind of "penal responsibility" was not included
at that time into international law.[24] He stressed how just the Kellogg-Briand
Pact, "for whose violation the London agreement establishes individual criminal responsibility," "does not forbid acts of private persons." The point was,
for Kelsen, that such a form of penal responsibility ended up providing a legal
justification to "retroactive punishment" of nazi criminals.[25] Kelsen's critique
was however not so much focused on the problem of "retroactive punishment" as on the fact that the judges of the Nuremberg Trials represented
only the war winners and "was imposed upon vanquished States," without,
for example, "Germany's consent."[26] In the light of this, even the "retroactive punishment" of the nazi officials seemed to be nothing to Kelsen's eyes
but the application of the "winner's justice," that is, the expression of a
"privilegium odiosum," which he hoped would not constitute "a precedent"
for international law. As correctly stressed, the particular conformation of
the Nuremberg Trials ended up, in Kelsen's view, embodying a dangerous
violation of the chief principle of "equality before the law."[27] Just this violation and thus the "asymmetrical" relationship between winners' and losers'
crimes underpinning, for him, the Nuremberg Trials revealed, according to
his interpretation, their fundamental "political" nature.[28]

With this, he had no intention of softening or limiting the severity of nazi
crimes. He wanted rather, in my opinion, to highlight what he thought was
the main flaw of the *ratio* behind the Trials. To him, the latter had changed
the principle of legal justice into a form of "revenge" of the Allies against
the Axis powers. He emphasized then how the conception and the category
of "revenge"—regardless of its motivations—did and could not belong to the
realm of Law. In my opinion, he was not making an apology of moral indifference toward atrocious and inhuman acts, as he seemed to recall attention
to the idea that there were no forms of justice fairer or better than others. In
other terms, he was asking to apply and enforce the principle of international
justice—so to say—*democratically.*

Along with stringent issues of international politics and law, Kelsen
maintained his interest and curiosity for politics and political theory, which
took shape, in my opinion, through two main aspects: he returned to reflect,

on the one hand, on bolshevik-communist theory and, on the other, on the meaning of real and representative democracy. We have already seen that Kelsen's interest in marxism and bolshevism dated back to the early 1920s: his American essays again proposed a series of reflections already developed, for example, in his *Sozialismus und Staat*.[29]

The Political Theory of Bolshevism. A Critical Analysis and *The Communist Theory of Law and State* (1948; 1955) aimed to attack the idea according to which marxism would be "scientific" and thus an objective concept of economics, society, and even law. In this sense, similarly to *Sozialismus und Staat* and to the first edition of *Vom Wesen und Wert der Demokratie*, Kelsen identified in the marxist critique of the "bourgeois" law as oppressive and unjust an "ethical" component, whereas in the "prophecy" of a future society of people perfectly equal and free, a sort of hidden "anarchic" tendency.[30] Against the communist and Soviet conception of law, Kelsen was evidently recalling just to his *Sozialismus und Staat*, when arguing that law was not the expression of the ruling class's interests (as marxism and the political movements deriving from it stated), because in history "law" had often been an effective instrument to improve and support the working class.[31] The point for me is not as much to recognize the fact that in the United States Kelsen maintained his view of marxism and bolshevism, as to highlight the connection between such a view and the historical-political context of that period. In my opinion, with his attack on communism and bolshevism, Kelsen wanted to undermine the Soviet legal school, which blamed in particular his legal theory and the Western legal system as a whole to be nothing but the expression of capitalist interests.[32]

In this sense, if it is true that in the 1920s and 1930s Kelsen's critique of bolshevism and marxism could be interpreted as an integrative part of his defense of parliamentary democracy, then in the 1940s and 1950s that same critique should be correctly situated within the Cold War ideological contrast between the West and the East. With regard to this aspect, between 1944 and 1955 Kelsen was one of those many European emigrés who were under the scrutiny of the F.B.I., which committed to identifying "commies" and potential enemies of the United States on the American soil. He was not a victim of the Cold War American anti-communist obsession but had to be very cautious, chiefly after being subjected to interrogation by an F.B.I. agent.[33] As an interesting example of how profoundly that obsession impacted postwar American society, the anti-Soviet connotation of Kelsen's work on the *Communist Theory of Law* was particularly appreciated, for example, by Professor Bernard Schwartz, director of the Comparative Law Institute of New York University Law School in 1956, who wrote a long and detailed review of the book. It is interesting to observe—just as an expression of the ideological battle at that time between the Western and Eastern bloc—that

Schwartz made a sort of preliminary distinction between Kelsen as a legal thinker with his *Reine Rechtslehre* and Kelsen as a strong critic of communist ideology and its conception of law. Schwartz's sympathies were all addressed toward the second of the two Kelsens.[34] The end of World War II and the reconfiguration of the global system according to the bipolar logic had enormous implications for democratic theory. The collapse of nazi and fascist regimes pushed many European intellectuals of different political orientation to question the roots of totalitarianism, as an ideology and as a political system, while posing a likewise stringent and crucial problem: how to reconstruct a stable and strong democracy, which logically implied again questioning the nature, the character, and the meaning of democracy.[35] The latter issue was particularly relevant—as Kelsen himself comprehended—in a period dominated by two superpowers, each of which claiming to embody and defend "true democracy."[36]

After the war, political thinkers and philosophers such as Raymond Aron, Karl Popper, Isaiah Berlin, Hannah Arendt, Jacob Talmon, and Friederich Von Hayek, just to mention some of the most famous, were all interested (despite their differences and peculiarities) in understanding why totalitarianism could triumph, while taking a clear stance in favor of democracy and liberties. Although she did not belong to Cold War liberalism, Arendt left a lasting impression on postwar political philosophy with her *Origins of Totalitarianism* (1951), which was a complex elaboration on the nature and internal dynamics of totalitarian systems (notably the nazi and the soviet ones). She argued that they were all characterized by the existence of one single political party, the annihilation of any form of true social, political, and idealistic pluralism, the total control of the party coinciding with the State over civil society, and an ideology which was assumed to be absolutely and objectively just and true.[37] The particular nature of totalitarian ideology was at the heart of Raymond Aron's philosophy too, in his *Démocracie et Totalitarisme* (*Democracy and Totalitarianism*) (1965). Here, the French philosopher and sociologist compared totalitarian ideologies to forms of "secularized religions" promising the realization on the earth of perfect human and political communities, in which the supreme ideal of equality or the supreme ideal of the pure race would finally become true. The promise of such perfection ended up turning, in his view, into the ultimate justification of violence, persecutions, massacres against those opposing to such great projects.[38] Both Arendt and Aron showed how totalitarian systems and ideologies destroyed any form of pluralism and the individual was reduced to the mere cog of a repressive and pervading power. The critique of the anti-pluralist and anti-individual connotation of totalitarianism with its mono-party rule and its all-explaining, all-embracing ideology was likewise present in the work of the philosopher of science Karl Popper, the economist Friederich

Von Hayek, and the political philosopher Jacob Talmon. The latter argued, in his *Les Origines de la Démocracie totalitaire* (*The Origins of Totalitarian Democracy*) (1952), how some aspects of the eighteenth-century philosophical legacy contributed to create the conditions which made the totalitarian mentality flourish. Talmon denounced, for example, the "totalitarian" implications of Rousseau's conception of democracy. The social contract and chiefly the Rousseauian contempt for the minority, his insistence on the "general will" as unitary and homogeneous entity, to Talmon, represented all illiberal and anti-pluralist aspects of the Genevan thinker's political philosophy.[39]

Isaiah Berlin, who was influenced by Talmon's work, was far from being an anti-Enlightenment intellectual, but he recognized in that particular tradition of thought, which had been however so relevant for the development of Western liberal-democratic theory and institutions, controversial elements which, in his view, had indirectly nurtured (totalitarian) monism. The eighteenth-century faith in science and mathematics, in the possibility to extend scientific methods to social and human reality had led, for Berlin, to the assertion of a "scientist" kind of mentality, according to which objectively true principles for organizing and reforming society, politics, and even human nature did exist. This kind of belief was potentially dangerous—Berlin argued—because it entailed, in his opinion, a basically "monist" assumption, according to which the objectively correct and true solution to social, political, and human problems could be identified (and applied).[40] Von Hayek shared a similar, although not coincidental, critical approach to some aspects of scientist Enlightenment with Isaiah Berlin. The claim of prominent eighteenth-century thinkers to consider social and human reality with the same approach of a scientist studying inanimate nature had generated an engineer's type of attitude, which presupposed that, once discovered, the laws underpinning both society and politics could be modeled and changed by a group of "the enlightened." As he argued in *The Abuse of Reason* (1952), those embracing this philosophical and epistemological vision reasoned in terms of plans, laws, processes, in which there was very little room for individuals as free and diverse subjects.[41] Although based on different theoretical assumptions, Karl Popper was of a similar belief. He thought that totalitarianism reflected in first instance human belief that absolute truth could be obtained. Once obtained, the primary duty was to impose it even to those reluctant to accept. The exact opposite to such *forma mentis* was, for Popper, a scientific one, which was instead based on the principle of "falsifiability," according to which a theory was scientific if it was "incompatible" with possible empirical observations.[42] In political terms—as we can read in his major work *The Open Society and Its Enemies*—his concept of falsifiability implied a critique of all those theories (notably, for Popper, scientific materialism) affirming to have identified the objective laws of social, economic, and political development, while taking a stand in favor of an anti-dogmatic, free, pluralist, and critical way of thinking. The latter was based on the consciousness, according to Popper, that empirical facts could not be altered or "bowed" simply to fit and "serve" a theory or a particular and pre-established view of life.[43]

All these thinkers, who impacted Western post–World War II political and social thought with their works, thus shared a profound intellectual interest in the origins of totalitarianism, the idea that the latter embedded in a particular way of conceiving human reality, which found its ultimate expression in ideologies claiming to represent the only just way of interpreting and changing the world. Nazism and soviet communism were—for all of the intellectuals mentioned so far—a perfect example of such a claim.[44] In the specific case of Aron, Berlin, Popper, Talmon, and Von Hayek (i.e., the so-called Cold War liberals), their reflection on totalitarianism was functional to elaborating a personal political view, which was pro-liberalism and pro-democracy. All of them believed, to different extents, that liberal democracy was the opposite of hard right and hard left totalitarian systems just because it was based on a well-defined world outlook : free, pluralist, anti-dogmatic, and recognizing all individuals as subjects of the same rights and freedoms. Obviously, each of these intellectuals had their own peculiarities and originality.[45]

Yet, looking at them from a general point of view, while emphasizing their affinities, allows me not only to situate them within the twentieth-century legacy of liberal and democratic thought, but also—and most importantly for me—to highlight two aspects. Even though—for example unlike Berlin, Talmon, and in part Von Hayek—Kelsen showed no critical attitude toward Enlightenment tradition, which he always considered the cradle of modernity and particularly modernity as the expression of a scientific mentality, there were, in my opinion, two main aspects of intellectual proximity between the political visions of the Cold War thinkers mentioned so far and that of Kelsen.[46] First, their anti-dogmatic approach, their mistrust and critique of absolute truth, and their stance in favor of pluralism resounded Kelsen's political and democratic theory.[47] Second, similar to Kelsen, such an approach was connected with a coherence, although to different degrees, on liberal democracy. As we are going to see, both aspects re-emerged from Kelsen's *Foundations of Democracy* itself. In the next part of my work, I will argue how in his 1955 essay Kelsen's anti-dogmatic, pluralist, liberal, and relativist vision of democracy revealed itself to be coherent with a procedural conception of democracy.

DEMOCRACY AS "GOVERNMENT FOR": A CRITIQUE

At a general glance, *Foundations of Democracy* seems to be a sort of overview of Kelsen's democratic theory. This is, however, only an impression:

along with topics already discussed during his European period, some interesting changes occur. First of all, this long essay was published for the journal *Ethics. An International Journal of Social, Political and Legal Philosophy* and was based on Kelsen's lectures at the University of Chicago, the Walgreen Lectures.[48] Also, as we are going to see, Kelsen's ideal and political targets were partly different. The targets changed, although the mind framework underpinning the essay, in my opinion, was profoundly similar to that of his previous works. He was trying to delineate an analysis of real democracy, while defending it both *against* the Soviet claims to represent true democracy and *against* a series of prominent intellectuals (from Eric Voegelin to Jacques Maritain and Friederich Von Hayek) who, in his opinion, offered a misinterpretation of democracy.[49]

In this sense, *Foundations of Democracy* did represent Kelsen's contribution to the intellectual debate on democracy in the post-totalitarian age.[50] The main point is, however, that Kelsen's critique to the Soviet system and to specific thinkers of his age allows us to identify another remarkable components of his political theory, which in some respects were, in my opinion, already implicit, for example, in both editions of *Vom Wesen und Wert der Demokratie*, that is, *proceduralism*. By procedural democracy, one means a particular way of conceiving democracy, according to which the latter would consist in a series of means, procedures, and techniques to make political decisions. What distinguishes this particular decision-making process is the fact that the government itself is chosen by the people, who are equally equipped with civil and political liberties.[51] In historical terms, this particular view of democracy asserted itself after the end of World War II. As a response to those supposed "universal truths" (racial superiority for example)—in the name of which totalitarian ideologies had violated the most basic principles of human co-existence—postwar intellectuals and many after them rather emphasized rather the fact that what legitimized democratic leaders to rule was their being elected by the people through specific instruments, through "fair procedures."[52]

If we look at Kelsen, it is quite easy to observe how already his pre–World War II political works seemed to possess a procedural connotation. His critique of philosophical and political absolutism and his insistence on the fact that democratic system was characterized by a series of decisional/ representative mechanisms that maximized civil and political freedom (the majority principle, the proportional voting system, etc.) show us how Kelsen elaborated on democracy in procedural terms before the end of World War II: that is, before the label "procedural" became successful.[53] We could thus state that—as a political thinker—Kelsen proved to have, already during the post–World War I period, a certain kind of sensitivity and a vision, which would be later defined as typical of a procedural conception of democracy.

Yet, the latter took shape with more clarity in *Foundations of Democracy*, through two well-defined lines of reasoning: in the first instance, through a direct controversy with the Soviet political system and more precisely with the Soviet view of "true democracy," and subsequently, through a similarly direct controversy with prominent thinkers of his age, such as Eric Voegelin, the "neo-jusnaturalist" Emil Brunner, Jacques Maritain, Karl Niebhur, Friederich Von Hayek, and also with the economist (and friend) Joseph A. Schumpeter.[54]

In the incipit of *Foundations of Democracy* Kelsen looked at the Soviet Union and Soviet communism as a powerful threat to democracy, not only politically speaking but also ideologically, because of the Soviet claim to have accomplished true democratic principles. Again, for Kelsen, a reflection on the meaning of democracy was needed: "in Soviet political theory," Kelsen wrote, "the dictatorship of the Communist Party, pretending to be the dictatorship of the proletariat, is presented as democracy. It is of the greatest importance to disclose the conceptual device through which this distortion of the symbol could be achieved."[55]

It has been said that Kelsen's political reflection during the European years was more "abstract" than in the United States, where he would prioritize the anti-Soviet critique.[56] Yet, it is likewise useful to remember that his European works were everything but abstract. They all addressed specific political targets (from bolshevism to nazism). Also, exactly like in his European writings, in *Foundations of Democracy* he posed himself the problem of elaborating on the significance of democracy against its opponents (or at least those figures and those theories on the meaning of democracy which he openly disagreed with), in this case, the Soviet regime. He argued in fact that the defeat of nazism did not imply that anti-democratic political systems would vanish.[57] When discussing about Soviet ideology, Kelsen primarily referred to the *Manifesto of the Communist Party* and to Lenin.[58] It was in Marx's popular work that Kelsen identified the ultimate source of that "distortion" of the meaning of democracy. Here—Kelsen observed—the creation of the dictatorship of the proletariat was conceived as a necessary "step" toward the triumph of a true democracy.[59]

For Kelsen, Lenin had adopted this core principle changing it into a powerful instrument to ideologically justify the bolshevik Revolution and the bolshevik concentration of the power into their hands. He stressed in fact how Lenin considered the dictatorship of the proletariat the highest form of democracy because it became a "democracy for the poor" against bourgeois democracy, that is, the merely formal and unjust one. Kelsen greatly insisted on Lenin's equation between dictatorship and democracy because he wanted to show that such an identification—for him absolutely paradoxical and "perverse"—was possible if one started from the assumption that democracy was a "government *for.*"[60] According to the latter perspective, the crucial parameter to identify the legitimacy of a system (in this case the democratic one) was the "who" and the "what" *for* which that government was established. For Lenin—Kelsen emphasized—the "who" and the "what" of Soviet communism were the proletariat and the "interests," the "good" of the proletariat itself, as revolutionary class. In this sense—Kelsen argued—even a dictatorship could be seen as a form of democracy.[61] Any "substantive" attempt to justify a government—and Lenin's identification of the proletarian dictatorship with true democracy because it carried out "the interests of the people" represented an example of such to Kelsen—was highly problematical and controversial for the Austrian legal theorist:

> This perversion of the concept of democracy from a government by the people, and that can mean in a modern state only by representatives elected by the people, to a political regime in the interest of the people is not only theoretically inadmissible because of a misuse of terminology, but it is also politically problematical. For it substitutes as the criterion of the form of government defined as democracy a highly subjective value judgment—the interest of the people—for the objectively ascertainable fact of representation by elected organs.[62]

Kelsen insisted on how the specific content of such "interest of the people" could not be "objectively" determined. Such argumentation echoed his aversion toward the belief in the existence of objective, universally valid and self-evident principles or truth, which—as previously discussed—was profoundly related to his harsh, positivist attack against natural law doctrine.[63] Most importantly since there was, for Kelsen, no "objective criterion" for determining "the interest of the people" or "the common good" (of the people itself), the latter could become and actually became "the ideological justification of any government whatsoever," including a dictatorship. It became the "ideological justification" of any leader, whoever that was, including a dictator.[64] The analogy between this argumentation and that present in *Vom Wesen und Wert der Demokratie* about the figure of the autocrat and the nature of autocracy (in contrast with democracy) is evident.[65] Here, in order to strengthen his reasoning, Kelsen reminded us how even the Nazis attacked the "formal" character of parliamentary democracy as their counterpart, while claiming to act and rule for the good of their people, for the "common good," for the "greatness and glory of Germany," that is, *for*, exactly like the Soviets.[66] As he had already clearly argued in *Verteidigung der Demokratie*, here Kelsen stressed again how, for him, the radical left and radical right shared the same aversion to parliamentary, "formal" democracy.[67] For Kelsen, however, Soviet communism was not the only ideology trying to justify democracy in terms of some allegedly superior and objectively just principle; that is, it was not the only ideology claiming that democracy was above all a government *for* (for the people, for "the interests of the people," for the "common good," etc.). During the later postwar period, there had been the resurgence of what Kelsen—with ill-concealed contempt—defined as "neo-jusnaturalism." The end of World War II was marked by a general critique, not to say condemnation, of legal positivism which with his motto "law is law" appeared to many as being co-responsible for the rise of totalitarian ideology. The Nazis and the perverse dis-humanization of their victims were read as the most radical and extreme outcome of a civilization which had lost any moral principle and the connection of law with ethics.[68]

Differently from the nineteenth and the first half of the twentieth century, the postwar period witnessed a renewed interest for natural law and an attempt to reflect on the nature of law and politics, while going beyond legal positivism itself. The Nuremberg Trials, which were criticized by Kelsen as a form of "winner's victory," have been interpreted, in a long-term historical perspective, as the symptom of a natural law renaissance. Behind the London Charter providing the International Criminal Court with the right to prosecute "crimes against humanity," there was a clear and well-defined rationale, which can be ascribed to a sort of natural law–oriented mindset. The principle of "*nullum crimen, nulla poena sine praevia lege*" had in fact not been applied to the Nazis prosecuted in Nuremberg because of the particular nature of their crimes, violating any basic moral standards. When affirming that law had "to serve justice," the German jurist Gustav Radbruch seemed to interpret and voice the ultimate *ratio* underpinning the Trials against Nazis.[69] The writing of the UN Charter of Universal Human Rights (1948) itself is commonly considered as another relevant expression of postwar natural law resurgence. Through the Charter, as scholars have stressed, a clear message was delivered: there were not only legal positive rights, which had to be granted and protected within the space of the nation-State, but also human rights, as rights belonging to everyone, as human beings.[70]

In his *Foundations of Democracy* Kelsen identified a series of figures—the theologists Emil Brunner, Karl Niebhur, and the political philosopher and pedagogist Jacques Maritain—as representatives of a natural law revival in the specific form of a reformulation of the meaning of democracy. The first two were protestant while the third one was catholic but, regardless of their belonging to different christian denominations, all of them—according to Kelsen—shared a basically common approach to democracy. They were all anti-positivist and considered legal positivism not only as a key characteristic of the prewar period but also as one of those cultural elements preparing the soil for the rise of totalitarianism. On such a basis, they sought instead to establish a direct connection between "democracy and christianity," more precisely with a conception of natural law having a strong christian connotation.[71] For Brunner, for example, the triumph of totalitarian ideologies and systems depended essentially on the detachment, operated by legal positivism, between law and justice, more precisely between law and christian justice. Kelsen stressed about how in Brunner's *Gerechtigkeit: Eine Lehre von Grundgesetze der Gesellschaftsordnung (Justice and Social Order,* 1943), christian justice was considered the ultimate reflection of the "absolute divine natural law."[72]

Brunner's theory of democracy was nothing but, for Kelsen, the expression of an attempt to link democracy to the principle of christian natural law, that is, to christian theology.[73] Although he took distance from the admission of an "absolute divine natural law," the protestant American theologist Karl Niebhur was likewise critical toward a purely positivist foundation of democracy because the latter would remove the concept of justice which, for Kelsen, exactly like Brunner was fundamentally christian justice.[74] Such a connection was even more strongly established by the French catholic Maritain who in *Christianity and Democracy* (1945) blamed legal positivism and secularization for nurturing that relativism which—in his opinion—opened the doors to totalitarianism. A "God-less" democracy, based on the separation between law and ethics (christian), was for Maritain the ultimate source of its debacle between the 1920s and the 1930s.[75]

On such premises—Kelsen observed—Maritain promoted to refound postwar democracy on the christian values embedded in the Gospel, which was interpreted by the catholic French as profoundly democratic with its recall to all people's equality.[76] To Kelsen, all these thinkers embodied a sort of philosophical and political rebellion against legal positivism in the name of christian natural law and more precisely in the name of a fundamentally "theological" conception of democracy.[77] The point here is not so much to understand who was right or who was wrong. Kelsen's critique of neo-jusnaturalists might be blamed for being ideological as much as Kelsen considered them ideological. Rather, I want to focus on the rationale behind Kelsen's argumentation. When connecting democracy and its legitimacy to christian theology and the values it expressed, Brunner, Maritain, and Niebhur were acting, for Kelsen, in a very similar way to the Soviets and their supporters. To Kelsen their *forma mentis* appeared fundamentally analogous. To him, neo-jusnaturalists had no interest in the way in which political decisions were made within a democratic government; they had no interest, for example, in the parliamentary process or in the parliamentary dialectic and how it worked. They were rather engaged in defining the essence of democracy in terms of enacting the principles of christian natural law doctrine (although Kelsen was the first to admit that such doctrine was not interpreted exactly in the same way by these three thinkers). In his view, they were seeking to justify democracy as a government in the name of a christian "absolute divine natural law" (Brunner); in the name of a christian natural law which was not "absolute" but had to precede and legitimate the positivist one (Niebhur); and in the name of "universal" and "democratic" natural law principles included in the Gospel (Maritain). Kelsen's declared intent was to prove that "there was no essential connection between democracy and christian religion."[78]

In controversy with Brunner, Kelsen wondered how a supposed absolute and thus immutable, eternal "divine and natural law" could serve as a superior criterion to determine and influence positive law which—as such—served to organize and regulate society, that is, something plural and changing per se.[79] In controversy with Niebhur, Kelsen highlighted how the idea of a "natural law" which had to prevail over the positive one, while being not completely "absolute," appeared as a sort of contradiction. If it was not totally absolute, it had to be considered, for Kelsen, as "relative," and if such, the Austrian legal theorist wondered on which basis Niebhur could advocate the primacy of natural law.[80] Finally, against Maritain, Kelsen responded that the principle of equality as we can read in the Gospel was far from corresponding to the modern one, that is, equality before the Law. The Gospel's equality was "transcendent"; it was equality in front of God. As such, the christian conception of equality could coexist—Kelsen affirmed—with the maximum of legal and civil inequality. It is evident how Kelsen was seeking to undermine the connection, established by the French philosopher, between democracy and the Gospel. With this objective, Kelsen stressed thus that the seed of modernity itself inside the Gospel—that is, the principle according to which there should be a separation between "Caesar" and the "God"—paradoxically ended up for being considered by Maritain as one of those elements hampering the connection between democracy and christianity.[81]

In my opinion, Kelsen elaborated two argumentations (the first against Soviet doctrine and the second against "neo-jusnaturalism") which ideally ran parallel. In the first instance, both theories failed, for Kelsen, to provide a consistent and sharable conception of democracy. With regard to Soviet communism, Kelsen emphasized how the idea of democracy as "government for" could and—in his opinion—was actually used as the ideological cover for a dictatorship. With regard to neo-jusnaturalists, Kelsen discussed what he considered the logical and philosophical weaknesses of their reflection in order to prove that they were not offering any truly and credible alternative theory of democracy in the post-totalitarian age. Also, and most importantly to me, both theories were depicted by Kelsen as deeply distant from the conception of democracy as "government by," that is, "government by the people."[82] Both Soviet communists and neo-jusnaturalism ended up, for Kelsen, sharing a "substantive" vision of democracy, because they were trying, to his eyes, to justify their conception of democracy in terms of the accomplishment of principles/objectives considered objectively true and valid. For me, Kelsen's argumentation on Brunner, Niebhur and Maritain was thus functional to show that their "neo-jusnaturalist" view of democracy was fundamentally based— similarly to the Soviet one—on the idea that democracy was not so much a "government by" as a "government for." Kelsen's preference was addressed to the first of the two definitions of democracy.[83]

So far, I have sought to identify some of the main reasons why Kelsen was critical toward the principle of democracy as "government for," but one question remains open: why his preference for democracy "as government by"? Any attempt at replying to such a key question implies investigating Kelsen's procedural conception of democracy. I will argue that the latter was perfectly coherent with the main components of his democratic theory discussed so far.

IN DEFENSE OF A PROCEDURAL CONCEPT OF DEMOCRACY

For Kelsen, identifying the essence of any government with its final purpose, which might have been the accomplishment of "people's interests," the "common good," or christian ideal of justice, put the issue of personal and political freedom into the background. He argued in fact that no substantial difference between autocracy and democracy could emerge if starting from the concept of "government for the people" as the main defining element of democracy. Autocracy could be a "government for the people" as well as democracy. The autocrat could self-depict as the one carrying out the supreme "common good," for example.[84] The latter, in other terms, could become the ideological instrument to legitimate a power with no limit. Also, Kelsen emphasized how there was no way to determine an "objectively ascertainable common good," not even within a democratic system.[85] Values, judgments, and opinions varied, changed, and above all were plural because—as he had already elaborated in his European writings—what one meant by the people was a plural entity itself as well as its so-called "will."[86]

In his opinion, the definition of democracy, which presupposed the full recognition of such complexity and plurality was, as a last resort, that of democracy as "government by the people." The latter did not presuppose any alleged "common good," any objectively true principle to carry out (the supreme revolutionary values, for soviet communism, or christian values for "neo-jusnaturalists") as the people, made up of citizens, exercised their political rights to participate in political life and elect their representatives. On the basis of equal rights (civil and political) and universal suffrage, the people—"adult individuals"—elected, within an indirect democracy, their representatives and their government. In this sense—Kelsen argued—democratic elections and political representation became the specific "relationship" between "the elected" and "the electors."[87] Differently from the concept of democracy as "government for," here the definitional focus moved from the "what" to the "how": democracy was no more a problem of "what," of which supreme value/principle to achieve or carry out as the problem of "how" the government and "the social order" were established, according to which "procedures," according to which "rules." Democracy as "the government by the people" had to be meant as a series of procedures and mechanisms in order to "create and apply the social order constituting the community."[88] The "how-centered" definition of democracy is to be carefully taken into account chiefly in relation to two specific topics discussed by Kelsen in his 1955 essay: Eric Voegelin's theory of representation and the relationship between democracy and economics, with a particular reference to the Soviet doctrine, on the one hand, and to Friederich Von Hayek's theory, on the other. Voegelin and Kelsen knew each other: the former was a student of Kelsen and one of his assistants at the University of Vienna. In the early 1950s both were distinguished emigré in the United States In 1952 Voegelin published *The New Science of Politics: An Introduction* on which Kelsen wrote a long review which he did not publish.[89] Until the mid-1960s Kelsen continued to write about and examine Voegelin's work. Also, they had a long correspondence, while living in America.[90] Although they were both interested in understanding how the postwar political order could be re-founded on stable basis, they were on the opposite sides of the barricade.[91]

Voegelin interpreted the rise of totalitarianism as the most radical and perverse effect of political ideologies (notably the nazi and the soviet one) which believed in creating a perfect kind of human community, on earth. This aspiration and promise, in the name of which anything, even the most ferocious crimes, could be justified, for Voegelin, represented the attempt to "immanentize" the "transcendence," to bring about the "heaven" on earth, which in depth implied the substitution of God with Man. Such a substitution had to be related to the aftermath of modern scientism, secularization, and positivism, which—for Voegelin—had contributed to the removal of any form of "transcendence," creating "secular religions."[92] Once it was removed, the principle of man's absolute capability to transform reality (social, political, even mental) according to one's views and aspirations—which, for Voegelin, was common to all totalitarian ideologies—could take shape and succeed.[93] Kelsen could not agree with his former student. As we have seen so far, all his legal and political theory was a clear and insistent rejection of any form of "transcendence," because in the latter he saw a form of absolutism (philosophical, religious, epistemic, and even political).[94] His critique of natural law doctrine in favor of a rigorous legal and philosophical positivism (legal and philosophical), his attack on christian neo-jusnaturalists, and the definition of autocracy itself should be interpreted in this sense. He could not accept a theory, just blaming the removal of "transcendence" elements as the ultimate source of totalitarianism. Also, he contested Voegelin's definition of ideologies—such as nazism and communism—as "secular religions." For Kelsen, that was nothing but an oxymoron, because a religion did exist *strictu sensu* only on the condition of believing in an ultra-earthly being. To his eyes Voegelin's work contained rather a dangerous (chiefly because, for him, intelligently disguised) critique of the legacy of modernity and Enlightenment, which were rather based, for him, on the consciousness of a fundamental and radical separation between religion and politics.[95] It is useful to take into account just such profound diversity of views when looking at the *Foundations of Democracy*, in which Kelsen directly and frontally attacked Voegelin on the issue of representation. For the Austrian political scientist, the postwar restoration of democracies had to go beyond the scheme of traditional representation, that is, political and parliamentary representation, which he defined in his *New Science of Politics*, as "elemental": Voegelin was suggesting to go beyond "formal" democracy.[96] "Elemental representation" had to be integrated with an "existential representation." The latter indicated the relationship between the ruler/s and "society as whole." It was just this relationship which, for Voegelin, avoided democracy being only a government in the formal or "constitutional" sense of the term. To him, if such relationship failed, democracy as a system failed too.[97] As stressed by scholars, behind the distinction between "elemental" and "existential" representation there was the even more fundamental one between "immanence" and "transcendence." In Voegelin, representation (as a key component of modern democracy) had to be re-formulated in terms of an "openness toward transcendence."[98]

In his essay of 1955, Kelsen briefly summarized Voegelin's theory of representation to identify what he thought were its most dangerous autocratic implications. If "existential representation" was more essential to democracy than the "elemental" one, once established that the ruler was in a relationship with the people, that is, that he "represents the people," the issue of how that ruler got the power, whether or not "elemental" representation was granted, and whether or not fundamental rights themselves were granted became of secondary relevance.[99] As a proof of that, Kelsen reminded how, for Voegelin, the dichotomy between party pluralism or party-monism was not crucial to distinguishing a democratic system from a dictatorship.[100] Kelsen could thus argue against Voegelin:

> Our analysis of the theory of representation advocated by the new science of politis shows that it is of the utmost importance to maintain as strictly as possible just the concept of representation which this science disparages as merely "elemental," [. . .] and to reject its replacement by a concept of "existential"

representation, which only obscures the fundamental antagonism between democracy and autocracy.[101]

For Kelsen, Voegelin's theory of representation ended up being paradoxically more functional to autocratic systems than to democratic ones. "Existential" representation, with its claim to create a connection between the ruler and the "society as a whole"—which for Kelsen was nothing but an attempt at applying the concept of "transcendence" to politics—for him put the issue of freedom to the background. That did not happen—Kelsen stressed—if considering democracy in procedural terms, that is, if one assumed that democracy was first of all a technique/means to establish a "government by the people": in other words if conceiving democracy from the perspective of the "how" rather than of the "what."[102] In my opinion, Kelsen adopted a substantially similar kind of argumentation to criticize the alleged essential relationship between democracy and economics. In the 1950s—as an effect of the Cold War—the contrast between the West and the East passed through the confrontation between those arguing that democracy needed a socialist kind of economics and those who instead argued that only within a capitalist system could democracy exist and prosper.[103] In Kelsen's view—as we are going to see—both parties were fundamentally misinterpreting the meaning of real democracy, which in his opinion was linked to no specific economic form, as well as not being linked to the accomplishment of an alleged "common good," or "people's interests," or a certain ideal of justice, and so on. Kelsen argued that soviet economic doctrine was based on the principle—already theorized by Marx[104]—according to which true democracy was possible only within a socialist economic regime. If it were true that behind the connection established by marxism between economics and politics there was the idea of the primacy of the former over the latter, the interpretation of the "transition" from capitalism to socialism and thus from "formal" to "substantial" or true democracy posed, for Kelsen, two main controversies.[105] First, he argued how the transformation of the proletariat into the "ruling group" in order to set up a socialist economy would take place through "political means" which might be "peaceful"—by conquering the political majority as professed by the Social Democrats, for example—or by means of a revolution—as actually done in Russia by Lenin and the Bolsheviks. In both cases—Kelsen thought—politics was more central than economics.[106] Second, he insisted again on the fact that, once the proletarian revolution broke out, a further step to take, according to marxist doctrine, was to establish a "proletarian dictatorship," that is,—in Kelsen's perspective—to "get rid of democracy" itself. He returned to his traditional anti-Marxist argumentation, which was already clearly present in his European works: regardless of the final ideal to achieve, for him, defining a dictatorship as a form of democracy meant to alter and pervert the meaning of the latter.[107]

Kelsen extended his critique to the Social Democrats too: he reminded how for them the creation of a socialist economy as an integrative component of a true democracy was hampered in capitalist states by the existence of a minority possessing the property of the means of production and exercising its influence over a large majority of the people. Only if the means of production were conferred to the government, "economic power" could be exercised in the interests of the people.[108] In such reasoning, Kelsen disputed the connection between a specific form of economic organization and the possibility of establishing a true democracy. He started from the (legal) assumption, according to which the economic system (the right of property, the contracts, etc., all characterizing a capitalist and "free economy") was essentially regulated by law. He stated thus that "freedom of economy is a legal freedom, a freedom guaranteed by law."[109]

Starting from such an assumption, Kelsen could argue that within modern states and particularly the democratic ones, the existing economic system was such because it was maintained and sustained by the "law-making" mechanism. The latter—in a democracy—was determined, albeit indirectly, by those who possessed political rights, including the working class. Against social democratic argumentation Kelsen replied thus that the particular conformation of modern and democratic states made "economic power and political rights" deeply intertwined: the prevailing economic system, capitalism, was such because it corresponded to the will of the majority of the people, which expressed itself through democratic elections and thus through the exercise of political rights. As a proof of that, Kelsen stressed how—despite the problems and limits of capitalism—the citizens of the major Western democracies, all provided with civil and political rights, had opted to maintain that kind of economics.[110] Yet, Kelsen's critique did not imply any one-sided apology for capitalism and not even a position in favor of those arguing a necessary correlation between capitalism and democracy, that is, between capitalism and civil, political freedom. Among "those," in *Foundations of Democracy* Kelsen targeted Friederich Von Hayek, the Austrian economist and political thinker. In his *The Road to Serfdom* (1944), Von Hayek identified capitalism as the proper economic system of a modern democracy because—unlike socialist systems, which consisted in a form of planned economy controlled by the government—it presupposed free individuals, equipped with full rights. For Von Hayek, a government interfering in the economic field inevitably interfered in the life and personal choices of citizens, restricting their civil and political freedom.[111]

Behind Von Hayek's economic doctrine there was a double assumption, that a free economic system would liberate and generate individuals' creative energy and above all that a planned economy would inevitably conflict with freedom, because it would lead to the creation of an élite of super-bureaucrats controlling the entire economic process and thus the individuals involved in it. The elimination of economic freedom would lead to the elimination of any other form of freedom.[112] With his work, Von Hayek thus provided a powerful justification of the Western block economic and political institutions. Kelsen developed his reply by following two key lines of reasoning. He commenced by arguing that capitalism as a character of democratic states was a "tendency" rather than an objective and universal "rule." Similarly, for Kelsen, from the fact that there had been historical examples of undemocratic states with planned economy, one could not infer that "inevitably" and "necessarily" this kind of economic organization would lead to the total and complete suppression of civil and political freedom.[113] In the light of this, Kelsen considered improper Von Hayek's idea that the "rule of the law" could not be maintained within a socialist state with a planned economy, because it necessarily served to grant freedom and thus it could only exist within a democracy.[114] In history—Kelsen stressed—the so-called "rule of the law" had primarily provided "security in the field of law," that is, that law-making and law-applying process were regulated by law and in the respect of the law: that they were "rationalized."[115] Although it had become an integral part of modern democracies, the "rule of the law"—Kelsen argued—did not thus deal essentially with guaranteeing freedom and democracy, as with a problem of power "rationalization."[116] Kelsen's argumentation partly contained a historical truth: in Europe, whether Continental or not, the "rule of the law" had in fact characterized constitutional-monarchic governments rather than democratic ones for a long time.[117]

Yet, in my opinion, Kelsen was underestimating the key role played by "the rule of law" in protecting citizens from the arbitrariness of the power. His main intent was in fact to prove, against Von Hayek, that there was not necessarily a link between the rule of the law and democracy and thus that there was no necessarily link between the rule of the law and capitalism as a hallmark of democracy. For Kelsen, Von Hayek's mistake was to consider the connection between capitalism and democracy as a sort of "law": the Austrian economist had universalized a kind of relation that was historical, empirical, and as such could change and vary.[118]

Regardless, with the evident ideological differences between the two points of view, both Von Hayek and his counterpart (the supporters of the soviet doctrine) linked, for Kelsen, the creation and the functioning of a true democracy to the accomplishment of certain economic principles (socialist or capitalist).[119] In other words, for Kelsen, both shared a similar approach to democracy: the meaning of the latter had to be defined through the "what" (the aftermath of a socialist or capitalist economy) rather than through the "how." Instead, from Kelsen's perspective, democracy as a form of government did not serve any specific ideological content. With this term, in my opinion, Kelsen equally meant the soviet doctrine of democracy, "neo-jusnaturalism," Voegelin's proposal to replace "elemental" with "essential" representation, those theories establishing a direct connection between democracy and socialism, and those claiming the exact opposite. To all of them, Kelsen opposed a theory of democracy, which was centered on the way in which political decisions were made rather than what was decided. From this point of view, the understanding of the specific character of the relationship between the rulers and the ruled became crucial to him.[120]

Kelsen focused in fact on elections and leaders' selection as a constitutive element of democracy: democracy did not signify the absence of leaders. Real democracy could not overcome the split between the rulers and the ruled. In this sense, there was no substantial difference between democracy and autocracy. Yet, it was the way in which leaders came to power in democracy which made the difference between the two. Democratic leaders were such because they had been chosen and voted by the people, and, most importantly—since the particular nature of their legitimacy—they remained in charge until new elections did decide their destiny. Their leadership was temporary and legitimized from below: the relationship between them and the people was thus "fluid," changing, not only because their "rulership" was not permanent but also because the ruled of today could become the rulers of tomorrow.[121] Elections (democratic) were thus the specific procedure to select leaders. Such a procedure was "rational, and publicly controllable."[122]

So far, Kelsen basically seemed to re-propose a kind of argumentation already developed in his European writings and notably in the second edition of *Vom Wesen und Wert der Demokratie*.[123] Yet, in *Foundations of Democracy*, two differences emerge: first, the reflection on the particular nature of (democratic) leaders should here be put within the context of the contraposition between democracy as "government for" and democracy as "government by." Most importantly, Kelsen systematically introduced the issue of elections and competition. By doing so, he could be directly compared with Joseph A. Schumpeter's democratic theory. Like Kelsen and Von Hayek, Schumpeter was Austrian and like the latter was an economist. With both, he shared the same destiny of emigré in the United States.[124] Before the end of the war, Schumpeter published his major study on *Capitalism, Socialism and Democracy* (1942).[125] Although Schumpeter's work should be correctly put within a greater debate at that time, involving prominent figures such as Polanyi and Von Hayek, "on the nature of capitalism and socialism," he addressed the meaning and the characters of modern and representative democracy, exactly like Kelsen.[126]

If we juxtapose *Foundations of Democracy* with part IV of Schumpeter's popular work, we can observe that both thinkers started from assuming the hiatus between the idea and the reality of democracy, between real and ideal democracy.[127] The latter had been conceptually developed, for Schumpeter, by the "classical theory of democracy," notably by Rousseau, with his *Contract social* relating the creation of a true democratic system to the accomplishment of "common good." For Schumpeter, a "common good" as objectively existing and rationally conceivable could not, however, exist within a continuously changing world subject to "the habits of the bourgeois society."[128] The political and ideological implications of Schumpeter's critique to the so-called "classical theory of democracy" are numerous.[129]

At this point, I would rather recall attention on two aspects, particularly significant for me: in Schumpeter like in Kelsen, there was not only the attempt to delineate a realistic theory of democracy but, maybe most importantly, a likewise clear critical and skeptical attitude toward the conception of "common good" (whatever this meant). In my opinion, for both thinkers, such a critique constituted the conceptual premise to define democracy not in terms of "what" as in terms of "how" and more precisely how political decisions were made in democracy. Like Kelsen, Schumpeter looked at the electoral mechanism as an intrinsic component of modern democracy. If the latter had to be realistically considered as "that institutional arrangement for arriving at political decisions," elections were—like for Kelsen—an essential element of that "institutional arrangement." I would like to point out how, exactly like Kelsen, Schumpeter stressed the fact that leaders—in democracy—were "removable": they were chosen from below and from below they could be "evicted."[130] If focusing on these aspects (the relevance of the "how" rather than the "what" for defining democracy; the key role played by the electoral mechanism; and leaders' temporary power position), Schumpeter and Kelsen seemed to share a fundamentally procedural vision of democracy. Yet, in his *Foundations of Democracy*, Kelsen referred to Schumpeter with critical words. The main element of controversy was, I believe, the different political significance assigned by the two thinkers to "political competition." Schumpeter's famous definition of "democratic procedure" "as that "institutional arrangement for arriving at political decisions in which the people acquired the power to decide by means of competitive struggle for the people's vote" appeared to Kelsen an overestimation of the actual meaning of "political competition" itself.[131] The Austrian economist set undoubtedly a great value on "political competition" as a means to select leaders, moreover in order to effectively stress how far real democracy was from its ideal.[132] Schumpeter held the same critical attitude toward ideal democracy as Kelsen. Like the Austrian legal theorist, he refused the idea of the people as a unitary and preexisting entity, but unlike the latter, he took such refusal to its extreme consequences, by rejecting even the principle of "government by the people."[133] I think that such an element of diversity between the two should be taken into account to better comprehend not only Schumpeter's emphasis on "political competition" but also Kelsen's reply.

By following Schumpeter's reasoning—Kelsen argued—democracy ended up becoming a "government by competition" rather than "government by the people."[134] More precisely, Kelsen contested the idea according to which "the kind of competition for leadership which is to define democracy entails free competition for a free vote."[135] In this way, for Kelsen, Schumpeter made "free elections" a mere function of "political competition": to him, the Austrian economist was misinterpreting the actual relationship between free elections and "political competition" by defining the latter as the "primary criterion" to define democracy.[136]

Against Schumpeter's procedural conception of democracy, Kelsen opposed his own: evidently recalling to his European writings, he affirmed first of all that the so-called "political competition" ceased to be so crucial after the elections. This perfectly corresponded to his idea of the legislative body as a political space within which a plurality of subjects (political parties) made political decisions through a complex game of reciprocal concessions and compromises. The latter evidently clashed with the principle of competition, race, and struggle.[137] Hence, according to Kelsen, Schumpeter did not realize that "free elections" and—connected with them—the electoral system were not democratic only and exclusively because they allowed "political competition" but, rather, because they were functional in reducing the split between the majority and the minority, in order to get as close as possible to the principle of "self-determination." As in fact already elaborated in both editions of *Vom Wesen und Wert der Demokratie*, the "most democratic" electoral system in this sense was, for him, the proportional one, described as the most functional to a political life based on compromises and dialogue, rather than on struggle and harsh competition.[138]

Schumpeter and Kelsen's vision of democracy had strong and undeniable procedural elements, although the two interpreted them differently. Schumpeter's proceduralism had an "elitist" connotation which was, in my opinion, fundamentally alien to Kelsen's. Schumpeter was primarily focused on the moment in which leaders competed with each other for people's votes,[139] whereas Kelsen was much more interested in what happened (within the legislative body) after the elections. Schumpeter emphasized the competitive nature of democracy, oriented to leaders' selection, whereas Kelsen emphasized the opposite, that is, its alleged conciliatory dynamics.[140] With regard to the latter aspect, by repeating that, for example, the proportional system served to soften the hiatus between the ruled and the rulers in order to have a better approximation to "self-determination," Kelsen was again posing the problem of the relationship between ideal and real democracy. Differently from Schumpeter's, Kelsen's democratic theory indeed assumed a continuous tension between ideal and reality. As a proof of that, Schumpeter and Kelsen had a substantially different approach to the figure of Rousseau. In *Capitalism, Socialism and Democracy*, Rousseau was essentially considered as the main representative of the so-called "classical democracy," that is, of a democratic theory centered on the principles of "common good" and "the will of the people" which, for Schumpeter, were totally "unrealistic." His judgment left no doubt: Rousseau's vision of democracy had to be refused.[141] Kelsen's attitude was less one-sided: although—like Schumpeter—his primary goal was to define what real democracy was, he remained of the same opinion he had expressed a long time before. Rousseau was, to him, the thinker who—better and most "effectively" than others—had identified "the problem of democracy," that is, the problem of "self-determination."[142]

In his American essay of 1955, Kelsen critically addressed Rousseau's conception of the minority as a threat to the unity of the "general will." Yet, unlike Schumpeter, he firmly believed that the starting point of a serious reflection on the meaning of modern democracy implied not so much to simply reject Rousseau's legacy *in toto* as to recognize the absolute centrality of the concept of "self-determination."[143] As seen so far, in *Foundations of Democracy* Kelsen traced a basically procedural theory of democracy against a series of specific targets: against the soviet doctrine, neo-jusnaturalists, the assumption of a necessary connection between democracy and capitalism, or even against Schumpeter's theory whose proceduralism was seen in a critical way by Kelsen because of the principle of "political competition." Yet, I think that the significance and the extent of Kelsen's procedural conception of democracy goes beyond his personal intellectual battle against a series of doctrines and personages, which he considered controversial at that time and also as going beyond the Cold War atmosphere which he surely breathed. The "substantive" conceptions of democracy, for Kelsen, shared the common belief that the crucial point was to identify the alleged true content and purpose of democracy: democracy as the accomplishment of social justice or democracy as the realization of christian values, and so on. Following such a perspective, for Kelsen, the problem of freedom, be it civil, individual, or political, became of secondary importance. Kelsen instead seemed to think that a theory of democracy focused on the "how" rather than on the "what" inevitably put that problem to the foreground, because democracy as a procedure to make political decisions and more precisely to select the rulers did exist and did work—Kelsen argued—just thanks to the provision of fundamental liberties.[144]

Here, we can see how Kelsen's proceduralism (much more, for example, than Schumpeter's one) had a clear liberal connotation. Without civil and political freedoms, for Kelsen, democracy as a technique to politically decide from below, albeit indirectly, would be simply inconceivable and practically unfeasible. In real democracy the split between the rulers and the ruled could not be avoided but, unlike autocracy, the former were chosen from the latter, because citizens were provided with full rights. Democracy as a procedure entailed the concept of freedom and concretely positive rights of freedom.[145] Just the latter were—as I have tried to argue in the previous chapters—a crucial presupposition of Kelsen's democratic theory. Pluralism (ideal, political, social) implied the recognition of freedoms and its promotion through specific institutions. Constitutional jurisdiction—as theorized by Kelsen between the 1920s and the 1930s—was seen as an efficient and rational means to grant a better protection of minorities' freedom (besides the unity of the Austrian Federal State). Relativism assumed a widespread guarantee of fundamental freedoms and implied individuals' responsibility to make decisions "about social values" rather than passively following the autocrat's *diktats*.[146]

To me, Kelsen sustained the procedural character of democracy not only (like, for example, Schumpeter) in terms of promoting a realistic theory of this particular form of government but also because—in his opinion—it served the principle of freedom much better that any other "substantive" theory of democracy. In the light of this, we can better grasp the sense of his words when he wrote in 1955 that "the problem of democracy is not the problem of the most effective government; others may be more effective. It is the problem of a problem guaranteeing the greatest possible amount of freedom."[147] Kelsen was justifying democracy with a liberal argumentation. After all, it was in *Foundations of Democracy* that Kelsen clearly put modern and real democracy in connection with "political liberalism."[148] He observed in fact that "modern democracy cannot be separated from political liberalism. Its principle is that the government must not interfere with certain spheres of interests of the individual, which are to be protected by law."[149] In this way, he was re-proposing the most ancient and popular definition of political liberalism as that doctrine aiming to understand how to protect individuals' life from abuses of power.[150] In my opinion, freedom became the ultimate discriminating and definitory element not only between democracy and autocracy but also between a procedural and a "substantive theory" of democracy, between "government for" and "government by."

KELSEN IN THE HISTORY OF POLITICAL THOUGHT: A REASONED OVERVIEW

Kelsen as a political thinker offers us a complex and articulated theory of democracy, which is pluralist, constitutional (in the particular sense, which

I attributed to this term in chapter 2 of this book), positivist, relativist, and procedural. His democratic theory cannot be interpreted without considering his legal theory. In this sense, I have concentrated my attention on his *Hauptprobleme der Staatsrechtslehre* (1911), which represents—in my opinion—a crucial text to understand Kelsen's political thought itself. The critique of the concept of the State as "legal person" and equipped with a "will" allowed him to reconsider the role of the Parliament and then of society itself. His legal theory, positivist and of neo-Kantian influence, also played a decisive role in the establishment of his anti-natural law critique and even of his relativist outlook.[151]

Against natural law doctrine, which in his view was conceptually based on the principle of inferring positive law from alleged absolute principles/values (embedded in the so-called "nature"), Kelsen delineated a positivist conception of law implying the recognition that law was above all a human product. As such, its content was not only immanent but reflected also values and interests, which changed over time.[152] Yet, as declared in the Introduction, I deliberately moved my focus to the historical-political dimension of his democratic theory. By doing so, I have shown how all Kelsen's writings devoted to the meaning and characteristics of modern democracy were not developed within a *vacuum*. I identified a series of concrete issues, problems, figures, and challenges, which—in my opinion—stimulated Kelsen to reflect on the essence and value of democracy. The collapse of the Habsburg Empire and the creation of a new institutional and political system was much more than a mere historical background for Kelsen's writings of the late 1910s and early 1920s. Faced with the Austrian constituent debate on the electoral system, Kelsen in fact expressed his position in favor of political and proportional representation, through a reflection which revealed most of his argumentation included in both editions of *Vom Wesen und Wert der Demokratie*.[153]

As a legal adviser for the Subcommittee of the Constitutional Assembly, he participated in the drafting of the constitution, initially sharing the Social Democrats' anti-federalist position. We have seen that in the first instance Kelsen's constitutional drafts reflected some key political inputs, which he received from Karl Renner, and which mainly concerned the complex issue of the relationship between the Constituent Assembly (i.e., the central institution of the new Austrian Republic) and the Länder. The making of the constitutional jurisdiction, which has always been considered as Kelsen's most relevant contribution to the first Austrian Republic, could not be fully comprehended without considering such an issue and thus the concrete political debate of that time. The creation of a Constitutional Court was above all determined by the urgent necessity to build a federal system, in which the Länder were not totally subordinated to the Federation, while providing the latter with the tools to prevent the Regions from acquiring too much autonomy. It was in the light of this problem that Kelsen's invention of the "ex officio procedure," which activated the Court as "impartial guardian" of the constitution, should be considered. For Kelsen, however, the birth of the new Austrian democratic Republic, as well as of other major democratic systems in the postwar period, was far from representing the definitive assertion of such form of government. If looking at Kelsen's two editions of *Vom Wesen und Wert der Demokratie* through the lens of an historian, we can observe how the 1920 edition, in many respects, embodied his response to the bolshevik doctrine and political experiment in Russia. The same applies to the extended edition of 1929, which could be seen as his reply to reactionary movements trying to rise to power in his country and which—in some cases, like in fascist Italy—had already accomplished their goal. In a continuous dialogue with his time and its major political challenges, Kelsen in the early 1930s published a series of brief writings, which sound like his last, personal attempt to defend democracy as the best and most human form of government in a historical period, which was rejecting it within a growing radicalization of politics.[154]

In the mid-1950s, he returned to democratic theory with *Foundations of Democracy*, which can be considered as Kelsen's personal contribution to the post–World War II debate on the meaning of democracy. The U.S. intellectual and political environment offered him new stimuli, while pushing him to face a different legal and political tradition to the European one. Yet, his *Foundations of Democracy*—similarly to his previous works on the same issue—was primarily conceived of as a critical reflection on those theories and figures who, in his opinion, continued, for him, to profess a distorted significance and interpretation of democracy, while embodying more or less effectively a threat to democracy itself.[155] Such a critique should be situated within a broader historical context: that characterized by the head-on struggle between two political-ideological sectors (the American and the Soviet one), both claiming to represent the true accomplishment of democratic principles. The undoubtedly relevant impact, which the historical-political dimension had on Kelsen's political and democratic reflection, does however not deplete the complexity of his work. Through the analysis of his major writings, aiming to contextualize them, I have sought to show how Kelsen elaborated a theory of democracy, starting from the capital distinction between real and ideal democracy. His search for a realistic understanding of democracy implied a critical reflection on Rousseau's political legacy and thus on freedom as "self-determination," which led Kelsen to argue that direct democracy was unfeasible. In the light of that, his aim became to reason on the meaning of representative and indirect democracy, to understand its *essence* and *value*. In Kelsen's perspective, real democracy was *pluralist* on two levels: first, he refused to consider the people as a unitary, uniform entity, while emphasizing its plural connotation, which turned into one of the theoretical conditions to justify political and party pluralism as an integrative component of modern and parliamentary democracy. The latter in fact, for him, was characterized by the existence of political and ideal pluralism finding its actual expression in the plurality of political parties. Yet, he did not confine himself to identifying a connection between parliamentary democracy and pluralism starting from the assumption of the plural character of the people. He related pluralism (and parliamentary democracy) to the *principle of freedom* (civil and political). Pluralism in its many forms had a sense, did exist, and could be preserved only if rights of freedom were granted for everyone, including the minority.[156]

A democracy renouncing the protection of the minority was not such any more: the minority was vital, according to Kelsen, for the democratic decision-making process itself. Laws issued by the legislative body were democratic, provided that they were not the mere *diktat* of the majority against the minority, as the result of a *compromise* between the two. To make political compromises work, the minority had to be provided with the same rights and freedoms as the majority. For Kelsen, two tools were, in particular, useful to strengthen the position of the minority within the democratic process: a proportional voting system and constitutional jurisdiction. The former had a double merit in Kelsen's view. It gave political voice to a plurality of political subjects, while respecting and reflecting the plural essence of the people itself. The particular character of the proportional system thus provided the minority with robust representation within the Parliament, allowing it to influence the majority decisions.[157] With regard to this specific aspect, Kelsen however seemed aware of the fact that rights of freedom and the adoption of the proportional were not sufficient to preserve democracy from the "tyranny of the majority." In his 1930s essays on constitutional theory and jurisdiction he interpreted in fact the making of the Austrian Constitutional Court and the "ex officio" procedure as two excellent (legal) instruments to grant protection to the minority, as well as the unity of the Austrian state against potential centrifugal thrusts from the Länder. The nullification of anti-constitutional laws and the obligation for the majority to have the consent of the minority in order to pass a constitutional reform appeared to Kelsen as a fundamental guarantee in favor of the minority and thus of his idea of democracy as based on the compromise between majority and minority.[158]

In this sense, constitutional jurisdiction also became—in a broader perspective—functional to the preservation of that pluralism which—along with the provision of freedoms—was, for Kelsen, a condition for the existence of democracy and parliamentary dialectics itself.

As a political thinker, Kelsen was not only interested in identifying the institutions characterizing, in his opinion, real democracy and making it work properly. In his main works, he elaborated also on the philosophical, ideal, and epistemological outlook underpinning democracy, that is, *relativism* in contrast with absolutism. Within well-structured reasoning on the main differences between democracy and autocracy, Kelsen defined relativism as that "Weltanschauung" rejecting dogmas—principles considered universally and objectively true, more generally refusing the existence of a transcendent Truth or immutable values from which human, social, political, and even legal conduct had to be inferred. Because of its particular nature, relativism (in the aforementioned sense of the term) enhanced precisely the concept of ideal, political, and social pluralism, that is, one of the key components, for Kelsen, of real democracy. Being a relativist meant, from his point of view, being aware of the fact that values and principles were a human product and as such they were immanent and mutable.

I have tried to stress how such a conception of relativism did not necessarily imply indifference to values or moral choices, as consciousness of the fact that it was individual responsibility to choose and opt for certain values rather than for others. In this sense, he seemed to connect relativism with the principle of *personal responsibility* and in the last instance with that principle which, for him, was the presupposition to personal responsibility itself: freedom, conceived both as an ideal and as a positive right.[159] Also, he argued that a relativist vision, with its pluralist component, contributed to stimulate a tolerant approach, a tolerant attitude toward other opinions. A relativist was that kind of person—Kelsen affirmed—who respected others' points of view and consequently others' right to express it, because he did not assume the existence of an absolute truth. He thus related relativism to *tolerance*. Both the principle of personal responsibility and tolerance were, to Kelsen, two aspects characterizing democracy and distinguishing it from its opposite, autocracy.[160]

Similarly to his argumentation in support of the pluralist and constitutional character of real democracy, here Kelsen observed that relativism (as a philosophical view) and tolerance would remain an unanswered letter unless full rights of freedom were provided to everyone, to the majority as well as to the minority. Kelsen's defense of relativism thus implied a defense of fundamental rights. Kelsen's aversion to the belief in the existence of absolute truth or objective principles (of whatever nature), determining what was right and what was wrong once and for all, played a relevant role in his conception of democracy as "government by (the people)" rather than "government for" too, which can be identified with the *procedural* character of his democratic theory. Since real democracy was, in Kelsen's view, pluralist and characterized by a relativist outlook of the world, the validity and ultimate legitimacy of its institutions could not consist of the accomplishment of a specific pro-gram or principle considered as objectively and universally true (Kelsen's favorite example was undoubtedly the doctrine of soviet democracy). Such legitimacy had rather to rely on the people, as a plural entity, who selected their leaders through elections, giving them the right to rule and make politi-cal decisions. In this sense, Kelsen looked at democracy as a procedure, a method to make political decisions assuming a fluid, dynamic relationship between the rulers and the ruled. Yet, again, democracy as a method, as "gov-ernment by the people," did exist and did work, for Kelsen, only provided that full rights of freedoms were legally recognized and protected: leaders' selec-tion from below would be not possible without rights of freedom Similarly, it would be impossible to remove them peacefully through new elections.[161]

I have tried to argue how all the major components of his democratic theory assumed one fundamental principle, that of freedom. On the basis of the analysis developed so far, I think that Kelsen interpreted that fundamental principle in two ways, which are profoundly intertwined in his whole theory and which, historically speaking, belong to two great traditions of thought: the democratic and the liberal. Since his very first writings on the meaning and function of democracy, Kelsen explicitly referred to Rousseau as the major, modern philosopher of democracy. As I have sought to stress, the author of the *Contract social* remained a key point of reference for Kelsen until *Foundations of Democracy*. All his democratic theory started from a twofold assumption: the distinction between ideal and real democracy and the identification of Rousseau as the one who, for Kelsen better than anyone else, defined ideal democracy as that form of State in which citizens were fully and democratically free because they could politically determine themselves ("self-determination"). Kelsen's particular way of "using" the Rousseauian conception of democratic freedom represents, in my opinion, one of the most interesting aspects of his political thought. We have seen how Kelsen, in search of a realistic comprehension and definition of democracy, immediately took his distance from the Rousseauian concept of democratic freedom as "self-determination." The latter clashed with social order, which was inevi-tably established, for the Austrian legal theorist, with the separation between the rulers and the ruled. The point is however that Kelsen never completely gave up Rousseau. All his democratic theory, with its realistic aspiration, looked at the Rousseauian principle of freedom, which Kelsen interpreted in terms of "self-determination," not as something to simply get rid of but, rather, as a final goal, which could not be reached but however which could be approached as much as possible.

From this assumption, Kelsen, in all of his works, posed himself the prob-lem of how to get closer to that principle within a parliamentary and repre-sentative democracy. The proportional voting system and the debate between the majority and the minority—both considered by him as efficient tools to reduce the gap between the rulers and the ruled—should be situated within a broader reflection aiming to justify freedom in a *democratic* way, that is, according to the principle of "self-determination." Yet, all Kelsen's works so far discussed seem to be underpinned by a similarly strong *liberal* justification and conception of freedom and democracy.

I have argued that all the major components of Kelsen's democratic theory imply the recognition (and guarantee) of rights of freedoms which are both political freedom par excellence, that is, the right to vote, as well as classical liberal freedoms such as freedom of thought, freedom of press, freedom of expression, and freedom of science. In my opinion, freedom and its preservation represent the ultimate and deepest significance (value maybe?) of Kelsen's democratic theory.

If behind his search to understand how to get closer to the ideal of democracy, Rousseau's shadow lengthens behind Kelsen's, it is likewise relevant to recall the importance—not to say primacy—of liberal freedoms which were the shadow of other, prominent figures, those of European political liberalism. Kelsen's concern for the tyranny of the majority and his insistence on the protection of the minority can be certainly related, in his works, to the democratic problem not to emphasize the split between the rulers and the ruled but most importantly can be related to the European tradition of liberalism. His defense of tolerance and freedoms of press, opinion, thought, and science is the quintessence of a *liberal sensitivity*. At the same time, *his anti-dogmatic attitude* as well as his critique of those theories and doctrines professing the existence of objective, absolute, immutable truths, or principles was also an interesting element of affinity in the latter postwar period with some exponents of Cold War liberalism itself.[162] Equally liberal was his trust in human rationality, in the human ability to make good choices through the use of reason, through dialogue and peaceful confrontation. This is certainly one of the most remarkable characters of all Kelsen's political theory, that is, the belief that within a pluralist political system, providing freedoms, and characterized by a general relativist outlook, people could make wise and efficient political decisions for the community. His emphasis on the importance of compromises as an integral part of a modern and parliamentary democracy in fact assumed a deep-rooted trust in human reason, to which he always remained loyal, and which historically speaking comes from a very ancient past, from that Enlightenment movement, which was one of the cradles of modern European liberalism and which Kelsen praised.[163]

The political events of his time, the polarization of politics, and the growth of the extreme right and the extreme left in the early postwar period seriously challenged that trust, which he however never abandoned and which continued to characterize his further works. The peculiarity was that Kelsen reaffirmed that trust by confronting himself, his whole life long with a series of specific and well-defined doctrines, events, and figures who, in his opinion, posed a serious challenge to what he meant by the "essence" and "value" of democracy. By doing so, he developed a theory and a defense of liberal and representative democracy.

NOTES

1. See: Jeremy Telman, "Introduction: Hans Kelsen for Americans," in *Hans Kelsen in America—Selective Affinities and the Mysteries of Academic Influences*, 1–13. On Kelsen in the United States see also: Johannes Fleichtinger, "Transantlantische Vernetzungen. Der Weg Hans Kelsens und seines Kreises in die Emigration," in *Hans Kelsen—Leben—Werke—Wirksamkeit*, 321–338; Thomas Olechowski, Stephan Wedrac, "Hans Kelsen und Washington," in *Hans Kelsen—Leben—Werke—Wirksamkeit*, 259–274. On Kelsen's relationship with the University of Cologne and more particularly on his moving to the United States, see also: Oliver Lepsius, "Hans Kelsen und Nationalsozialismus," in *Hans Kelsen—Leben—Werke—Wirksamkeit*,271–287.

2. Carl Landauer, "Antinomes of the United Nations: Hans Kelsen and Alf Ross on the Charter," *European Journal of International Law* 14 (2003): 771.

3. Telmann, "Introduction: Hans Kelsen for Americans," 3–4. Also, Brian Bix, "Kelsen in the United States: Still Misunderstood," in *Hans Kelsen in America— Selective Affinities and the Mysteries of Academic Influences*, 25–27.

4. Paolo Carrozza, "Kelsen and Contemporary Constitutionalism: The Continued Preference of Kelsenian Themes," *Estudios de Deusto* 67/1 (enero-junio 2019): 62. The author stresses how the core of Kelsen's constitutional theory dates back to the European period and notably between the 1920s and the 1930s. Ibid., 57–62. On this point: see chapter 2.

5. Métall, *Hans Kelsen. Leben und Werk*, 75–76.

6. See: Kelsen, *Peace through Law*, 1944; Hans Kelsen, *Society and Nature. A Sociological Inquiry* (New Jersey: Lawbook Exchange Ltd, 2009).

7. In the second part of *General Theory of Law and State*, Kelsen devoted the whole Chapter IV to "democracy" and "autocracy" as "forms of government." It is interesting to observe that he discussed about both through a series of argumentations, already developed in most of his European works.

8. See: Kelsen, *General Theory of Law and State*, 2006; Hans Kelsen, *The Law of the United Nations. A Critical Analysis of Its Fundamental Problems* (New York: Frederick A. Praeger Inc., 1950).

9. In the last part of his life, Kelsen continued to show a clear interest for democratic and political theory. In 1945 he published—as we have already seen—*General Theory of Law and State*; in 1948 his essay on *Absolutism and Relativism in Philosophy and Politics*, previously discussed; in the same year he published two works on communist and bolshevik theory with *The Political Theory of Bolshevism* and *The Communist Theory of Law*. In 1955 he published an essay on *Democracy and Socialism*, whereas

two years later it was the time of the already analyzed *What Is Justice?* In 1963, he gave a last contribution to the topic with *Politics, Ethics, Religion and Law.* Within this series of works—all of them more or less directly referring to democratic theory—*Foundations of Democracy* was, in my opinion, the most important one.

10. Jochen Von Bernstorff, "Peace and Global Justice through Prosecuting the Crime of Aggression? Kelsen and the Morgenthau on the Nuremberg Trials and the International Judicial Function," in *Hans Kelsen in America—Selective Affinities and the Mysteries of Academic Influences*, 85–86.

11. See: chapter 1.

12. Kelsen, *Peace through Law*, 9 ff. On this point see: Zolo, "International Peace through International Law," chiefly: 309–311. Four years before publishing *Peace through Law*, Kelsen delivered a series of Lectures (Harvard Lectures at the Harvard Law School), which were later edited as a book on *Law and Peace in International Relations*, 1948. Here his critical view toward an international order based on the primacy of nation-states clearly emerged. On Kelsen as scholar and theorist of international law in the second postwar period: Hauke Brunkhorst, "Hans Kelsens Werk zwischen Krieg, Revolution und Neugründung der internationalen Gemeinschaft," in *Hans Kelsen und die Europäische Union: Erörterungen moderner (Nicht-) Staatlichkeit*, hrsg. Tamara Ehs (Baden-Baden: Nomos Verlag, 2008), 27–49.

13. Kelsen, *Peace through Law*, 56–67.

14. Ibid.

15. Sévane Garibian, "Crimes Against Humanity and International Legality in Legal Theory after Nuremberg," *Journal of Genocide Research* 9, no. 1 (2007): 93.

16. Like Kant, Kelsen imagined a "Federation," while stating that the assertion of the primacy of international law and the elimination of nation-states sovereignty would lead to the creation of a "universal" legal community of men and women who would become true citizens of the world. Kelsen, *Peace through Law*, 3–9. In this sense, for example according to Danilo Zolo, his pacifist theory seemed to echo Christian Wolff's idea of a "civitas maxima." Zolo, "International Peace through International Law," 309–310.

17. For a detailed analysis of Kelsen's use of the German Christian Wolff's conception of "civitas maxima" see: Peter Langford and Ian Bryan, "From Wolff to Kelsen," in *Hans Kelsen and the Natural Law Tradition*, 261 ff.

18. On Kelsen, Bobbio and Habermas as chief exponents of the so-called "cosmopolitan" or "legal pacifism": Danilo Zolo, *I signori della pace. Una critica del globalismo giuridico* (Roma: Carocci, 2008).

19. Kelsen, *The Law of the United Nations: a Critical Analysis of its Fundamental Problems*, XIII–XVII; 15–17; 27–50.

20. Landauer, "Antinomes of the United Nations: Hans Kelsen and Alf Ross on the Charter," 771–772.

21. Ibid., 780–783.

22. Andrea Gattini, "Kelsen, Hans," in *The Oxford Companion to International Criminal Justice*, ed. Antonio Cassese (Oxford: Oxford University Press, 2009), 403.

23. Bernstorff, "Peace and Global Justice through Prosecuting the Crime of Aggression? Kelsen and the Morgenthau on the Nuremberg Trials and the International Judicial Function," 93.

24. Hans Kelsen, "Will Judgment in the Nuremberg Trial Constitute a Precedent in International Law?," *The International La Quarterly* 1, no. 2 (1947): 161.

25. Ibid., 155; 161.

26. Ibid., 170.

27. As observed by Bernstorff, "Peace and Global Justice through Prosecuting the Crime of Aggression? Kelsen and the Morgenthau on the Nuremberg Trials and the International Judicial Function," 95.

28. Kelsen, "Will Judgment in the Nuremberg Trial Constitute a Precedent in International Law?," 167–171.

29. See chapter 1.

30. See: Kelsen, *The Political Theory of Bolscevism. A Critical Analysis* (New Jersey: The Lawbook Exchange, 2011). This book was considered by the F.B.I. as the proof of Kelsen's true anti-communist spirit. Oliver Rathkolb, "Hans Kelsen und da F.B.I während des Macarthysmus in den U.S.A.," in *Hans Kelsen—Leben—Werke—Wirksamkeit*, 339–348.

31. See: Hans Kelsen, *The Communist Theory of Law and State* (New York: Frederick A. Praeger, 1955), 1–51.

32. Kelsen's work on the *Communist theory of Law* was attacked by one of the most prominent soviet legal theorists of that time, Andrej Vishinsky. For the latter, Kelsen's conception of law was the expression of the interests of capitalist system. In Kelsen's opinion, Vishinsky's was likewise the expression of the interests of Soviet regime. Bobbio, *Studi generali sulla teoria del diritto*, 101 and generally Denys De Béchillon, *Qu'est—ce qu'une règle de Droit?* (Paris: Odilé Jacob, 1997), 77–78.

33. Mario G. Losano, "Kelsen criptocomunista e l'F.B.I. In margine al suo libro postumo *Religione secolare*," *Sociologia del diritto* no. 1 (2017): 145–150.

34. Bernard Schwartz, "Review of the Communist Theory of Law," *The University of Chicago Law Review* 23 (1956): 354–356.

35. Müller, "Fear and Freedom. On Cold War Liberalism," 45–64.

36. Kelsen, "Foundations of Democracy," 1955, 250–252.

37. See: Hannah Arendt, *The Origins of Totalitarianism* (Boston: MHM, 1973).

38. See: Raymond Aron, *Democracy and Totalitarianism. A Theory of Political Regimes* (New York: Praeger, 1968).

39. See: Talmon, *The Origins of Totalitarian Democracy*, 1986.

40. See: Berlin, "Historical Inevitability," 1969.

41. See: Friederich Von Hayek, *Counter-Revolution of Science: Studies on the Abuse of Reason* (United Kingdom: Liberty Press, 1979).

42. See: Karl Popper, *The Logic of Scientific Discovery* (London, New York: Routledge, 2002).

43. See: Popper, *The Open Society and Its Enemies*, vol. I and vol. II.

44. Müller, "Fear and Freedom. On Cold War Liberalism," 45–64; More generally, on Cold War Liberalism see also: Haddock, *A History of Political Thought*, 240–251.

45. I am well aware of the major differences between the thinkers mentioned. For sure, Arendt cannot be ascribed to Cold War liberalism. Her political reflection aimed to reformulate politics as active and conscious citizens' participation in public

life, while being profoundly critical toward the traditional liberal view of freedom, conceived as mainly non-interference from the State into individuals' life. The latter was instead defended by Berlin, who insisted on the moral aspects of freedom, that is, as freedom of choice. In turn, the British thinker was also distant from Popper's appreciation for technocratic elements as well as from Aron's interest, with realistic connotation, for international relations. Also, neither Berlin nor Popper identified a direct connection between capitalism and freedom like Von Hayek. Yet, Popper and Von Hayek's—both Austrian—intellectual formation cannot be fully understood if the Vienna circle experience is overlooked. Instead, in the case of Berlin, he initially flirted with Ayer's logical positivism at Oxford, to later take distance from it and embrace the history of ideas. Instead, Aron had a debt toward the tradition of French moralists, while showing an affinity with a thinker such as Eric Voegelin since both defined nazism, fascism, and soviet communism as forms of "secular religions" characterized by intrinsically totalitarian components. Besides their abovementioned major works, to have an effective outlook of their peculiar intellectual profiles see: Richard Allen, "Hayek and Liberty Under Law," in *Beyond Liberalism: The Political Thought of F. A. Hayek & Michael Polany*, ed. Richard Allen (New Brunswick: J. Transaction, 1998), 47–66; Crowder, *Liberalism and Value Pluralism*, 2002; Gerda Bohmann, "Politische Religionen" (Eric Voegelin und Raymond Aron)—Ein Begriff zur Differenzierung von Fundamentalismus?," *Österreichische Zeitschrift für Soziologie* 34, no. 1 (2009), 3–22; Malachi Hacohen, "Karl Popper, the Vienna Circle and Red Vienna," *Journal of the History of Ideas* 59, no. 4 (1998): 711–73; Bhikhu Parekh, *Hannah Arendt and the Search for a New Political Philosophy* (London and Basingstoke: Macmillan, 1981).

46. On Kelsen's attitude toward modernity as expression of the Enlightenment movement: Clemens Jabloner, "In Defense of Modern Times: A Key-note Address," in *Hans Kelsen—Leben—Werke—Wirksamkeit*, 331–342.

47. Yet, it useful to point out that Kelsen was critical both to Talmon's specific definition of "totalitarian democracy" and to Von Hayek's theory of an essential correlation between capitalism and liberal democracy.

48. Kelsen delivered the Walgree Lectures on invitation of his friend, the political scientist, Hans Morgenthau. Daniel F. Rice, "Kelsen and Niebhur on Democracy," in *Hans Kelsen in America—Selective Affinities and the Mysteries of Academic Influences*, 135.

49. It is interesting to observe how in his work, Kelsen praised compromises and conciliation between opposite views but as political thinker he frontally attacked and criticized those diverging from his position, in no uncertain terms.

50. Yet, as stressed by scholars, Kelsen's essay had no serious echo in the United States maybe because at that time most of American political science departments "were dominated by methodological behaviorism." Urbinati, "Editor's Preface," 3–4.

51. Maria Paula Saffon and Nadia Urbinati, "Procedural Democracy, the Bulwark of Equal Liberty," *Political Theory* 41, no. 3 (2013): 441–442.

52. Gerry Mackie, "The Values of Democratic Proceduralism," *Irish Political Studies* 26, no. 1 (2011): 439–453.

53. See: chapters 1 and 3.

54. Kelsen, "Foundations of Democracy" 307 ff.

55. Ibid., 250–251.

56. Herrera, "Science et Politique chez Hans Kelsen," 104–105.

57. Kelsen, "Foundations of Democracy," 250.

58. Exactly like in the first edition of *Vom Wesen und Wert der Demokratie* and in *Sozialismus und Staat*, Kelsen referred to Lenin's *State and Revolution*. On this topic see: chapter 1.

59. Kelsen, "Foundations of Democracy," 256. On this topic see: Marx and Engels, *The Manifesto of the Communist Party*, (Moscow: Progress Publishing, 1952).

60. The italics are mine.

61. Kelsen, "Foundations of Democracy," 256–257.

62. Ibid., 257.

63. See: chapter 3.

64. Kelsen, "Foundations of Democracy," 257.

65. See: chapter 3.

66. Kelsen, "Foundations of Democracy," 258.

67. See: chapter 3.

68. Johannes Messner, "Postwar Natural Law Revival and its Outcome," *Natural Law Forum* paper 41 (1959): 101 ff; see also: Gerhard Oestreich, *Die Idee der Menschenrechte in ihrer geschichtlichen Entwicklung* (Berlin: Landeszentrale für Politische Bildung, 1961).

69. Stanley L. Paulson, "Lon L. Fuller, Gustav Radbruch and the Positivist Theses," *Law and Philosophy* 13, no. 3 (1994): 315–317.

70. On this topic see: Samuel Moyn, *The Last Utopia. Human Rights in History* (Cambridge, Massachusetts, London: Harvard University Press, 2010). For a concise overview of the natural law revival, see also: Franz Fillafer und Johannes Fleichtinger, "Natural Law and the Vienna School: Hans Kelsen, Alfred Verdross and Eric Voegelin," in *Hans Kelsen and the Natural Law Tradition*, 425–460.

71. Rice, "Kelsen and Niebhur on Democracy," 2016, 136. Rice's essay contains an interesting reply to Kelsen's attack on Niebhur's conception of democracy.

72. See: Heinrich Emil Brunner, *Gerechtigkeit: Eine Lehre von der Grundgesetzen der Gesellschaftsordnung* (Zürich: Zwingli Verlag, 1943). On Brunner's work, see: Paul King Jewett, *Emil Brunner: An Introduction to the Man and His Thought* (Illinois: Intervarsity Press, 1961).

73. Kelsen, "Foundations of Democracy," 310–320.

74. See: Karl P. R. Niebhur, *The Children of Light and Children of Darkness: A Vindication of Democracy and a Critique of its Traditional Defense* (New York: Scribner, 1944). On this aspect: Kelsen, "Foundations of Democracy," 327–331.

75. See: Jacques Maritain, *Christianisme et democratie* (Paris: Paul Harmattan, 1945). On Maritain's thought, see: Deal W. Hudson and Matthew Mancini, *Understanding Maritain: Philosopher and Friend* (Macon, GA: Mercer University Press, 1987).

76. Kelsen, "Foundations of Democracy," 340–347. For Maritain's (not explicit) reply to Kelsen, see: Jacques Maritain, *Truth and Human Fellowship* (Princeton: Princeton University Press, 1957).

77. Kelsen, "Foundations of Democracy," 307–308.
78. Ibid., 308.
79. Ibid., 315–320.
80. Ibid., 331–340.
81. Ibid., 344–347.
82. Ibid., 250–251.
83. Ibid., 251–258.
84. Ibid., 251.
85. Ibid.
86. Ibid., 252.
87. Ibid.
88. Ibid., 252–253.
89. Bert Van Roermund, "Kelsen, Secular Religion and the Problem of Transcendence," *Netherlands Journal of Legal Philosophy* 44, no. 2 (2015): 100–101. Also: Fleichtinger, "Transantlantische Vernetzungen. Der Weg Hans Kelsens und seines Kreises in die Emigration," 324, 330 ff.
90. See: Eric Voegelin, *Selected Correspondence 1950–1984*, vol. 30, ed. Thomas A. Hollweck (Columbia, Missouri: University of Missouri Press, 2007).
91. This powerfully emerges if comparing Voegelin's *The New Science of Politics* with Kelsen's posthumous *Secular Religion: a Polemic against misinterpretations of Modern Social Philosophy, Science and Politics as "New Religions."* See: Eric Voegelin, *The New Science of Politic. An Introduction* (Chicago, Illinois: The University of Chicago Press, 1952) and Kelsen, *Secular Religion: A Polemic against Misinterpretations of Modern Social Philosophy, Science and Politics as "New Religions,"* hrsg. Robert Walter, Clemens Jabloner, and Klaus Zeleny (Wien; New York: Springer, 2012).
92. The term and concept of "secular religion" was common to Voegelin and Aron.
93. Voegelin, *The New Science of Politics*, 107 ff. See: Ellis Sandoz, *The Voegelian Revolution. A Biographical Introduction* (New York: Routledge, 2000).
94. See also on this point: Jabloner, "In Defense of Modern Times," 332 ff.
95. See: Kelsen, *Secular Religion: a Polemic against misinterpretations of Modern Social Philosophy, Science and Politics as "New Religions,"* in particular: 47–83 and 251–270. On Kelsen's critique of what he though was Voegelin's true ideological intent underpinning his theory on the origins of totalitarianism see: Richard Potz, "Introductory Remarks," in *Secular Religion: a Polemic against misinterpretations of Modern Social Philosophy, Science and Politics as "New Religions,"* VII–X; Clemens Jabloner, Klaus Zeleny, and Gerhard Donhauser, "Editorial Remarks," in *Secular Religion: a Polemic against misinterpretations of Modern Social Philosophy, Science and Politics as "New Religions,"* XI–XV; Iain Stewart, "Kelsen, the Enlightenment and the Modern Premodernists," *Austrian Journal of Legal Philosophy* 37 (2013): 251 ff. On the same topic, see also: Fillafer and Feichtinger, "Natural Law and the Vienna School: Hans Kelsen, Alfred Verdross and Eric Voegelin," 439–447. On the dispute between Voegelin and Kelsen see also: Van Ooyen, *Der Staat der Moderne. Hans Kelsens Pluralismustheorie*, 223–234 and Van

Ooyen, "Totalitiarismustheorie gegen Kelsen und Schmitt: Eric Voegelins 'Politische Religionen' als Kritik des Rechtspositivismus und politischer Theologie," *Zeitschrift für Politik* 49, no. 1 (2002): 62–68. Here, the author stresses how Voegelin's theory of "secular religions" as the source of totalitarianism contains a critique of Kelsen's legal positivism. It is interesting to observe that Kelsen contested the use of "secular religion" to Raymond Aron too. On this specific aspect: Kelsen, *Secular Religion: A Polemic against Misinterpretations of Modern Social Philosophy, Science and Politics as "New Religions,"* 22 ff; 26.

96. Voegelin, *A New Science of Politics*, 52 ff.

97. Ibid.

98. On this aspect, see: Nicoletta Stradaioli, "Monisms and Pluralism: Eric Voegelin's Contribution," in *Monisms and Pluralisms in the History of Political Thought*, ed. Andrea Catanzaro and Sara Lagi (Novi Ligure: Epoké, 2016), 99 ff.

99. Kelsen, "Foundations of Democracy," 266–268.

100. Ibid., 263.

101. Ibid., 268.

102. This is, in my opinion, the core concept underpinning the whole paragraph against Voegelin's "New Doctrine of Representation." Kelsen, "Foundations of Democracy," 258–269.

103. See: John Lewis Gaddis, *The Cold War. A New History* (New York: Penguin books, 2007) .

104. See: Marx and Engels, *The Manifesto of the Communist Party*.

105. Kelsen, "Foundations of Democracy," 348–348.

106. Ibid., 249.

107. Ibid., 349–350.

108. Ibid., 353–354.

109. Ibid., 353.

110. Ibid., 354–355.

111. Von Hayek, *The Road to Serfdom*, chiefly 44 ff.

112. Ibid., 66 ff. See on Hayek's work as political thinker and economist: Roland Kley, *Hayek's Social and Political Thought* (Oxford: Oxford University Press, 1994) and also Lawrence J. Connin, "Hayek, Liberalism and Social Knowledge," *Canadian Journal of Political Science* 23, no. 2 (1990): 297–315. The latter discusses the complexity of the particular epistemological foundations both of his liberal political theory and his neoliberal economic theory.

113. Kelsen, "Foundations of Democracy," 357–359.

114. Ibid., 360. On this point see: Friederich Von Hayek, *The Road to Serfdom* (London: Ark paperbacks, 1986).

115. Kelsen, "Foundations of Democracy," 361.

116. Ibid., 361–362.

117. See: Costa and Zolo ed., *The Rule of Law*, 2007. Also: Trevor Robert S. Allan, *The Rule of Law: Freedom, Constitution, Common Law* (Oxford: Oxford University Press, 2013).

118. Kelsen, "Foundations of Democracy," 365–366.

119. Ibid., 366.

120. Ibid., 290 ff.

121. Ibid., 290–292.

122. Ibid., 291. In *Foundations of Democracy* Kelsen emphasized the "rationalistic" character of leadership selection in a democratic system as well as the fact that the relationship between the ruled and the rulers could be by analogy compared with that between equal individuals rather than between father and son. The latter was, in his opinion, more typical of an autocracy. Here, the autocrat was in fact superior to his subjects. With the first kind of argumentation, Kelsen again seemed to affirm that the way we think and comprehend reality had an impact on political and social forms of organization. The second kind of argumentation seemed instead to re-echo his European studies on Freud and the psychology of the masses. Kelsen, "Foundations of Democracy," 288 ff. On Kelsen and Freud see: chapter 3.

123. See: chapters 1 and 3.

124. See: Richard Swedberg, *J. A. Schumpeter. His Life and Work* (Cambridge: Cambridge University Press, 1991).

125. Schumpeter's work became in the second half of the twentieth century a major point of reference for American political scientists.

126. See: Joseph A. Schumpeter, *Capitalism, Socialism and Democracy* (London, New York: Routledge, 1994), in particular Part IV, Chapter XXI, Chapter XXII, Chapter XXIII.

127. This aspect is stressed by Lagerspetz, "Kelsen on Democracy and Majority Decision," 155–157.

128. Schumpeter, *Capitalism, Socialism and Democracy*, 245–254.

129. In this sense see: Richard Bellamy, "Schumpeter and the Transformation of Capitalism, Liberalism and Democracy," *Government and Opposition* 26, no. 4 (1991): 500–519; John Medearis, "Schumpeter, the New Deal and Democracy," *American Political Science Review* 91, no. 4 (1997): 819–832 and Gerry Mackie, "Schumpeter's Leadership Democracy," *Political Theory* 37, no. 1 (2009): 128–153.

130. Schumpeter, *Capitalism, Socialism and Democracy*, 272.

131. Kelsen, "Foundations of Democracy," 369–371.

132. Schumpeter, *Capitalism, Socialism and Democracy*, 269 ff.

133. Ibid., 271–273.

134. Kelsen, "Foundations of Democracy," 370.

135. Schumpeter, *Capitalism, Socialism and Democracy*, 271.

136. My intent is to stress the constitutive elements of Kelsen's critique of Schumpeter's theory. It is however to be recognized that, in the heat of the dispute, Kelsen accurately avoided mentioning those passages of *Capitalism, Socialism and Democracy*, in which Schumpeter argued how, to correctly function, a real democratic system needed a certain amount of tolerance and fundamental rights such as freedom of press and speech. On this point see: Schumpeter, *Capitalism, Socialism and Democracy*, 272.

137. Kelsen, "Foundations of Democracy," 370.

138. Ibid., 370–371.

139. This might be a good reason why Schumpeter's work became so popular among political scientists (American political scientists in particular).

140. On the "elitist" component of Schumpeter's democratic theory see: John E. Elliott, "Joseph A. Schumpeter and the Theory of Democracy," *Review of Social Economy* 52, no. 4 (1994): 284 ff.

141. Schumpeter, *Capitalism, Socialism and Democracy*, 250 ff.

142. Kelsen, "Foundations of Democracy," 277–278.

143. Ibid., 278–282.

144. Ibid., 253–258; 287–288; 291–293.

145. Kelsen, "Foundations of Democracy," 293.

146. See: chapters 1, 2 and 3.

147. Kelsen, "Foundations of Democracy," 293.

148. Ibid., 287.

149. Ibid.

150. De Ruggiero, *History of European Liberalism*, 1927 and Sabine, *A History of Political Theory*, 1945.

151. See: chapters 3 and 4.

152. See: chapter 1.

153. Ibid.

154. See: chapters 1 and 3.

155. See: this chapter.

156. See: chapter 1.

157. See: chapters 1 and 2.

158. See: chapter 3.

159. Ibid.

160. Ibid.

161. See: chapter 4.

162. Ibid.

163. See: John Gray, *Liberalism: Essays in Political Philosophy* (New York: Routledge, 1989). See also: Sabine, *A History of Political Theory*, 1945.

Bibliography

HANS KELSEN'S WORKS:

Kelsen, Hans. *Die Staatslehre des Dante Alighieri* (1905). San Bernardino: Ulan Press.

———. "Wählerlisten und Reklamationsrecht" (1907). In Hans Kelsen, *Veröffentlichte Schriften 1905–1910 und Selbstzeugnisse*, hrsg. von Matthias Jestaedt, 301–330. Tübingen: Mohr Siebeck, 2007.

———. *Die Hauptprobleme der Staatsrechtslehre entwickelt aus der Lehre vom Rechtssatze*. Tübingen: Mohr Siebeck, 1911.

———. "Politische Weltanschauung und Erziehung" (1913). In Hans Kelsen, *Die Wiener Rechtstheoretische Schule*, Bd. 2, hrsg. von Hans R. Klecatsky, René Marcic und Herbert Schambeck, 1501–1524. Stuttgart: Franz Steiner Verlag, 2010.

———. *Eine Grundlegung der Rechtssoziologie*. Wien: C. B. Mohr, 1914.

———. "Ein einfaches Proportionalwahlsystem." *Arbeiter Zeitung* (November 24, 1918): 2–3.

———. "Der Proporz im Whalordunungsentwurf." *Neue Freie Presse* (December 1, 1918): 3–4.

———. "Das Proportionalwahlsystem." *Der österreichische Volkswirt* (December 7, 1918): 115–118.

———. "Vom Wesen und Wert der Demokratie. Vortrag vor der Wiener juristischen Gesellschaft am 5. November 1919." *Juristische Blätter* 48 (1919): 376–389.

———. *Das Problem der Souveränität und die Theorie des Völkerrechts. Beitrag zu einer Reinen Rechtslehre*. Tübingen: Mohr Siebeck, 1920.

———. "Der Vorentwurf der österreichischen Verfassung" (1920). In *Die Vorentwürfe Hans Kelsens für die Österreichische Verfassung*, hrsg. von Gerald Schmitz, 1–33. Wien: Manz Verlag, 1981.

———. "Vom Wesen und Wert der Demokratie" (1920). In Hans Kelsen, *Verteidigung der Demokratie*, hrsg. von Matthias Jestaedt und Oliver Lepsius, 1–33. Tübingen: Mohr Siebeck, 2006.

———. "Der Begriff des States." *Imago* VIII (1922): 97–141.

———. "God and the State" (1922/1923). In *Essays in Legal and Moral Philosophy*, Ttranslated by Peter Heath and selected by Ota Weinberger, 61–82. Dortrecht: Reidel, 1973.

———. "Die Stellung der Länder in der künftigen Verfassungs Deutsch-österreichs" (1922–1923). In Felix Ermacora, *Die Entstehung der Bundesverfassung 1920. Die Sammlungen der Entwürfe zur Staats- bzw. Bundesverfassung*, 125–143. Wien: Braumüller, 1990.

———. *Österreichisches Staatsrecht. Ein Grundriss entwicklungsgeschichtlich dargestellt.* Tübingen: J. B. C. Mohr, 1923.

———. *Die Hauptprobleme der Staatsrechtslehre entwickelt aus der Lehre vom Rechtssatze.* Tübingen. Mohr Siebeck, 1923.

———. *Sozialismus und Staat: eine Untersuchung der politischen Theorie des Marxismus*, 2. Erw. Aufl. Leipzig: C. L. Hirschfeld, 1923.

———. "Verfassungs und Verwaltungsgerichtsbarkeit im Dienste der des Bundesstaate, nach der neuen österreichischen Verfassung." *Zeitschrift für Schweiz. Recht* 52 (1923): 161–198.

———. "Allgemeine Staatslehre" (1925). In Hans Kelsen, *Verteidigung der Demokratie*, hrsg. von Matthias Jestaedt und Oliver Lepsius, 34–114. Tübingen: Mohr Siebeck, 2006.

———. "Demokratie" (1926). In Hans Kelsen, *Verteidigung der Demokratie*, hrsg. von Matthias Jestaedt und Oliver Lepsius, 115–148. Tübingen: Mohr Siebeck, 2006.

———. "Zur Soziologie der Demokratie." *Der Österreichische Volkswirt* 19 (1926): 209–211.

———. *Die Grundlagen der Naturrechtslehre und des Rechtspositivismusm.* Charlottenburg: R. Heise, 1928.

———. "La garantie jurisdictionelle de la constitution." In *Annuaire de L'Institut Internationelle de droit publique*, 52–201. Paris: Les Presses Universitaires de France, 1929.

———. "Der Drang zur Verfassungsreform." *Neue Freie Presse* (October 6, 1929): 29–30.

———. "Die Grundzüge der Verfassungreform." *Neue Freie Presse* (October 20, 1929): 6–7.

———. "Vom Wesen und Wert der Demokratie" (1929). In Hans Kelsen, *Verteidigung der Demokratie*, hrsg. von Matthias Jestaedt und Oliver Lepsius, 149–228. Tübingen: Mohr Siebeck, 2006.

———. "Verteidigung der Demokratie" (1932). In Hans Kelsen, *Verteidigung der Demokratie*, hrsg. von Matthias Jestaedt und Oliver Lepsius, 229–237. Tübingen: Mohr Siebeck, 2006.

———. "Kelsen on the Judgment of Staatsgerichtshof 25 October 1932." In *The Guardian of the Constitution. Hans Kelsen and Carl Schmitt on the Limits of Constitutional Law*, edited by Lars Vinx, 228–253. Cambridge: Cambridge University Press, 2015.

———. *Staatsform und Weltanschauung.* Tübingen: J.B.C. Mohr (Paul Siebeck Verlag), 1933.

————. *Reine Rechtslehre: Einleitung in die rechtswissenschaftliche Problematik. Studienausg. der 1.er Aufl. 1934*, hrsg. von Matthias Jestaedt. Tübingen: Mohr Siebeck, 2008.

————. "Wissenschaft und Demokratie" (1937). In Hans Kelsen, *Verteidigung der Demokratie*, hrsg. von Matthias Jestaedt und Oliver Lepsius, 238–247. Tübingen: Mohr Siebeck, 2006.

————. "Platonic Justice" (1938). In Hans Kelsen, *What is Justice? Justice, Law, Politics in the Mirror of Science. Collected Essays*, 82–109. Berkeley and Los Angeles: University of California Press, 1957.

————. *Peace Through Law*. Chapel Hill: The University of North Carolina Press, 1944.

————. *General Theory of Law and State* (1945), with a new Introduction by A. Javier Trevino. London and New York: Routledge, 2006.

————. "Selbstzeugnisse" (1947). In Hans Kelsen, *Veröffentlichte Schriften 1905–1910 und Selbstzeugnisse*, hrsg. von Matthias Jestaedt, 29–91. Tübingen: Mohr Siebeck, 2007.

————. "Will Judgment in the Nuremberg Trial Constitute a Precedent in International Law?" *The International Law Quarterly* 1, no. 2 (1947): 153–171.

————. *The Political Theory of Bolshevism. A Critical Analysis* (1948). New Jersey: The Lawbook Exchange, 2011.

————. "Absolutism and Relativism in Philosophy and Politics" (1948). In Hans Kelsen, *What is Justice? Justice, Law, Politics in the Mirror of Science. Collected Essays*, 1–24. Berkeley and Los Angeles: University of California Press, 1957.

————. "Law, State and Justice in the Pure Theory of Law." *The Yale Law Journal* 57 (1948): 377–390.

————. "The Natural Law Before the Tribunal of Science" (1949). In Hans Kelsen, *What is Justice? Justice, Law, Politics in the Mirror of Science. Collected Essays*, 137–173. Berkeley and Los Angeles: University of California Press, 1957.

————. "The Natural Law Before the Tribunal of Science" (1949). In Hans Kelsen, *What is Justice? Justice, Law, Politics in the Mirror of Science. Collected Essays*, 1–24. Berkeley and Los Angeles: University of California Press, 1957.

————. *The Law of the United Nations. A Critical Analysis of the Fundamental Problems*. New York: Frederick A. Praeger Inc., 1950.

————. *The Communist Theory of Law*. New York: Frederick A. Praeger, 1955.

————. "Foundations of Democracy" (1955). In Hans Kelsen, *Verteidigung der Demokratie*, hrsg. von Matthias Jestaedt und Oliver Lepsius, 248–286. Tübingen: Mohr Siebeck, 2006.

————. "What is Justice?" (1957). In Hans Kelsen, *What is Justice? Justice, Law, Politics in the Mirror of Science. Collected Essays*, 137–173. Berkeley and Los Angeles: University of California Press, 1957.

————. *Secular Religion: A Polemic against misinterpretations of Modern Social Philosophy, Science and Politics as "New Religions,"* hrsg. von Robert Walter, Clemens Jabloner, and Kalus Zeleny. Wien, New York: Springer, 2012.

SECONDARY LITERATURE

Ableitinger, Alfred. "Die Grundlegung der Verfassung." In *Österreich 1918–1938. Geschichte der ersten Republik Zwei Bände*, hrsg. von Erika Weinzierl, and Kurt Skalnik, 147–194. Graz, Wien: Styria Verlag, 1983.

Alexy, Robert. "Law and Morality and the Existence of Human Rights." *Ratio Juris* 25, no. 1 (1995): 2–14.

Allan, Trevor Robert S. *The Rule of Law: Freedom, Constitution, Common Law.* Oxford: Oxford University Press, 2013.

Allen, Richard. 1998. "Hayek and Liberty Under Law." In *Beyond Liberalism: The Political Thought of F. A. Hayek & Michael Polanyi*, edited by Richard Allen, 47–66. New Brunswick: J. Transaction, 1998.

Anderson, George. *Federalism: An Introduction.* Oxford: Oxford University Press, 2008.

Angelis De, Gabriele. "Ideals and Institutions. Hans Kelsen's Political Theory." *History of Political Thought* 30, no. 3 (Autumn 2009): 524–546.

Aron, Raymond. *Democracy and Totalitarianism. A Theory of Political Regimes.* New York: Praeger, 1969. (Original edition 1965).

Bárcena, Josu Miguel de, Tajadura Javier. *Kelsen versus Schmitt: política y derecho en la crisis del constitucionalismo.* Escolar y Mayo: Pozuelo de Alarcón, 2018.

Barth, Boris. *Europa nach dem grossen Krieg: die Krise der Demokratie in der Zwischenkriegszeit 1918–1938.* Frankfurt-New York: Campus Verlag, 2016.

Baume, Sandrine. *Kelsen and the Case for Democracy.* Bruxelles: ECPR, 2012.

———. "Rehabilitating Political Parties: An Examination of Writings of Hans Kelsen." *Intellectual History Review* 28 (January 24, 2018): 425–449.

Baumert, Renaud. "Audiautur ataltera pars: justice constitutionelle et decision démocratique dans le pensée de Hans Kelsen." In *La controverse sur "le gardien de la Constitution" et la justie onstitutionelle. Kelsen contre Schmitt*, sous la direction de Olivier Beaud et Pasquale Pasquino, 127–149. Paris: Editon Panthéon-Assas, 2007.

Béchillon De, Denys. *Qu'est – ce qu'une règle de Droit?* Paris: Odilé Jacob, 1997.

Beetham, David. "Michels and his Critics." *European Journal of Sociology* 22, no. 1 (1981): 81–99.

Beiser, Frederick C. *Hermann Cohen: An Intellectual Biography.* Oxford: Oxford University Press, 2018.

Bellamy, Richard. "Schumpeter and the Transformation of Capitalism, Liberalism and Democracy." *Government and Opposition* 26, no. 4 (1991): 500–519.

———. *Liberalism and Modern Society. An Historical Argument.* London: Blackwell Publishers, 1992.

———. *Political Constitutionalism. A Republican Defence of the Constitutionality of Democracy.* Cambridge: Cambridge University Press, 2007.

———. "Constitutional Democracy." In *The Encyclopedia of Political Thought*, edited by Michael Gibbons, 1–15. New Jersey: John Wiley & Sons, 2015.

Bendereski, Joseph W. "Carl Schmitt and the Weimar Right." In *The German Right in the Weimar Republic. Studies in the History of German Conservatism, Nationalism and Antisemitism*, edited by Larry Eugene Jones, 268–290. New York; Oxford: Berghahn, 2014.

Berger Peter, Bischof Günter, and Plasser Fritz, eds. *From Empire to Republic: Post World War I Austria*. Innsbruck: Innsbruck University Press, 2010.

Berlin, Isaiah. "Historical Inevitability." In Isaiah Berlin, *Four Essays on Liberty*, 41–117. Oxford: Oxford University Press, 1969. (Original edition 1953).

———. "Two Concepts of Liberty." In Isaiah Berlin, *Four Essays on Liberty*, 118–172. Oxford: Oxford University Press, 1969. (Original edition 1958).

———. *Tra filosofia e storia delle idee. La società pluralista e i suoi nemici. Intervista autobiorgrafica e filosofica* (It. trans.), a cura di Steven Lukes. Firenze: Ponte alle Grazie, 1994.

Bernstorff, Jochen Von. "Peace and Global Justice through Prosecuting the Crime of Aggression? Kelsen and the Morgenthau on the Nuremberg Trials and the International Judicial Function." In *Hans Kelsen in America – Selective Affinities and the Mysteries of Academic Influences*, edited by Jeremy Telman, 85–99. Netherlands: Springer, 2016.

Bisogni, Giovanni. *La politicità del giudizio sulle leggi. Tra le origini costituenti e il dibattito giusteorico conteüporaneo*. Torino: Giappichelli, 2017.

Bix, Brian H. "Kelsen in the United States: Still Misunderstood." In *Hans Kelsen in America – Selective Affinities and the Mysteries of Academic Influences*, edited by Jeremy Telman, 17–29. Netherlands: Springer, 2016.

Blum, Mark E., and Smaldone William T, eds. *Austro-Marxism: The Ideology of Unity*. Leiden; Boston: Brill, 2015.

Bobbio, Norberto. *Diritto e potere. Saggi su Kelsen*. Milano: Edizioni di Comunità, 1992.

———. *Studi generali sulla teoria del diritto*. Torino: Giappichelli, 2012.

Böckenförde, Ernst-Wolfgang. "The Concept of the Political: A Key to Understanding Carl Schmitt's Constitutional Theory." *Canadian Journal of Law and Jurisprudence* 10, no. 1 (1997): 5–19.

Bongiovanni, Giorgio. *Reine Rechtslehre e dottrina giuridica dello Stato. Hans Kelsen e la Costituzione austriaca del 1920*. Milano: Giuffré, 1998.

Boogman, Hans and Van der Plaat, Gees N, eds. *Federalism: History and Current Significance of a Form of Government*. Netherlands: Springer, 1980.

Boudëc Le, Nathalie. "Le role de le pensee de Gustav Radbruch dans la refondation de l'État de droit démocratique après 1945." *Revue d'Allemagne* 46, no. 1 (2014): 83–94.

Brauneder, Wilhelm. *Österreichische Verfassungsgeschichte. Einführung in Entwicklung und Strukturei*. Wien: Manzsche Verlag, 1992.

Breuer, Stefan. *Georg Jellinek und Max Weber. Von der sozialen zur soziologischen Staatslehre*. Baden-Baden: Nomos Verlag, 1999.

Brunkhorst, Hauke. "Hans Kelsens Werk zwischen Krieg, Revolution und Neugründung der internationalen Gemeischaft." In *Hans Kelsen und die Europäische Union: Erörterungen moderner (Nicht-) Staatlichkeit*, hrsg. von Tamara Ehs, 27–49. Baden-Baden: Nomos Verlag, 2008.

Brunner, Emil H. *Gerechtigkeit: Eine Lehre von den Grundgesetzen der Gesellschaftsordnung.* Zurich: Zwingli Verlag, 1943.

Busch, Jürgen, and Bersier Ladavac, Nicoletta. "Zwischen zwei Welten." In *Hans Kelsen – Leben – Werke – Wirksamkeit*, hrsg. von Robert Walter, Werner Ogris, and Thomas Olekowski, 167–192. Vienna: Manz, 2009.

Busino, Giovanni. "The Signification of Vilfredo Pareto's Sociology." *Revue européenne de sciences sociales* XXXVIII, 117 (2000): 217–228.

Bussjäger, Peter, Shramek, Christoph and Johler, Mirella M. "Federalism and Recent Dynamics in Austria." *Revista d'Estudis Autonomics I Federals* 28 (2018): 74–100.

Caldwell, Peter C. *Popular Sovereignty and the Crisis of German Constitutional Law.* Durham, North Carolina: Duke University Press, 1997.

Calsamiglia, Alberto. *Contribución a un estudio crítico de la teoria kelseniana.* Madrid: Servicio de Publicaciones, 1979.

Canovan, Margaret. "Arendt, Rousseau and Human Plurality in Politics." *The Journal of Politics* 45, no. 2 (May, 1983): 286–302.

Capua, Raimondo De. *Hans Kelsen e il problema della democrazia.* Roma: Carocci, 2003.

Carrino, Agostino. *Kelsen e il problema della scienza giuridica (1910–1935).* Napoli: Edizioni scientifiche italiane, 1987.

Carrozza, Paolo. "Kelsen and Contemporary Constitutionalism: The Continued Preference of Kelsneian Themes." *Estudios de Deusto* 67/1, enero-junio (2019): 55–82.

Carsten, Francis L. *The First Austrian Republic 1918–1938.* Aldershot: Gower Publishing Company, 1986.

Caserta, Marco. *La forma e l'identità. Democrazia e costituzione in Hans Kelsen.* Torino: Giappichelli, 2005.

Connin, Lawrence J. "Hayek, Liberalism and Social Knowledge." *Canadian Journal of Political Science* 23, no. 2 (1990): 297–315.

Constant, Benjamin. *Principles of Politics Applied to all Governments.* Indianapolis: Liberty Fund Inc., 2003. (French edition 1815).

Crowder, George. *Liberalism and Value Pluralism.* London; New York: Continuum, 2002.

Czeike, Felix. *Historische Lexikon.* Wien: Kremayr und Sherian, 1994.

Dard, Olivier. "The Action Française in a Transnational Perspective." In *Reactionary Nationalists, Fascists and Dictatorships in the Twentieth Century against Democracy*, edited by Ismael Saz, Zira Box, Toni Morant, and Julián Sanz, 29–47. Berlin: Springer Verlag, 2019.

Dogliani, Patrizia. "Fascism and Fascists in Italy." In *Reactionary Nationalists, Fascists and Dictatorships in the Twentieth Century against Democracy*, edited by Ismael Saz, Zira Box, Toni Morant, and Julián Sanz, 125–143. Berlin: Springer Verlag, 2019.

Douglass, Robin. "Rousseau's Critique of Representative Democracy: Principled or Pragmatic?" *American Journal of Political Science* 57, no. 3 (July 2013): 735–747.

Dreier, Horst. *Rechtslehre, Staatssoziologie und Dmokratietheorie bei Hans Kelsen.* Baden-Baden: Nomos Verlag, 1986.

———. *Hans Kelsen im Kontext. Beiträge zum Werk Hans Kelsens und gistverwandter Autoren*, hrsg. von Matthias Jaestedt, and Stanley L. Paulson. Tübingen: Mohr Sieeck, 2019.

Duverger, Maurice. *Les constitutions de la France*. Paris: Presses Universitaires de France, 2004.

Dyzenhaus, David. "Why Positivism is Authoritarian." *The American Journal of Jurisprudence* 1, no. 1 (1992): 83–112.

———. *Law and Politics. Carl Schmitt's Critique of Liberalism*. Durham, North Carolina: Duke University Press, 1998.

———. *Legality and Legitimacy. Carl Schmitt, Hans Kelsen and Hermann Heller in Weimar*. Oxford: Oxford University Press, 1999.

Dziadzio, Andrzej. "The Role Played by the Constitutional Tribunal in Preserving the Liberal Nature of the Habsburg Monarchy in the Turn of the 19th Century." In *Constitutional Developments of the Habsburg Empire in the Last Decades before its Fall*, edited by Kazimierz Baran, 25–32. Krakow: Jagiellonan University Press, 2010.

Ehrlich, Eugen. *Grundlegung der Soziologie des Rechts*. München und Leipzig: Verlag Duncker & Humblot, 1913.

Ehs, Tamara. *Hans Kelsen und die politische Bildung im modernen Staat: Vorträge in der Wiener Volksbildung. Schriften zu Kritikfähigkeit und Rationalismus*. Wien: Manz, 2007.

———. "Erziehung zur Demokratie: Hans Kelsen als Volksbildner." In *Hans Kelsen – Leben – Werke – Wirksamkeit*, hrsg. von Robert Walter, Werner Ogris, and Thomas Olekowski, 81–95. Vienna: Manz, 2009.

———. "Felix Frankfurter, Hans Kelsen and the Practice of Judicial Review." *Zeitschrift für Öffentliches auslandisches Recht und Völkerrecht* 73 (2013): 451–481.

Elliott, John E. "Joseph A. Schumpeter and the Theory of Democracy." *Review of Social Economy* 52, no. 4 (1994): 280–300.

Ermacora, Felix. *Quellen zum österreichischen Verfassungsrecht (1920). Die Protokolle des Unterausschusses des Verfassungsausschusses*. Wien: Österreichisches Staatsarchiv, 1967.

———. *Die Bundesverfassung und Hans Kelsen. Analyse und Materialen*. Wien: Universitätsbuchhanlung, 1981.

———. *Österreichische Föderalismus vom patrimonialen zum kooperativen Bundesstaat*. Wien: Wien Braumüller, 1989.

———. *Die Entstehung der Bundesverfassung 1920. Die Sammlungen der Entwürfe zur Staats- bzw. Bundesverfassung*. Wien: Braumüller, 1990.

Estlund, David M., emy Waldron, Jeremy, Grofman, Bernard and Feld, Scott L. "Democratic Theory and the Public Interest." *The American Political Science Review* 83, no. 4 (December 1989): 1317–1340.

Favuzzi, Pellegrino. "Hans Kelsen's and Ernst Cassirer's Conception of Natural Law." In *Hans Kelsen and the Natural Law Tradition*, edited by Peter Langford, Ian Bryan and John McGarry, 327–371. Leiden: Brill, 2018.

Fawcett, Edmund. *Liberalism. The Life of an Idea*. Princeton, New Jersey: Princeton University Press, 2015.

Ferrajoli, Luigi. *La democrazia costituzionale*. Bologna: Il Mulino, 2016.

———. *La logica del diritto. Dieci aporie nell'opera di Hans Kelsen*. Roma-Bari: Laterza, 2017.

Ferrell, Jason. "The Alleged Relativism of Isaiah Berlin." *Critical Review of International Social and Political Philosophy* 11, no. 1 (2008): 41–54.

Fillafer, Franz, and Fleichtinger Johannes. "Natural Law and the Vienna School: Hans Kelsen, Alfred Verdross and Eric Voegelin." In *Hans Kelsen and the Natural Law Tradition*, edited by Peter Langford, Ian Bryan, and John McGarry, 425–460. Leiden: Brill, 2018.

Fioravanti, Maurizio. *Costituzione*. Bologna: Il Mulino, 1998.

———. *La costituzione democratica. Modelli e itinerari del diritto pubblico del Ventesimo secolo*. Milano: Giuffrè, 2018.

Fleichtinger, Johannes. "Transantlantische Vernetzungen. Der Weg Hans Kelsens und seines Kreises in die Emigration." In *Hans Kelsen – Leben – Werke – Wirksamkeit*, hrsg. von Robert Walter, Werner Ogris, and Thomas Olekowski, 321–338. Vienna: Manz, 2009.

Frosini, Vittorio. *Saggi su Kelsen e Capograssi. Due interpretazioni del Diritto*. Milano: Giuffré, 1988.

Gallagher, Michael, and Paul Mitchell, eds. *The Politics of Electoral Systems*. Oxford: Oxford University Press, 2008.

Galli Della Loggia, Ernesto. "Le ceneri di Gramsci." *Mondo Operaio* 7 (1977): 69–91.

Galston, William. "Realism in Political Theory." *European Journal of Political Theory* 9, no. 4 (October 2010): 385–411.

García Amado, Juan Antonio. *Hans Kelsen y la norma fundamental*. Madrid: Pons, 1996.

García Berger, Mario. "The Legal Norm as a Function: the Influence of Ernst Cassirer an the Margburg Neo-Kantians on Hans Kelsen." *Problema anuario de filosofía y teoría del derecho* (online) 12 (2018): 239–262.

García-Salmones, Ravira. "On Kelsen's Sein. An Approach to Sociological Themes." *No Foundations: Journal of Extreme Legal Positivism* 8 (2011): 41–70.

Garibian, Sévane. "Crimes Against Humanity and International Legality in Legal Theory after Nuremberg." *Journal of Genocide Research* 9, no. 1 (2007): 93–111.

Gattini, Andrea. "Kelsen, Hans." In *The Oxford Companion to International Criminal Justice*, edited by Antonio Cassese, 402–404. Oxford: Oxford University Press, 2009.

Gazzolo, Tommaso. *Essere/Dover Essere. Saggio su Hans Kelsen*. Milano: Franco Angeli, 2016.

Gennet, Tim. *Der Fremde im Krieg. Zur politischen Biographie von Robert Michels 1876–1936*. Berlin: Akademie Verlag, 2012.

Gerber, Carl Friedrich Von. *System des privaten Rechtes*. Jena: F. Mauke, 1850. (Original edition 1848).

Goyard-Fabre, Simone. "L'inspiration kantienne de Hans Kelsen." *Revue de Métaphisyque et de Morale* 83, no. 2 (1978): 204–233.

Gozzi, Gustavo. "Rechtstaat and Individual Rights in German Constitutional History." In *The Rule of Law. History, Theory and Criticism*, edited by Pietro Costa and Danilo Zolo, 237–259. Berlin: Springer Verlag, 2007.

Gray, John. *Liberalism*. Minneapolis: Minneapolis University Press, 1986.
———. *Liberalism: Essays in Political Philosophy*. New York: Routledge, 2009.
Gümplova, Petra. *Sovereignty and Constitutional Democracy*. Baden-Baden: Nomos Verlag, 2011.
———. "Hans Kelsen's Critique of Sovereignty." In *Jurisprudence and Political Philosophy in the 21st Century*, vol. 2, edited by Miograd A. Jovanovič and Bojan Spaič, 101–113. Frankfurt am Main: Peter Lang, 2012.
Gulick, Charles A. *Austria. From Habsburg to Hitler*. Berkeley, California: California University Press, 1984.
Hacohen, Malachi. "Karl Popper, the Vienna Circle and Red Vienna." *Journal of the History of Ideas* 59, no. 4 (1998): 711–734.
Haddock, Bruce. *History of Political Thought. 1789 to the Present*. Cambridge: Polity Press, 2005.
———. *History of Political Thought. From Antiquity to Present*. Cambridge: Polity Press, 2008.
Hanisch, Ernst. *Österreichische Geschichte 1890–1990. Der lange Schatte des Staates. Österreichische Gesellschaftsgeschichte im 20. Jahrhundert*. Wien: Carl Überreuter, 1994.
Harris, David. "European Liberalism in the 19th Century." *The American Historical Review* 60, no. 3 (1955): 501–526.
Hatier, Cécile. "Berlin and the Totalitarian Mind." *The European Legacy* 9, no. 6 (2004): 767–782.
Haybäck, Michael, ed. *Carl Schmitt und Hans Kelsen in der Krise der Demokratie in der Zwishenkriegszeit: eine rechtsphilosophische und historishe Analyse*. Dissertation, Salzburg, 1990.
Hayek, Friederich Von. *The Road to Serfdom*. London: Ark paperbacks, 1986 (Original edition 1944).
———. *The Counter-Revolution of Science. Studies on the Abuse of Reason*. Indianapolis: Liberty Press, 1979. (Original edition 1952).
Hebeisen, Michael W. *Die Souveränität im Frage gestellt: die Souveränitätslehre von Hans Kelsen, Carl Schmitt und Hermann Heller im Vergleich*. Baden-Baden: Nomos Verlag, 1995.
Heller, Hermann. "Die Souveränität. Ein Beitrag zur Theorie des Staates und Völkerrechts" (1927). In Hermann Heller, *Gesammelte Schriften*, Bd. 2, hrsg. von Christoph Müller. Leiden: A. W. Sijthoff, 1971.
———. "Politische Demokratie und soziale Homogenität" (1928). In Hermann Heller, *Gesammelte Schriften*, Bd. 3, hrsg. von Christoph Müller, 421–434. Leiden: A. W. Sijthoff, 1971.
———. "Rechtsstaat oder Diktatur?" (1929). In Hermann Heller, *Gesammelte Schriften*, Bd. 3, hrsg. von Christoph Müller, 443–462. Leiden: A. W. Sijthoff, 1971.
Herrera, Carlos Gustavo. "La polemica Schmitt-Kelsen sobre el guardian de la constitucion." *Revista de Estudios Politicos* 86 (Octubre Deciembre 1994): 195–227.
———. "Kelsen et le libéralisme." In *Le droit, le politique. Autour de Max Weber, Hans Kelsen, Carl Schmitt*, sous la direction de Carlos Miguel Herrera, 60–80. Paris: L'Harmattan, 1995.

————. "Science et politique chez Hans Kelsen." In *Hans Kelsen. Forme du droit et politique de l'autonomie*, sous la direction de Olivier Jouanjan, 99–133. Paris: Presses Universitaire de France, 2010.

Hinghofer-Szalkay, Stephan G. "The Austrian Constitutional Court: Kelsen's Creation and Federalism's Contribution?" *Féderalism Régionalisme* 17 (2017): https://popups.uliege.be:443/1374–3864/index.php?id=1671.

Holmes, Stephen. "Kelsen, Hans". In *The Encyclopedia of Democracy*, edited by Seymour M. Lipset, 689–690. London: Routledge, 1995.

Hudson, Deal W. and Mancini, Matthew J. *Understanding Maritain: Philosopher and Friend*. Macon, GA: Mercer University Press, 1987.

Invernizzi-Accetti, Carlo. "Reconciling Legal Positivism and Human Rights: Hans Kelsen's Argument from Relativism." *Journal of Human Rights* 17, no. 2 (2018): 215–228.

Jabloner, Clemens. "Kelsen and the Viennese Years." *European Journal of International Law* 9, no. 2 (1998): 368–385.

————. "Die Gerichtshöfe des öffentlichen Rehts im Zuge des Staatsumbaues 1918 bis 1920." In *Beiträge zur Rechtsgeschichte Österreichs*, Bd. 2, hrsg. von Thomas Olechowski, 213–222. Wien: Verlag der Österreichischen Akademie der Wissenschaft, 2011.

————. "In Defense of Modern Times: A Key-note Address." In *Hans Kelsen in America – Selective Affinities and the Mysteries of Academic Influence*, edited by Jeremy Telman, 331–342. Netherlands: Springer, 2016.

————, Zeleny, Klaus and Donhauser, Gerhard. "Editorial Remarks." In Hans Kelsen, *Secular Religion: A Polemic against Misinterpretations of Modern Social Philosophy, Science and Politics as "New Religions,"* edited by Robert Walter, Clemens Jabloner, and Kalus Zeleny, XI–XV. Wien, New York: Springer, 2012.

———— and Olechowski, Thomas, hrsg. *Methodenreinheit und Erkenntnisvielhaft: Aufsätze zur Rechtstheorie, Rechtsdogmatik und Rechtsgeschichte*. Wien: Manz, 2013.

————, Olechowski, Thomas and Zeleny, Klaus, hrsg. *Das internationale Wirken Hans Kelsens*. Wien: Manz, 2016.

————. *Hans Kelsen in seiner Zeit*. Wien: Manz, 2019.

Jellinek, Georg. *Das System der öffentlichen subjektiven Rechte*. Freiburg: Akademische Verlagsbuchhandlung von J. C. B. Mohr, 1892.

————. *Die Erklärungen der Bürger und Menschenrechte*, Neue Auflage. Düsseldorf: Verlag Dr. Müller, 2006. (Original edition 1895).

————. *Allgemeine Staatslehre*, 3. Auflage. Berlin: Verlag von O. Häring, 1914. (Original edition 1900).

Jenks, William A. *The Austrian Electoral Reform of 1907*. New York: Columbia University Press, 1950.

Jestaedt, Matthias, and Lepsius, Oliver. "Der Rechts- und Demokratietheoretiker Hans Kelsen. Eine Einführung." In Hans Kelsen, *Verteidigung der Demokratie*, hrsg. von Matthias Jestaedt und Oliver Lepsius, VII–XXIX. Tübingen: Mohr Siebeck, 2006.

———. "Von den Hauptprobleme zur Erstauflage der Reinen Rechtslehre." In *Hans Kelsen – Leben – Werke – Wirksamkeit*, hrsg. von Robert Walter, Werner Ogris, and Thomas Olekowski, 114–135. Vienna: Manz, 2009.

———. "La science comme vision du monde: science du droit et conception de la démocratie en Hans Kelsen." In *Hans Kelsen. Forme du droit et politique de l'autonomie*, sous la direction de Olivier Jouanjan, 171–220. Paris: Presses Universitaire de France, 2010.

———, hrsg. *Hans Kelsen und die deutsche Staatsrechtslehre*. Tübingen: Mohr Siebeck, 2016.

Jewett, Paul K. *Emil Brunner: An Introduction to the Man and His Thought*. Illinois: Inter-varsity Press, 1961.

Kalvyas, Andreas. "The Basic Norm and Democracy in Hans Kelsen's Legal and Political Philosophy." *Philosophy and Social Criticism* 32, no. 5 (July 2006): 573–599.

Kann, Robert A. *A History of the Habsburg Empire 1526–1918*. California: California University Press, 1974.

Karlhofer, Ferdinand and Bischof, Günther, eds. *Austrian Federalism: History, Perspectives, Change*. Innsbruck: Innsbruck University Press, 2015.

Kelly, Duncan. "Revisiting the Rights of Man: Georg Jellinek on Rights and the State." *Law and History Review* 22, no. 3 (Autumn 2004): 493–529.

Kennedy, Ellen. "Introduction: Carl Schmitt's *Parlamentarismus* in Historical Context." In Carl Schmitt, *The Crisis of Parliamentary Democracy* (Eng. Trans. 1st ed. and 2nd ed.), edited and translated by Ellen Kennedy, XIII–L. Cambridge, Massachusetts, and London, England: MIT Press, 1988.

Kersten, Jens. *Georg Jellinek und die klassische Staatslehre*. Tübingen: Mohr Siebeck, 2000.

Klein, Martin D. *Demokratisches Denken bei Gustav Radbruch*. Berlin: Berliner Wissenschafts-Verlag, 2007.

Kley, Roland. *Hayek's Social and Political Thought*. Oxford: Oxford University Press, 1994.

Koch, Hans Joachim W. *A Constitutional History of Germany in the 19th and 20th Century*. London: Longman, 1984.

Laband, Paul. *Deutsches Reichsstaatsrecht*. Tübingen: J.C.B. Mohr (Paul Siebeck), 1907. (Original edition 1838).

Lacché, Luigi. "Rethinking Constitutionalism between History and Global World: Realities and Challenges." *Giornale di Storia Costituzionale/Journal of Constitutional History* 32, no. 2 (2016): 5–31.

Ladavac Bersier, Nicoletta. "Hans Kelsen (1881–1973). Biographical Note and Bibliography." *European Journal of International Law* 9, no. 2 (1998): 391–400.

Lagerspetz, Eerik. "Kelsen on Democracy and Majority Decision." *Archiv für Rechts und Sozialphilosophie* 103, no. 2 (March 2017): 155–179.

Lagi, Sara. *El pensamiento político de Hans Kelsen (1911–1920). Los origines de "De la esencia y valor de la democracia"*. Madrid: Biblioteca Nueva, 2007.

Lamego, José. *A Teoria pura do dereito de Kelsen*. Lisboa: AAFDL Editora, 2019.

Landauer, Carl. "Antinomes of the United Nations: Hans Kelsen and Alf Ross on the Charter." *European Journal of International Law* 14 (2003): 767–799.

Langford, Peter, and Bryan, Ian. "Introduction: the Kelsenian Critique of Natural Law." In *Hans Kelsen and the Natural Law Tradition*, edited by Peter Langford, Ian Bryan, and John McGarry, 1–55. Leiden: Brill, 2018.

———. "From Wolff to Kelsen: the Transformation of the Notion of Civitas Maxima." In *Hans Kelsen and the Natural Law Tradition*, edited by Peter Langford, Ian Bryan, and John McGarry, 161–187. Leiden: Brill, 2018.

Lepsius, Oliver. "Der Hüter der Verfassung demokratisch betrachtet." In *La controverse sur "le gardien de la Constitution" et la justice onstitutionelle. Kelsen contre Schmitt*, sous la direction de Olivier Beaud et Pasquale Pasquino, 103–126. Paris: Editon Panthéon-Assas, 2007.

———. "Hans Kelsen und Nationalsozialismus." In *Hans Kelsen – Leben – Werke – Wirksamkeit*, hrsg. von Robert Walter, Werner Ogris, and Thomas Olekowski, 271–287. Vienna: Manz, 2009.

———. "Kelsens Demokratielehre." In *Hans Kelsen. Eine politikwissenschaftliche Einführung*, hrsg. von Tamara Ehs, 73–90. Wien: Manz, 2009.

———. "Hans Kelsen's on Dante Alighieri's Political Thought." *European Journal of International Law* 27, no. 4 (November 1, 2016): 1153–1167.

Leser, Norbert. "Austro-Marxism. A Reppraisal." *Journal of Contemporary History* 11, no. 2/3 (July 1976): 133–148.

———. "Kelsens Verhältnis zum Sozialismus und Marx." In *Ideologiekritik und Demokratietheorie bei Hans Kelsen*, hrsg. von Peter Koller, Werner Krawietz, und Ernst Topitsch, 423–438. Berlin: Duncker & Humblot, 1982.

———. *Genius Austriacus. Beiträge zur Geschichte und Geistesgeschichte Österreichs*. Wien, Köln, Graz: Hermann Böhlhaus Nachf, 1986.

Lijoi, Federico. *La positività del diritto. Saggio su Hans Kelsen*. Roma: Aracne, 2011.

Lindemann, Albert S. *A History of European Socialism*. New Haven: Yale University Press, 1983.

Long, Graham M. "Relativism in Contemporary Liberal Political Philosophy." In *A Companion to Relativism*, edited by Stefen D. Hales, 307–325. New Jersey: Blackwell Publishing, 2011.

Losano, Mario G. "Il problema dell'interpretazione in Hans Kelsen." *Rivista internazionale di filosofia del diritto* XLV (1968): 524–542.

———. *Forma e realtà in Kelsen*. Milano: Edizioni di Comunità, 1981.

———. "La trilogia su Umberto Campagnolo (1904–1976). Kelsen, il federalismo, la guerra giusta e la guerra europea." *Accademia delle Scienze Torino* 145 (2011): 45–59.

———. "Hans Kelsen criptocomunista e l'F.B.I. al tempo del maccartismo. In margine al postumo *Religione secolare*." *Sociologia del diritto* no. 1 (2017): 140–160.

Lumowa, Valentino. "Benjamin Constant on Modern Freedom: Political Liberty and the Representative System." *Ethical Perspectives* 17, no. 3 (2010): 391–405.

Mackie, Gerry. "Schumpeter's Leadership Democracy." *Political Theory* 37, no. 1 (2009): 128–153.

———. "The Values of Democratic Proceduralism." *Irish Political Studies* 26, no. 11 (2011): 439–453.

Manin, Bernard. *The Principles of Representative Government*. Cambridge: Cambridge University Press, 2010.

Margiotta-Broglio, Costanza. "La Corte costituzionale italiana e il modello kelseniano." *Quaderni costituzionali* 2 (Agosto 2000): 333–370.

Maritain, Jacques. *Christianisme et democratie*. Paris: Paul Hartmann, 1945.

Martinelli, Claudio. "Gaetano Mosca's Political Theories: A Key to Interpret the Dynamics of Power." *Italian Journal of Public Law* 1 (2009): 1–21.

Martins, Antonio. "Sobre o Pensamiento politico de Hans Kelsen. Notas marginais a Da Essencia e valor da democracia (1920)." Paper for *Poética da Razão. Homenagem a Leonel Ribeiro dos Santos*, organized by Adriana Veríssimo Serrão et al., 591–599. Lisboa: Centro de Filosofia de Universidade de Lisboa, 2013.

Marx, Karl, and Friederich Engel. *Manifesto of the Communist Party*. Moscow: Progress Publishers, 1952. (Original edition 1848).

Mastellone, Salvo. *Storia delle democrazia in Europa. Da Montesquieu a Kelsen (XVIII–XX)*. Torino: UTET, 2004.

Mayer, Robert. "The Quest for Evolutionary Socialism: Eduard Bernstein and Social Democracy." *History of European Ideas* 23, nos. 2–4 (1997): 137–141.

Mccormick, John. *Carl Schmitt's Critique of Liberalism. Against Politics of Theology*. Cambridge: Cambridge University Press, 2009.

Medeiras, John. "Schumpeter, the New Deal and Democracy." *American Political Science Review* 91, no. 4 (1997): 819–832.

Merlino, Antonio. *Kelsen im Spiegel der Italienischen Rechtslehre*. Salzburg: Peter Lang, 2013.

Messner, Johannes. "Postwar Natural Law Revival and its Outcome." *Natural Law Forum* paper 41 (1959): 101–105.

Métall, Rudolf Aladar. *Hans Kelsen. Leben und Werk*. Wien: Deuticke, 1969.

Michels, Robert. *Zur Soziologie des Parteiwesens in der modernen Demokratie*. Stuttgart: Alfred Kröner Verlag, 1989.

Mill, John S. *On Liberty*. W. W. Norton: New York, 1975. (Original edition 1859).

———. *Considerations on Representative Government*. Oxford: Oxford University Press, 1975. (Original edition 1861).

Möllers, Christoph. "We are (afraid of) the People: Constituent Power in German Constitutionalism." In *The Paradox of Constitutionalism: Constituent Power and Constituent Form*, edited by Martin Loughlin and Neil Walker, 87–106. Oxford: Oxford University Press, 2008.

Mommsen, Hans. *The Rise and Fall of Weimar Democracy*. Frankfurt am Main-Berlin: The University of North Carolina Press, 1996.

Montesquieu, Charles Louis Baron de Secondat. *L'Esprit de Lois*. Paris: Classiques Garnier, 2011. (Original edition 1748).

Montoya-Brand, Alberto M., and Nataly Restrepo Montoya (Editores y compiladores). *Hans Kelsen. El reto contemporáneo de sus ideas politicas*. Medellín: EAFIT, 2011.

Moyn, Samuel. *The Last Utopia. Human Rights in History*. Cambridge, Massachusetts and London: Harvard University Press, 2010.

Mozetič, Gerald. "Hans Kelsen als Kritiker des Austromarximusm." In *Ideologiekritik und Demokratietheorie bei Hans Kelsen*, hrsg. von Peter Koller, Werner Krawietz und Ernst Topitsch, 445–458. Berlin: Duncker & Humblot, 1982.

Müller, Jan Werner. "Fear and Freedom. On 'Cold War Liberalism'." *European Journal of Political Theory* 7, no. 1 (2008): 45–64.

———. *Contesting Democracy: Political Ideas in the Twentieth Century*. New Haven: Yale University Press, 2011.

———. "Militant Democracy." In *The Oxford Handbook of Comparative Constitutional Law*, edited by Micheal Rosenthal and András Sajó, 1257–1258. Oxford: Oxford University Press, 2012.

Niebhur, Karl P. R. *The Children of Light and Children of Darkness: A Vindication of Democracy and a Critique of its Traditional Defense*. New York: Scribner, 1944.

Öhlinger, Theo. "Räpresentative, direkte und parlamentarische Demokratie." In *Ideologiekritik und Demokratietheorie bei Hans Kelsen*, hrsg. von Peter Koller, Werner Krawietz, und Ernst Topitsch. 215–237. Berlin: Duncker & Humblot, 1982.

———. "Verfassungsgerichtsbarkeit und parlamentarische Demokratie." In *Im Dienste an Staat und Recht. Festschrift für Erwin Melichar*, hrsg. von Hans Schäffer, 125–148. Wien: Manz Verlag, 1983.

Oestreich, Gerhard. *Die Idee der Menschenrechte in ihrer geschichtlichen Entwicklung*. Berlin: Landeszentrale für Politische Bildung, 1961.

Olechowski, Thomas. "Von der Ideologie zur Realität der Demokratie." In *Hans Kelsen. Eine politikwissenschaftliche Einführung*, hrsg. von Tamara Ehs, 113–123. Wien: Manz, 2009.

———. "Kelsens Rechtslehre im Überblick." In *Hans Kelsen. Eine politikwissen-schaftliche Einführung*, hrsg. von Tamara Ehs, 47–62. Wien: Manz, 2009.

———, and Wedrac, Stefan., hrsg. "Hans Kelsen und Washington." In *Hans Kelsen – Leben – Werke – Wirksamkeit*, hrsg. von Robert Walter, Werner Ogris, and Thomas Olekowski, 321–338. Vienna: Manz, 2009.

———, and Zeleny, Klaus hrsg. *Hans Kelsen in seiner Zeit*. Wien: Manz, 2019.

Ooyen, Robert C. Van. "Totalitarismustheorie gegen Kelsen und Schmitt: Eric Voegelins Politische Religionen als Kritik des Rechtspositivismus und politischer Theologie." *Zeitschrift für Politik* 49, no. 1 (2002): 56–82.

———. *Der Staat der Moderne: Hans Kelsens Pluralismustheorie*. Berlin: Duncker & Humblot, 2003.

———. *Hans Kelsen und die offene Gesellschaft*. Berlin: Duncker & Humblot, 2010.

Opalek, Kazimierz. "Kelsens Kritik der Naturrechts." In *Ideologiekritik und Demokratietheorie bei Hans Kelsen*, hrsg. von Peter Koller, Werner Krawietz und Ernst Topitsch. 71–86. Berlin: Duncker & Humblot, 1982.

Parekh, Bhikhu. *Hannah Arendt and the Search for a New Political Philosophy*. London and Basingstone: Macmillan, 1981.

Pasquino, Pasquale. "Penser la démocrtie: Kelsen en Weimar." In *Le droit, le politique. Autour de Max Weber, Hans Kelsen, Carl Schmitt*, sous la direction de Carlos Miguel Herrera, 211–225. Paris: L'Harmattan, 1995.

———. "Verfassungsgerichtsbarkeit und Demokratielehre." In *La controverse sur "le gardien de la Constitution" et la justie onstitutionelle. Kelsen contre Schmitt*, sous la direction de Olivier Beaud, Pasquale Pasquino, 20–31. Paris: Editon Panthéon-Assas, 2007.

———. "Condorcet, Kelsen et la régle de la majoritè." *Journal of Interdisciplinary History of Ideas* 7, no. 14 (2018): 1–18.

Paulson, Stanley L., hrsg. *Die Rolle des Neukantianismus in der Reine Rechtslehre: eine Debatte zwischen Sander und Kelsen*. Aalen: Scientia Verlag, 1988.

———. "Lon L. Fuller, Gustav Radbruch and the Positivist Theses." *Law and Philosophy* 13, no. 3 (1994): 315–317.

———. "Arguments conceptuelles de Schmitt à l'encontre du controlle de constitutionalité et response de Kelsen. Un aspect de l'affrontement entre Schmitt et Kelsen sur le gardien de la constitution." In *Le droit, le politique. Autour de Max Weber, Hans Kelsen, Carl Schmitt*, sous la direction de Carlos Miguel Herrera, 244–262. Paris: L'Harmattan, 1995.

———. "Radbruch on Unjust Laws: Competing Earlier and Later Views." *Oxford Journal of Legal Studies* 15, no. 3 (1995): 489–500.

———. "Some Issues in the Exchange between Kelsen and Kaufmann." *Scandinavian Studies in Law* 48 (2005): 269–290.

———. "Hans Kelsen and Carl Schmitt. Growing Discord Culminating in the "Guardian" Controversy." In *The Oxford Handbook of Carl Schmitt*, edited by Jens Meiierheinrch and Oliver Simons, 510–546. Oxford: Oxford University Press, 2016.

Paz, Reut Y. "Kelsen's Pure Theory of Law as a Hole in Time." *Dans Monde(s)* 1, no. 7 (2015): 74–94.

Pecora, Gaetano. *La democrzia di Hans Kelsen*. Torino: UTET, 1995.

Peterson, Brian. "Workers' Councils in Germany, 1918–1919: Recent Literature on the Rätebewegung." *New German Critique* 4 (winter 1975): 113–124.

Peuckert, Detlev J. K. *The Weimar Republic. The Crisis of Classical Modernity*. New York: Farrar, Starus, Giroux, 1993.

Pintore, Anna M. "Democracia sin derechos. En torno al Kelsen democratico." *Doxa* 23 (2000): 119–144.

Popper, Karl. *The Logic of Scientific Discovery*. London, New York: Routledge, 2002. (Original edition 1935).

———. *The Open Society and its Enemies*, vol. 1 and 2. London: Routledge, 1952. (Original edition 1945).

Potz, Richard. "Introductory Remarks." In Hans Kelsen, *Secular Religion: A Polemic against Misinterpretations of Modern Social Philosophy, Science and Politics as "New Religions,"* edited by Robert Walter, Clemens Jabloner, and Kalus Zeleny, VII–X. Wien, New York: Springer, 2012.

Radbruch, Gustav. "Goldbilanz und Reichsverfassung." *Die Gesellschaft* 1 (1924): 57–69.

———. "Gesetzliches Unrecht und übergesetzliches Recht." *Süddeutsche Juristen-Zeitung* 1, no. 5 (1946): 105–108.

Ragazzoni, David. *Il Leviatano democratico. Parlamento, partiti e capi tra Weber e Kelsen.* Roma: Edizioni di Storia e Letteratura, 2016.

———. "An Overlooked Puzzle in Kelsen's Democratic Theory." In *Compromise and Disagreement in Contemporay*, edited by Christian Rostball, and Theresa Scavenius, 96–118. New York: Routledge, 2017.

Rathkolb, Oliver. "Hans Kelsen und das F.B.I während des McCarthysmus in the U.S.A." In *Hans Kelsen – Leben – Werke – Wirksamkeit*, hrsg. von Robert Walter, Werner Ogris, and Thomas Olekowski, 339–348. Vienna: Manz, 2009.

Renner, Karl. *Staat und Parlament. Kritische Studie über die österreichische Frage und das System der Interessenvertretung.* Wien: GenossenschaftsBuchdruckerei, 1901.

———. *Das Selbstbestimmungsrecht der Nationen.* Leipzig, Wien: J. Deuticke, 1917.

Rennhofer, Friederich. *Ignaz Seipel. Mensch und Staatsmann. Eine biographische Dokumentation.* Wien: Hermann Böhlaus Nachf, 1978.

Riccobono, Francesco. *Antikelsenismo italiano.* Torino: Giappichelli, 2017.

Rice, Daniel F. "Kelsen and Niebhur on Democracy." In *Hans Kelsen in America – Selective Affinities and the Mysteries of Academic Influences*, edited by Jeremy Telman, 135–159. Netherlands: Springer, 2016.

Rigaux, François. "Hans Kelsen and International Law." *European Journal of International Law* 9, no. 2 (1998): 325–343.

Rizzi, Lino. "Il problema della legittimazione democratica in Kelsen e Rousseau." *Il Politico* 57, no. 2 (aprile-giugno 1992): 225–258.

Robertson, David. *The Judge as Political Theorist: Contemporary Constitutional Review.* Princeton, New Jersey: Princeton University Press, 2010.

Roermund Van, Bert. "Kelsen, Secular Religion and the Problem of Transcendence." *Netherlands Journal of Legal Philosophy* 44, no. 2 (2015): 100–115.

Roman, Eric. *Austria-Hungary and Successor States: A Reference Guide from the Renaissance to the Present.* New York: Fact on File Inc, 2003.

Roshwald, Ariel. *Ethnic Nationalism and the Fall of the Empires. Central Europe, Russia and the Middle East 1914–1923.* London and New York: Routledge, 2000.

Rousseau, Jean-Jacques. *Du Contract Social. Ou Principes du Droit Politique.* Paris: Flammarion, 2012. (Original edition 1762).

Ruggiero, Guido De. *The History of European Liberalism.* London: Peter Smith Pub. Inc, 1977. (Italian edition 1927).

Ryan, Alan. *The Making of Modern Liberalism.* Princeton, New Jersey: Princeton University Press, 2012.

Sabine, George. *A History of Political Thought.* New York: Henry Holt Company, 1951.

Saffon, Maria Paula, and Nadia Urbinati. "Procedural Democracy, the Bulwark of Equal Liberty." *Political Theory* 41, no. 3 (2013): 441–481.

Salvadori, Massimo L., ed. *European Liberalism.* New York: John Wiley and Sons Ltd., 1972.

Sandoz, Ellis. *The Voegelian Revolution. A Biographical Introduction.* New York: Routledge, 2000.

Schmitt, Carl. "Preface to the Second edition" (1926). In Carl Schmitt, *The Crisis of Parliamentary Democracy* (Eng. Trans. 1st ed. and 2nd ed.), edited and translated by Ellen Kennedy, 2–17. Cambridge, Massachusetts, and London, England: MIT Press, 1988.

———. *Der Begriff des Politischen. Ein kooperativer Kommentar* (1928). Berlin: Walter De Gruyter, 2016.

———. *Der Hüter der Verfassung.* Tübingen: Verlag von J.C.B Mohr (Paul Siebeck), 1931.

———. "Prussia Contra Reich: Schmitt's Closing Statement in Leipzig" (1932). In *The Guardian of the Constitution. Hans Kelsen and Carl Schmitt on the Limits of Constitutional Law,* edited by Lars Vinx, 222–227. Cambridge: Cambridge University Press, 2015.

———. *Legality and Legitimacy* (1932). Translated by Jeffrey Seitzer and with an Introduction of by John McCormick. Durham and London: Duke University Press, 2004.

Schmitz, Gerald. *Die Vorentwürfe Hans Kelsens für die Österreichische Verfassung.* Wien: Manz Verlag, 1981.

———. *Karl Renners Briefe aus St. Germain und ihre rechtspolitischen Folgen.* Wien: Manzsche Verlag und Universitätsbuchhandlung, 1991.

———. "The Constitutional Court of the Republic of Austria." *Ratio Juris* 16, no. 2 (June 2003): 240–265.

Schulmann, Jason. *Rosa Luxemburg: Her Life and Legacy.* New York: Palgrave and Macmillan, 2013.

Schumpeter, Joseph A. *Capitalism, Socialism, Democracy.* London, New York: Routledge, 1994. (Original edition 1942).

Schwartz, Bernard. "Review of the Communist Theory of Law." *The University of Chicago Law Review* 23 (1956): 354–356.

Scuto, Filippo. *La democrazia interna dei partiti: profile costituzionali di una transizione.* Torino: Giappichelli, 2017.

Smaldone, William. *Confronting Hitler: German Social Democrats in Defense of the Weimar Republic.* Lanham, MD: Rowman & Littlefield, 2009.

Stewart, Iain. "The Critical Legal Science of Hans Kelsen." *Journal of Law and Society* 17, no. 3 (January 1991): 273–308.

———. "Kelsen, the Enlightenment and the Modern Premodernists." *Austrian Journal of Legal Philosophy* 37 (2013): 251–278.

Stolleis, Michael. *Geschichte des öffentlichen Rechts in Deutschland. Staatsrechtslehre und Verwaltungswissenschaft 1800–1914,* Bd. 2. München: Verlag C. B. Beck, 1992.

———. *Geschichte des öffentlichen Rechts in Deutschland. Staatsrechtslehre und Verwaltungswissenschaft 1800–1914,* Bd. 3. München: Verlag C. B. Beck, 1999.

———. *Der Methodenstreit der Weimarer Staatsrechtslehre – ein abgeschlossenes Kapitel der Wissenschaftgeschichte?* Stuttgart: Franz Steiner Verlag, 2011.

Stone-Sweet, Alec. *Governing with the Judges. Constitutional Politics in Europe.* Oxford: Oxford University Press, 2000.

———. "Constitutional Courts and Parliamentary Democracy." *West European Politics* 25, no. 1 (January 2002): 77–100.

Stradaioli, Nicoletta. "Monisms and Pluralism: Eric Voegelin's Contribution." In *Monisms and Pluralisms in the History of Political Thought*, edited by Andrea Catanzaro and Sara Lagi, 95–104. Novi Ligure: Epoké, 2016.

Sully, Melanie A. *Continuity and Change in Austrian Socialism. The Eternal Quest for the third Way.* New York: Columbia University Press, 1982.

Swedberg, Richard. *Joseph A. Schumpeter. His Life and Work.* Cambridge: Polity Press, 1991.

Talmon, Jacob. *The Origins of Totalitarian Democracy.* London: Secker & Walburg, 1952.

Telman, Jeremy. "Introduction: Hans Kelsen for Americans." In *Hans Kelsen in America – Selective Affinities and the Mysteries of Academic Influences*, edited by Jeremy Telman, 1–16. Netherlands: Springer, 2016.

Thoma, Richard. "Sinn und Gestaltung des deutschen Parlamentarismus." In Richard Thoma, *Recht und Staat*, hrsg. von Bernhard Harms, vol. 1, 98–126. Berlin: Reimar Hobbing, 1929.

Tocqueville, Alexis De. *Democracy in America*, Vol. 1 and 2. London: Forgotten Books, 2012. (Original editions 1835, 1840).

Topitsch, Ernst. "Hans Kelsen – Demokrat und Philosoph." In *Ideologiekritik und Demokratietheorie bei Hans Kelsen*, hrsg. von Peter Koller, Werner Krawietz und Ernst Topitsch, 11–30. Berlin: Duncker & Humblot, 1982.

Treves, Renato. "Intorno all concezione del diritto in Hans Kelsen." *Rivista internazionale di filosofia del diritto* XXIX (1952): 117–197.

———. "Sociologia del diritto e sociologia dell'idea di giustizia nel pensiero di Kelsen." *Sociologia del diritto* 3 (1981): 160–175.

Triepel, Heinrich. *Die Staatsverfassung und die politische Parteien.* Berlin: Druck der Preuissischen Druckerei und Verlags-Aktiengesellschaft, 1927.

Troper, Michel. "Hans Kelsen et la jurisprudence." *Archives de philosophie du droit* 30 (1985): 83–94.

———. "Kelsen et la cour constitutionelle." In *La controverse sur "le gardien de la Constitution" et la justice constitutionelle. Kelsen contre Schmitt*, sous la direction de Olivier Beaud et Pasquale Pasquino, 83–98. Paris: Editon Panthéon-Assas, 2007.

Urbinati, Nadia. "Editor's Preface." In Hans Kelsen, *The Essence and Value of Democracy*, edited by Nadia Urbinati, and Carlo Invernizzi-Accetti, 1–25. Lanham, MD: Rowman & Littlefield Pub. Inc., 2013.

Vaihinger, Hans. "Mitteilungen über das dem Kongress überreichte Werk '*Die Philosophie des Als ob.*'" In *Atti del IV Congresso internazionale di Filosofia*, 297–309. Modena: Formiggini, 1911.

Vinx, Lars. *Hans Kelsen's Pure Theory of Law: Legality and Legitimacy.* Oxford: Oxford University Press, 2006.

———. "Introduction." In *The Guardian of the Constitution. Hans Kelsen and Carl Schmitt on the Limits of Constitutional Law*, edited by Lars Vinx, 1–21. Cambridge: Cambridge University Press, 2015.

Voegelin, Eric. *The New Science of Politics. An Introduction*. Chicago, Illinois: The University of Chicago Press, 1952.

———. *Selected Correspondence 1950–1984* Vol. 30, edited by Thomas A. Hollweck. Columbia, Missouri: University of Missouri Press, 2007.

Wall, Steven. "Introduction." In *The Cambridge Companion to Liberalism*, edited by Steven Wall, 1–19. Cambridge: Cambridge University Press, 2015.

Walter, Robert. *Hans Kelsen. Ein Leben im Dienste der Wissenschaft*. Wien: Manz, 1985.

———. *Hans Kelsen als Verfassungsrichter*. Wien: Manz, 2005.

Wandruska, Anton. *Österreichspolitische Struktur. Die Entwicklung der Parteien und politischen Bewegungen*. Wien: Verlag für Gesellaschaft und Politik, 1954.

Weber, Max. "Parlament und Regierung in neugeordneten Deutschland." In Max Weber, *Gesammelte Politischen Schriften*, hrsg. von Johannes Winckelmann. Tübingen: Mohr Siebeck, 1988. (Original edition 1918).

Weinberger, Ota. "Introduction: Hans Kelsen as Philosopher." In *Hans Kelsen: Essays in Legal and Moral Philosophy*, edited by Ota Weinberger, IX–XXVIII. Dortrecht and Boston: D. Reidel Publishing Company, 1973.

Williamson, Peter. *Varieties of Corporatism: A Conceptual Discussion*. Cambridge: Cambridge University Press, 1985.

Zagrebelski, Vladimiro. *Il "crucifige!" e la democrazia*. Torino: Einaudi, 2007.

Zalewska, Monika. "Some Misunderstandings Concerning Hans Kelsen's Concepts of Democracy and the Rule of Law." In *Jurysprudencja*, edited by Bartosz Wojciechoski, Tomasz Bekrycht, Carolina M. Cerm 8 (2017): 104–118.

Zolo, Danilo. "Hans Kelsen: International Peace through International Law." *European Journal of International Law* 9, no. 2 (1998): 306–324.

———. *I signori della pace. Una critica del globalismo giuridico*. Roma: Carocci, 1998.

Name Index

Ableitinger, Alfred, 17n84
Allen, Richard, 165n45
Angelis, Gabriele De, 47n67, 48n78
Arendt, Hannah, 136, 164n37, 165n45
Aron, Raymond, 136, 138, 164n38,
    165n45, 167n92, 168n95

Barth, Boris, 51n108
Baume, Sandrine, 4, 12n26, 43n13,
    52n125, 53n143, 91n107
Beaud, Olivier, 3, 12n15, 88n71,
    90n101, 93n149
Béchillon, Denys De, 164n32
Bellamy, Richard, 88nn77–78, 89nn95–
    96, 126n79, 169n129
Benderesky, Joseph W, 128n106
Berger, Mario G., 43n16
Berger, Peter, 51n110
Berlin, Isaiah, 109–11, 126nn84–85,
    136–38
Bernatzik, Edmund, 15, 42nn1–3
Bernstorff, Jochen Von, 163n10
Bersier Ladavac, Nicoletta, 51n116,
    120n4
Bischof, Günther, 84n16
Bluntschli, Johann Caspar, 36
Bobbio, Norberto, 2, 11n10, 48n84, 133,
    163n18, 164n32
Böckenförde, Ernst Wolfgang, 129n131

Bohmann, Gerda, 165n45
Boogman, John, 83n14
Boudëc Le, Nathalie, 128n107
Breuer, Stefan, 43n10
Brunner, Emil, 140, 143–45, 165n48,
    166n71, 167n74
Bryan, Ian, 3
Busino, Giovanni, 47n70

Caldwell, Peter C., 42n7, 52n118,
    90n103, 92n141, 93nn145, 148
Calsamiglia, Alberto, 3, 12n20
Campagnolo, Umberto, 120n6
Canovan, Margaret, 46n50
Capua, Raimondo De, 4, 12n25
Carrino, Agostino, 2, 11n11
Carrozza, Paolo, 162n4
Carsten, Francis, 47n63, 51nn110, 116
Caserta, Marco, 4, 12n25
Cohen, Hermann, 17, 43n16, 44
Conant, James B., 119
Connin, Lawrence J., 168n112
Constant, Benjamin, 76, 91n121
Costa, Pietro, 45n33, 169n117
Crowder, George, 51n106, 127n92,
    165n45

Dard, Olivier, 127n101
Dogliani, Patrizia, 127n102

191

Swedberg, Richard, 169n124

Talmon, Jacob, 48n94, 85n126, 136–38, 164n39, 165n47
Telman, Jeremy, 3, 12n19, 162nn1, 3, 163n10, 165nn46, 48
Tocqueville, Alexis de, 9, 13n35, 31–32, 50n101, 108, 126n119
Topitsch, Ernst, 11n6, 43n14, 45n34, 49n88, 51n116, 123n37, 129n122
Treves, Renato, 2, 11n10, 44n26, 51n115, 121n18
Triepel, Heinrich, 35–37, 51n118, 52n127, 90n103
Troper, Michel, 3, 11n14, 82n3

Urbinati, Nadia, 4, 12n28, 50n96, 166nn50–51

Vaihinger, Hans, 28, 48nn85–86
Vinx, Lars, 3, 12n17, 44n20, 48nn76–77, 90n101, 92nn142, 144, 93n146
Vishinsky, Andrej, 164n32

Voegelin, Eric, 6, 139–40, 146–48, 151, 165n45, 166n70, 167nn90–93, 96, 98, 102

Waldron, Jeremy, 49n94
Wall, Steven, 13nn33, 37, 40
Walter, Robert, 2, 11n5, 92n132, 120n4, 124n42, 129n131, 162n1, 164n30, 167n91, 168n95
Wandruskka, Anton, 82n5
Weber, Max, 10, 12n26, 13n28, 18, 28–29, 38, 43n10, 48n84, 50n106, 90n101
Weinberger, Ota, 122, 123n32, 169n1
Williamson, Peter, 53n140
Windelband, Wilhelm, 17
Wolff, Christian, 44, 133, 163n17

Zagrebelsky, Gustavo, 125n70
Zalewska, Monika, 120n8
Zeleny, Klaus, 2, 11nn7–8, 167n91, 168n95
Zolo, Danilo, 45n33, 163nn12, 16, 18, 169n117

About the Author

Sara Lagi is associate professor of history of political thought at the University of Turin (Italy). Her research interests are history of European liberalism and democratic thought. She has published works on Hans Kelsen's, Georg Jellinek's, and Isaiah Berlin's political thought. She is a member of the European Association for the History of Political Thoughts and of the Northeastern Political Science Association.

www.ingramcontent.com/pod-product-compliance
Lightning Source LLC
Chambersburg PA
CBHW022315280326
41932CB00010B/1107